TRIBUNALS ON TRIAL

Tribunals on Trial

A Study of Decision-Making under the Mental Health Act 1983

JILL PEAY

CLARENDON PRESS · OXFORD
1989

Oxford University Press, Walton Street, Oxford OX2 6DP
Oxford New York Toronto
Delhi Bombay Calcutta Madras Karachi
Petaling Jaya Singapore Hong Kong Tokyo
Nairobi Dar es Salaam Cape Town
Melbourne Auckland
and associated companies in
Berlin Ibadan

Oxford is a trade mark of Oxford University Press

Published in the United States
by Oxford University Press, New York

© Jill Peay 1989

All rights reserved. No part of this publication may be reproduced,
stored in a retrieval system, or transmitted, in any form or by any means,
electronic, mechanical, photocopying, recording, or otherwise, without
the prior permission of Oxford University Press

British Library Cataloguing in Publication Data
Peay, Jill
Tribunals on trial: a study of decision-making under
Mental Health Act 1983.
1. England. Mental illness hospitals. Compulsorily
detained patients. Discharge. Law
I. Title
344.204'44
ISBN 0-19-825249-8

Library of Congress Cataloging in Publication Data
Peay, Jill
Tribunals on trial: a study of decision-making under the Mental
Health Act 1983 / Jill Peay.
"An inquiry carried out at the Centre for Criminological Research,
University of Oxford."
Bibliography   Includes index.
1. Mental health laws—Great Britain. 2. Insane—Commitment and
detention—Great Britain. I. Title.
KD3412.P43   1989   344.41'044—dc20   [344.10444]   89-3433
ISBN 0-19-825249-8

Typeset by Latimer Trend & Company Ltd, Plymouth
Printed in Great Britain
by Biddles Ltd
Guildford and King's Lynn

Preface

In 1984 I was commissioned by the DHSS to undertake a study of certain aspects of the newly constituted tribunal system. I had previously conducted research under the Mental Health Act 1959, and the findings of this earlier study had contributed to a growing dissatisfaction with the existing Act. Indeed, as one of the main safeguards against the unjustified detention of psychiatric patients, Mental Health Review Tribunals, as they operated under the 1959 Act, were widely regarded as deficient. The enhancement of their role and methods of working was promoted as a critical feature of the package of improvements in mental health legislation brought about by the passage of the 1983 Act. Yet, were these changes to make a real difference to the process of review prior to discharge in the cases of detained psychiatric patients? Or, were the difficulties evident in this arena so deep-rooted as to be insusceptible even to systemic changes? The tribunal system was on trial, both in respect of its elevated role and because those responsible for working the system were prepared to submit themselves to the strictures of independent research. This book is based around the findings of that inquiry, conducted over three years and benefiting from the full co-operation of all those involved in making decisions to release detained patients.

The need to find out how the tribunals were working and the bases on which decisions were taken had two principal justifications. First, it was desirable that tribunal members should be informed about the practices of their colleagues; any individual member will have only limited knowledge as to how the tribunals work as a whole. Almost certainly, they will have no experience of how other members, legal, medical, or lay, within their panel operate, since no two members from the same group would sit on a tribunal together. A shared understanding of how tribunals do and should operate would seem to be a prerequisite to attaining consistency in decision-making. Moreover, the advantages to patients, their legal representatives, and the multiplicity of others involved in providing information to the tribunal, of gaining a clearer understanding of the true functioning of tribunals hardly needs stating. The second justification extends the 'need to know' to policy-makers. Revisions to the 1983 Act were effected with intent; those responsible should be informed as to the specific consequences of the changes made and whether the aims behind the reforms had been achieved. Together, these two types of feedback provide the basis for what Gottfredson and Gottfredson (1980: 356) have called 'the evolutionary process of learning'.

Chapter 1 sets out in greater detail the historical background to the research and poses the key themes to be addressed. The objectives, design, and working context of the research are dealt with in Chapter 2, which also briefly reviews the rationale for the methodology chosen. The following six chapters constitute the empirical heart of the research. The first three deal respectively with the interviews with patients, Responsible Medical Officers, and the judicial members of the tribunal. They provide a context for the subsequent chapters which attempt a detailed analysis of the tribunals' decision-making strategies based on observations of hearings in individual cases. As might be expected, the last chapter draws the findings together and makes some circumspect recommendations for reform.

It will readily become apparent that a tribunal hearing constitutes a complex and dynamic setting, at which information from a variety of sources is presented in both written and oral forms. No two tribunal hearings will follow exactly the same course, but they are likely to share a number of common features. Therefore, in order to assist the reader, a detailed description is presented within the appendices of the format of a typical tribunal dealing with a restricted case. This sets out the range of the formal information sources available to the tribunal and clarifies some of the terms which appear repeatedly throughout the book.

I have incurred many debts of gratitude in completing this work; most recently to the British Academy, for providing financial support to assist with the preparation of the manuscript. I am also indebted to the DHSS, who commissioned the original research and were generous with their support throughout. I am especially grateful to Dr Mary Dastgir of the Office of the Chief Scientist, who provided both warm encouragement and stimulation to me. She was, moreover, invaluable in smoothing the passage of the research behind the scenes in ways I could not pretend fully to grasp.

Members of the DHSS, both within the Mental Health Division and at the tribunal offices, where I spent long hours ploughing through files, made my task much more pleasurable than I could have hoped. C3 Division at the Home Office, despite coming in for some flak, were also helpful and prompt in their response to my inquiries; members of the Lord Chancellor's Department were of similar assistance. A special note of thanks is due to Mr Justice Hodgson, who acted to oversee the judicial aspects of the research in what might otherwise have been a tricky field.

Without doubt, I am most indebted to all of those people who volunteered to take part in the research—amongst whom were patients, psychiatrists, hospital staff, legal representatives and, of course, tribunal members in all of their manifestations. I cannot name them because I have guaranteed their anonymity; they are selectively protected from the accusatorial finger, but equally denied praise. For these individuals not only gave their time and their ideas, but did so with considerable frankness. Their willingness to expose themselves to criticism, at least some of which I hope they will find constructive, was, to me, indicative of the seriousness with which they approached their responsibilities.

Finally, the Centre for Criminological Research at Oxford did more than merely house the research and provide technological support in the form of a well-known soft fruit; my colleagues there were ever present with their support and nurture. But, my thanks are due particularly to the Director of the Centre, Roger Hood, for his long term patronage and to Andrew Ashworth and Sarah McCabe. All painstakingly read drafts and must be credited for their comments and their fortitude—but most of all for their inspiration.

J.P.

1 October 1988

CONTENTS

Abbreviations   xiv

1. The Tribunal System: Evolution and Objectives   1
   - I. Tribunals under the Mental Health Act 1959   3
   - II. The New Provisions   5
     - A. The Mental Health Act 1983   5
       - (i) Non-restricted cases   5
       - (ii) Restricted cases   6
     - B. The Mental Health Review Tribunal Rules (SI 1983 No 942)   10
     - C. The Membership of Tribunals in Restricted Cases   11
       - (i) The impetus for change   11
       - (ii) Appointing judicial members to the tribunal   13
       - (iii) The role of the regional chairmen   15
   - III. Conclusions   16

2. The Research Setting   19
   - I. Theoretical Context   20
   - II. Research Objectives   22
     - A. Methodology   23
       - (i) Procedures   23
       - (ii) Problems   24
       - (iii) Context   25
     - B. The Working Context of the Research   28
       - (i) Informal contact   29
       - (ii) Formal contact   30
     - C. Locative Context   31
       - (i) Acheland's patient population   31
       - (ii) Patient subsample: Characteristics   33
       - (iii) Acheland Hospital: Conflicting images of an institution's population   35

Contents

3. Praying Patience: The Patients' Perspectives ... 37
   I. Patients' Relationships with Their Responsible Medical Officers ... 38
      A. The Quantity and Quality of the Relationship ... 38
      B. Implications ... 40
   II. Patients' Views about the Tribunals ... 41
      A. New and Improved? ... 41
      B. Why Patients Apply ... 44
      C. Preparing for the Tribunal: The Role of the Representative ... 45
      D. Patients and their Reports: Is Seeing Believing? ... 47
   III. Patients, Their Treatment and the Impact of Acheland ... 50
      A. Coming to Acheland ... 50
      B. Treatment ... 51
      C. Leaving Acheland ... 52
   IV. Conclusions ... 54

4. The Responsible Medical Officers ... 58
   I. The Role of the RMO: Therapist and Custodian ... 58
      A. RMOs and the Tribunals ... 64
      B. Tribunals: Administrative Burden or Therapeutic Tool? ... 65
         (i) Contact ... 65
         (ii) Disclosure ... 66
         (iii) Professional relationships ... 68
         (iv) Decision-making with responsibility ... 68
         (v) Reflective v. reflexive decision-making ... 70
      C. Time for Crime: The Moral Threshold ... 71
   II. Conclusions ... 75

5. The Influence of the Judicial Approach ... 79
   I. The Rationale for Judicial Appointments ... 80
      A. The Judicial View: Caution and Constraint ... 82
         (i) Criteria ... 84
         (ii) Powers ... 85
         (iii) Evidence ... 87
         (iv) Systemic difficulties ... 89
         (v) Experience of members with release decisions ... 90

Contents

II. Rules and Procedures: Interpretation and Application	91
A. The Judicial Style	91
(i) Prehearing reviews	92
(ii) Disclosure of medical evidence	92
(iii) Timing of the medical member's report to the tribunal	93
(iv) The conduct of the hearing	95
B. Applying the Decision Criteria	95
C. Additional Information	96
III. Conclusions	98
6. Patients with Classifications of Psychopathic Disorders	**101**
I. Psychopathic Disorder: Definitions and Diagnosis	102
II. The Tribunals' Decisions: Outcome Measures	105
III. The Tribunals' Decisions: Rationale	108
A. Straightforward No Discharge Decisions	109
B. Classic Dilemmas	110
(i) Equity and treatability: The unequal exchange	111
(ii) True to form: Tribunals as regressive/passive decision-makers	112
(iii) The tribunal as ratifiers	114
(iv) Interactive issues	116
(v) Against the grain	124
C. Dischargeable Cases	124
(i) The impact of the RMO in facilitating change	126
(ii) Impact of legal member of the tribunal	130
D. Diagnostically Difficult Cases	132
IV. Conclusions	136
7. Patients with Classifications of Mental Illness	**141**
I. Recurrent Themes in the Tribunals' Reasoning	142
A. Insight	142
B. Medication and Stability	143
C. Remorse	144
D. The Absence of Disorder?	145
II. The Tribunal's Decisions: Outcome Measures	146
III. The Tribunals' Decisions: Rationale	147
A. No Discharge Cases	147

B. Intermediate Decisions		154
(i) Systemic problems		154
(ii) Departmental pressure: Home Office		155
(iii) Departmental Pressure: DHSS		157
(iv) A lack of impetus		157
(v) Means and ends: Pragmatism and the law		159
C. Discharges		161
(i) Against the grain: Declining to be cautious		161
(ii) Muddied waters: The unavoidability of evidence and law		163
(iii) Outcome triumphing over evidence		166
(iv) Restriction direction cases: The use of advisory powers		169
IV. Conclusions		172

8. Tribunals outside the Special Hospitals — 176

I. Observed Hearings	177
A. Non-Restricted Cases	179
(i) 'Hopeless' cases	179
(ii) Borderline cases	180
(iii) A strict application of the law?	184
B. Restricted Cases	186
(i) Borderline cases	187
(ii) Towards discharge: The influence of real options	189
II. Retrospective Decisions: The Use of S72(2)	191
A. Reasons for Discharge	193
B. A Rigorous Application of the Law?	195
III. Conclusions	197

9. Conclusions — 201

I. The Limitations of Legalism	201
A. Legalism Enshrined?	203
B. Is the Effectiveness of the Legal Approach Context-Specific?	204
C. The Impact of the System Personnel	206
D. The Assessment of Risk	207
II. The Transformation of Choice into Constraint	209
A. The Decisions of Tribunals	209

Contents

B. Understanding the Reasoning Process ... 210
  (i) Use of the statute ... 211
  (ii) Abuse of the statute ... 212
  (iii) Lack of options ... 213
  (iv) Deferral ... 213
  (v) Quiescent patients and passive tribunals ... 214
  (vi) Sign-posting ... 214
  (vii) Undermining the source rather than the content of evidence ... 214

C. Deliberations ... 216

D. Beyond the Legal Safeguard: Other Roles for the Tribunal ... 221

III. The Way Forward? ... 226

Appendix 1 ... 233
Appendix 2 ... 237
Appendix 3 ... 244
References ... 246
Index ... 252

ABBREVIATIONS

1983 Act	The Mental Health Act 1983
1959 Act	The Mental Health Act 1959
The Rules	The Mental Health Review Tribunal Rules 1983
Tribunal	The Mental Health Review Tribunal
RMO	Responsible Medical Officer
IP	Independent Psychiatrist
IPR	Independent Psychiatric Report
S	Section
R	Rule
RSU	Regional Secure Unit
MSU	Medium Secure Unit
ISU	Interim Secure Unit

The 1983 Act confers powers on the Secretary of State, commonly referred to as the Home Secretary; the two terms are accordingly employed interchangeably throughout the book. It would, however, have been more accurate to have referred to the Parliamentary Under-Secretary of State, who, in practice, assumed the role.

1. The Tribunal System: Evolution and Objectives

> Measures which subject individuals to the substantial and involuntary deprivation of their liberty are essentially punitive in character, and this reality is not altered by the facts that the motivations that prompt incarceration are to provide therapy or otherwise contribute to the person's well-being or reform. As such, these measures must be closely scrutinized to insure that power is being applied consistently with those values of the community that justify interferences with liberty for only the most clear and compelling reasons.
>
> Francis Allen (1971: 325)

There are numerous areas in which individual rights come into conflict with those of society as a whole. Few such conflicts can be more poignant or pose more imponderable dilemmas than those which arise when people who are deemed to be mentally disordered are compulsorily confined for psychiatric treatment. Loss of liberty is the bottom line in the muddied arena of individual rights. Although there may be grounds for legitimate dispute about the pre-eminence of a whole series of other so-called individual rights, the right to liberty should trump other general interests or collective goals.[1] However, where compulsory treatment is merited in the context of both psychiatric disorder and a history of offending, the critical issue will not solely concern whether absolute rights should outweigh questions of mere utility. Rather, the issue becomes whether and how one individual's immediate rights should be traded off against the—potentially collective— rights of other individuals to be protected from harm. The probability of this harm may, in reality, be quite low, but its expression, in respect of the rights of any specific potential victim, is powerful. The dilemma becomes acute where the diagnosis of disorder is not clear cut or where the benefits of treatment are

[1] See generally Waldron (1984) and specifically therein R. Dworkin 'Rights as Trumps' pp. 153–67.

arguable, yet society's interest in effecting some change is pressing because of the individual's past actions in seriously endangering the lives of others. The equation may be evenly balanced. How far should an individual's rights be transgressed in this arena in pursuit of some wider, but ill-defined societal good, which may derive, for example, from a diminution in future offending? Moreover, should account be taken of the need to protect the individual rights of potential victims?

Resolving these questions would, even in theory, be no easy task. Refereeing their practical resolution is often left to the law. Yet this task is further confounded by the setting in which decisions are made. For even where the bargaining is confined to the patient's rights versus utilitarian societal goals, such individual rights are frequently also moderated by considerations of a patient's therapeutic interests. For any individual, fulfilment of his or her legal rights may, in some instances, only be achieved at the expense of these therapeutic interests. For example, the right to discharge may prevent the completion of a beneficial treatment programme. The issues, therefore, are not clear cut; nor is the ground firm. Indeed, the shifts which take place in resolving opposing interests parallel those which have already occurred in the debate about compulsory confinement—from the right to refuse treatment to the right to receive treatment.[2]

This book addresses the efficacy of the law, first, to cope with the competing demands which derive from society and its mentally disordered members; and secondly, to resolve the conflicts inherent for all patients between their individual interests and their rights. This is achieved through an examination of the operation of the Mental Health Review Tribunal system. These tribunals constitute what is arguably the most important provision for the release of detained patients in a complex package of arrangements under the Mental Health Act 1983.[3] Under the terms of this Act, individuals who are considered to be mentally disordered, whether they have offended or not, can be compulsorily confined in hospital on non-punitive grounds. Tribunals have the authority to discharge certain categories of patients from their detention orders against the wishes of the psychiatrists responsible for their treat-

---

[2] See Gordon R. and Verdun-Jones S. (1983) and Gordon (1989)
[3] For a comprehensive discussion of these provisions see Hoggett (1984) and Gostin (1986).

ment in hospital. Their decisions therefore can have far reaching implications for the safety of the public.

Yet, the tribunals' fundamental role has been succinctly summarized as 'a safeguard for the liberty of the individual and to insure against unjustified detention in hospital' (Aarvold Report 1973, para. 35). In theory therefore, tribunals are not charged with achieving the difficult balance between individual and societal interests. Rather, they constitute one element (with a patient-primacy orientation) in a dynamic package of mental health legislation which has been designed to accommodate both sets of interests. But in practice, tribunals frequently attempt to achieve just such a satisfactory balance and thereby encounter a series of irresolvable dilemmas. This book will be concerned with an empirical examination of those issues.

1. TRIBUNALS UNDER THE MENTAL HEALTH ACT 1959

Mental Health Review Tribunals were established under the Mental Health Act 1959. As a form of review, the tribunals were heralded as an innovation. Decisions were to be made jointly by a lawyer, a lay person, and a psychiatrist, all of whom were independent from those responsible for detaining patients. It had been claimed that tribunals would act as a safeguard against both improper admission and unduly protracted detention.[4] However, it was readily apparent that they would be unable to fulfil the high expectations generated for them.

In respect of their role as a safeguard against improper admission, tribunals were largely ineffective, since review only took place *after* the implementation of compulsory procedures. Of course, the very existence of tribunal review may have had a deterrent impact, encouraging the professionals concerned to consider the issues more carefully when compulsory measures were envisaged. But, if such was the case, this would have been an unintentional consequence of the legislation. The tribunals' effectiveness in preventing unduly protracted detention also proved to be limited, especially in relation to patients with restriction orders attached to their discharge (those who had committed more

---

[4] As outlined by Derek Walker-Smith, the Minister of Health during the passage of the 1959 Act through Parliament (*Parl. Debates*, HC, vol. 598, col. 713, 26 Jan 1959).

serious offences and from whom the public were thought to be at risk of future offending). In these cases the tribunal had no power to discharge, and their function was merely to advise the Home Secretary about the patient's suitability for discharge, transfer, or trial leave. He acted as final arbiter and enjoyed the exclusive right to discharge.

The methods of working and inherent fairness of the tribunal system were also widely questioned. The tribunals' powers and procedures were criticized (Gostin 1975, 1977; Gostin and Rassaby 1980). Research demonstrated that there were significant variations between the fifteen tribunal regions in their discharge rates (Greenland 1970). Compounding these criticisms, Fennell (1977) argued that tribunal decisions were being influenced more by common-sense factors than by the statutory criteria which were supposed to govern their decisions.[5] The latter were described as providing no more than organizing boundaries within which a number of subordinate, non-legal categories were subsumed. In support of this, it was demonstrated that in reaching decisions the 'over-riding factor to the tribunal was the personality of the patient' (Hepworth 1985: 162). Hence, subjective assessments or gut reactions were found to be as, if not more, important than objective factors in assessing the crucial factor of perceived dangerousness, and thus fitness for discharge. Finally, a wide-ranging study of the operation of the tribunal system under the 1959 Act (Peay 1980) revealed significant individual differences between tribunal members in their attitudes towards, and knowledge about, mental health matters. It was a matter of concern that these differences in attitude and knowledge were found to have a systematic effect on the nature of decisions being made.

Thus, the very assumptions upon which tribunals had been promoted were being challenged. Although predicated on the notion that a professional consensus would be reached in making decisions if medical, legal, and lay perspectives were brought to bear on the complex problem of whether continued detention was necessary, research showed the decisions of the tribunals were not immune from the preferences and prejudices of individual members. Nor were these personal perspectives neutralized in the group decision-making process. The final blow was the failure of the statutory criteria to constrain the decisions. The system was felt to be fundamentally flawed. Tribunal members might apply

[5] S123 Mental Health Act 1959.

the law compassionately, yet their decisions could be characterized as neither just nor efficacious (Peay 1981). The impetus for reform of the system was overwhelming.

II. THE NEW PROVISIONS

A. *The Mental Health Act 1983*

(i) Non-restricted cases With the passage of the Mental Health (Amendment) Act 1982, consolidated by the Mental Health Act 1983, the government sought to counter a number of the general criticisms which had been levelled at tribunals. Indeed, they claimed to have achieved a 'significant improvement' in the system (*Department of Health and Social Security*, 1981, para. 23). Eligibility for review was extended to patients on twenty-eight-day orders, there were to be more frequent opportunities to apply for hearings, and a system of automatic hearings was introduced for those who lacked 'the ability or initiative to make an application' (ibid. para. 24). The criteria governing the tribunals' decisions (Mental Health Act 1983, S72) were also revised to make it clear that the only patients who could continue to be compulsorily detained were those whose mental disorder made it appropriate for them 'to be liable to be detained in a hospital for medical treatment' (S72(1)(*b*)(i)) *and* where such treatment was 'necessary for the health or safety of the patient or for the protection of other persons' (S72(1)(*b*)(ii)).[6]

In non-restricted cases tribunals were to continue to enjoy a complete discretionary power to discharge, but they were also to have regard to two additional factors, namely whether patients were found to be treatable, and for those suffering from mental illness or severe impairment, whether a criterion of viability outside of hospital could be satisfied (S72(2)(*a*)and(*b*)).[7] The behavioural basis of these additional criteria was intended to provide some element capable of more objective quantification than an assertion of medical need, thereby permitting lay people to have a greater say in determining the necessity for compulsory treatment and counterbalancing the dominance of medical criteria under the 1959 Act. The tribunal's powers in non-restricted cases

---

[6] See Appendix 1 for the full statutory criteria governing tribunals' powers in both non-restricted and restricted cases, under S72 and S73 of the 1983 Act.
[7] Ibid.

were also extended so as to make it possible to direct discharge on a future specified date and to recommend that patients be transferred to another hospital or into guardianship, or given leave of absence. Finally, the extension of legal aid, to include the costs entailed by a lawyer appearing for patients at hearings, meant that representation was likely to become the norm rather than the exception.

(ii) Restricted cases The most fundamental change brought about by the 1983 Act, which gave tribunals the power to discharge restricted cases, was not the direct result of a government initiative. Rather, it was a response to the ruling of the European Court of Human Rights in *X. v. the United Kingdom* (1981).[8] This decision found the United Kingdom Government to be in breach of Article 5(4) of the Convention because there was no court to which restricted patients could apply to consider the substantive (as opposed to procedural) justification for their detention, and, indeed, to order their discharge if there were no longer any substantive justification.[9] The court ruled that detained patients must have a right of periodic access to a judicial body to determine those issues. In order to comply with this, tribunals were given limited powers to discharge restricted patients, either absolutely or conditionally, and to defer a direction for a conditional discharge. These powers are, however, considerably narrower than those of the Home Secretary, who continues to enjoy a great deal of discretion in respect of restricted cases.[10] Not only can he authorize patients' transfer between institutions and grant permission for trial leave, but he also enjoys the power to add to any conditions imposed by the tribunal or to vary any conditions, whether imposed by the tribunal or by himself. He alone has the

---

[8] Application No 6998/75 (1981) 4 EHHR 181. See also Peay (1982*a*).

[9] For further discussion of Article 5(4) see Gostin (1982, p. 783).

[10] Tribunals in restricted cases have no discretionary power to discharge under any circumstances as they do under S72 for non-restricted cases; they have no power to order trial leave, or leave of absence; they have no power to lift the restriction order and leave patients subject solely to a hospital order; they have no statutory power to recommend transfer to another hospital, or indeed even to recommend to the Home Secretary that a patient be so transferred. See *Grant v. Mental Health Review Tribunal* and *R. v. Mersey Mental Health Review Tribunal, Ex parte O'Hara, The Times*, 28 Apr. 1986.

authority to recall conditionally discharged restricted patients to hospital.[11]

The statutory criteria are precise as to the circumstances in which the tribunals are under a duty to discharge patients.[12] They comply with the basic principles enunciated in the earlier European Court case of *Winterwerp*.[13] In this judgment, handed down in 1979, the Court stated that according to Article 5(i)(e) there were three minimum conditions to be satisfied in order to ensure that persons of unsound mind were lawfully detained: namely, the individual must reliably be shown to be of unsound mind on the basis of objective medical expertise; the mental disorder must be of a kind or degree warranting compulsory confinement; and the validity of continued confinement must depend upon the persistence of such a disorder. Under the 1983 Act, if patients are not suffering from a mental disorder of a nature or degree which makes it appropriate for them to be detained for medical treatment, they are entitled, as a minimum, to a conditional discharge.[14] It should be stressed that this entitlement exists independently of whether treatment (and detention) is necessary either for their health or safety or for the protection of other persons.[15]

In shifting the responsibility for the discharge of restricted patients away from the exclusive discretion of the Home Secretary, the European Court's decision achieved no small measure. Indeed, the changes incorporated by the 1983 Act were remarkable in the light of the recommendations of the Butler Committee, which constituted the most comprehensive and recent examination of the law relating to mentally abnormal offenders.[16] They had advocated the very reverse: namely that there should be established a new form of indeterminate sentence for dangerous mentally disordered

---

[11] The powers of the Secretary of State in respect of restricted patients are set out in S42 of the 1983 Act. S42(3) deals with the power to recall conditionally discharged patients.
[12] S72 Mental Health Act 1983 as applied by S73.
[13] *Winterwerp* Judgement of the ECHR, 24 Oct. 24 1979.
[14] See also Gostin (1982).
[15] See the use of 'or' in S73(1)(a).
[16] Home Office and DHSS (1975). At the time of the Butler Report, the release of restricted patients still lay within the sole discretion of the Home Secretary. The Report notably recommended that all restricted patients in Special Hospitals should be referred first to the Advisory Board (para 4.22) set up on the recommendation of the Aarvold Committee thereby further refining the mode of executive review.

offenders, from which release would lie within the complete discretion of the Home Secretary, given a positive recommendation by the Parole Board (para. 4.45). Moreover, release would be 'dependent entirely on the issue of dangerousness' (para. 4.39). Yet, to reiterate, the 1983 Act enhanced judicial rather than executive discretion and based the release of restricted patients on the issue of mental disorder at the expense of considerations of dangerousness. Ironically, proposals for reforming restriction orders prior to *X. v. the United Kingdom*, namely by fixing the duration of an order in proportion to the gravity of the offence committed, had also been couched in terms diametrically opposed to those finally adopted.[17] The earlier recommendation would have required the trial judge to have applied similar principles for both mentally normal and mentally abnormal offenders. However, the decision in *X. v. the United Kingdom*, reflected in S73, is based on the presumption that 'detention of a person of unsound mind' remains lawful only whilst the unsoundness of mind continues (Gostin 1982). The effective length of a restriction order ought now to be determined by clearly limited therapeutic considerations not retributive ones, thus clearly differentiating the bases for continued confinement for mentally abnormal and normal offenders.

Yet there is, under the 1983 Act, a notable mismatch between the criteria that it is necessary for patients to satisfy before a restriction order is made and those criteria that have to be satisfied before making a discharge decision.[18] The former require an assessment that it is necessary to impose the order to protect the public from serious harm, whilst the latter may be complied with solely by medical/therapeutic considerations. Indeed, at the point of discharge the requirement that tribunals be satisfied that treatment is not necessary 'for the protection of other persons' appears merely as a third arm to criteria oriented around the patient's needs; even if they are positively convinced that the patient requires to be detained in the interests of protecting others, this will not constitute a sufficient basis in the absence of medical

[17] See, for example, Gostin (1977).
[18] S41(1) of the Mental Health Act 1983, which deals with the power of the higher courts to restrict discharge from hospital, states: 'Where a hospital order is made ... and it appears to the court, having regard to the nature of the offence, the antecedents of the offender and the risk of his committing further offences if set at large, that it is necessary for the protection of the public from serious harm so to do, the court may ... order ... 'a restriction order''.

need.[19] Similarly, a dangerousness criterion appears only in a rarely used section of the Act.[20] Finally, the mismatch between admission and discharge criteria will be most exaggerated for those patients for whom Special Hospital care is recommended, since they will have to satisfy the additional criterion before admission that they require treatment under conditions of special security because of their 'dangerous, violent or criminal propensities'.[21]

The position of restricted patients under the 1983 Act is therefore anomalous. In theory, utilitarian considerations govern the fate of offenders found to be disordered at the point of sentence, and their need for treatment (or its absence) continues to trump any subsequent retributive or protective interventions. In receiving hospital orders these offender-patients will be diverted irrevocably into the therapeutic system, where therapeutic precepts hold sway. Yet offenders who are only disturbed at the time of their offence, or who develop disorders after sentence whilst in custody, will have entirely different principles applied to their passage through the criminal justice system.[22] Although the few offenders found unfit to plead or not guilty by reason of insanity will be given similar disposals to those allotted to restricted patients, those employing a defence of diminished responsibility and initially given custodial disposals or those who are transferred to hospital from prison under S47/49 of the 1983 Act, may subsequently experience the rigours of the parole system, where punishment, deterrence, and protective considerations can be active and legitimate considerations. Thus, the criminal law employs a complex set of principles and procedures to deal with normal or borderline disordered offenders or those whose disturbances are untimely. By comparison, the approach of the 1983 Act is a model of principled simplicity. Yet, it is evident that in the lottery of the sentencing process questions concerning who receives what, and where they go, can be critical to the timing of their ultimate release.

The upshot is that tribunals dealing with restricted applicants are in a unique position. They determine the effective length of an indeterminate psychiatric detention order in accordance with

[19] S72(1)(b)(ii) Mental Health Act 1983
[20] See S72(1)(b)(iii), 1983 Act. This section applies in non-restricted cases where the RMO has barred the patient's nearest relative from exercising their right to discharge the patient.
[21] S4 National Health Service Act 1977.
[22] See Hoggett (1984: pp. 156–85)

statutory criteria. The only other body faced with comparable dilemmas, namely the Parole Board, enjoys considerable flexibility as its decisions are not governed by fixed criteria. Moreover, the Board merely acts in an advisory capacity; it does not have the final responsibility for releasing offenders on parole, for this rests with the Home Secretary. As noted above, since a proportion of patients on restriction orders reviewed by the tribunal have committed very serious crimes and may indeed have avoided a life prison sentence because of their mental disorder, determining whether to discharge will be of significant interest to applicants, the public, and sentencers.

B. The Mental Health Review Tribunal Rules (SI 1983, No. 942)

As already mentioned, under the 1959 Act, tribunals had been criticized because research established that the way they carried out their tasks varied both between and within regions. Discrepancies in the procedures adopted were felt to be contrary to the rules of natural justice since patients and their representatives could not prepare themselves adequately for the type of informal approach their particular tribunal was to adopt. Indeed, the Council on Tribunals in its Annual Report for 1974–5 found fault with the tribunals' proceedings for contravening many of the provisions of natural justice.

The rules of natural justice should be observed by any body or individual having the duty to act judicially (*de* Smith 1980). They may be summarized by two cardinal principles: *nemo judex in causa sua*, that no person should be judge in his own cause, and *audi alteram partem*, that no person should be condemned unheard. In 1967 a new concept, the duty to act fairly, emerged in *Re K.(H.) (an infant)*(1 All ER 226, 94,99). This has generally been interpreted as the duty to observe certain aspects of the rules of natural justice and has been thought to apply in the exercise of administrative rather than judicial functions. Although under the 1959 Act it could be argued that the tribunals fulfilled a combination of administrative and judicial functions, under the 1983 Act, with their new powers in restricted cases, they were more clearly cast in a judicial mould.

The Mental Health Review Tribunal Rules 1960, which provided the code of procedure to be followed in tribunal proceedings, had been the focus for much of the criticism levelled at tribunals. These rules were accordingly reviewed by a committee which subsequently recommended their extension and clarification.[23] The committee hoped that revamping the rules would lead to greater consistency in their application. The new rules were introduced in conjunction with the Mental Health Act 1983. Amongst others, there were provisions which made it necessary to disclose all the relevant reports to patients (unless the tribunal concluded that such disclosure would 'adversely affect the health and welfare of the patient or others' R12(2)), and to give patients the decision in writing with reasons.

C. *The Membership of Tribunals in Restricted Cases*

(i) The impetus for change Under the Mental Health Act 1959 there was no distinction between the membership of the panels dealing with restricted cases and non-restricted cases. Both types of tribunal were presided over by legal members with 'such legal experience as the Lord Chancellor considers suitable'—normally barristers or solicitors of some local standing.[24] In 1982 it was announced that the government proposed both to extend the tribunals' powers in restricted cases and also to strengthen their membership, by ensuring that restricted tribunals would be chaired by lawyers with 'substantial judicial experience in the criminal courts'.[25] Lord Belstead argued that the power to release restricted patients who might have been convicted of very serious crimes carried with it a 'formidable responsibility'.[26] It was therefore felt to be essential that the power to discharge should be vested in those who had the 'confidence of the public and of the judiciary'.[27] Since alteration in the tribunals' membership was not strictly necessary for the new legislative provisions to comply with the European Court's judgment in *X. v. the United Kingdom* it clearly requires some further explanation.

The crux of the European Court's criticism was that restricted patients had no right of access to have the lawfulness of their detention determined by a court. What was meant by a court was

---

[23] See the unpublished discussion paper by the Committee on Mental Health Review Tribunal Procedures. DHSS (1978).
[24] Mental Health Act 1959, Schedule 1(*a*).
[25] Lord Belstead, *Parl. Debates*, HL, vol. 426, col. 761, 25 Jan. 1982.
[26] Ibid.   [27] Ibid.

not entirely clear; it did not necessarily signify a court of law of the classic kind, but certainly required a body with judicial character which afforded the minimum procedural guarantees and was independent of the executive and of the parties to the case. And what was meant by the term 'judicial'? One of the principal characteristics of judicial power is that proceedings terminate in an order or decision which is binding and conclusive on both parties; the precise nature of the judicial procedure may be flexible provided that it is appropriate to the kind of deprivation of liberty in question.

Tribunals as constituted under the 1959 Act, acting merely in an advisory capacity, did not have the characteristics of a court, nor were their proceedings judicial. However, once given the power to discharge restricted cases, as proposed under the new legislative provisions, the tribunals satisfied both criteria seemingly required by the European Court's decision.[28] Yet this posed a clear dilemma. How might the government ensure, if the tribunals were to share with the Home Secretary the responsibility for determining whether restricted patients were entitled to be released, that the public would be placed at no greater risk than under the existing system?

Questions relating to the public's safety have been a predominant concern of successive Home Secretaries. The Home Secretary may properly be regarded as the 'guardian of the public interest'.[29] Indeed, it has been argued in the House of Lords that the Secretary of State is 'the *only* party capable of representing any interest the public may have in opposing an application for discharge' (emphasis added).[30] Acting in an executive capacity when discharging restricted patients, it is clearly not inappropriate for Home Secretaries to take full account of any lingering doubts there may be about the consequences of a decision to discharge for the public's safety, particularly since restriction orders are imposed primarily on protective grounds. Yet, even before the 1983 Act, if patients were *not* suffering, there would have been no

---

[28] The recent case of *Associated Newspaper Group plc* (see Appendix 3) controversially found the tribunal not to be a 'court' for the purposes of the Contempt of Court Act 1981.

[29] See the High Court cases of *Campbell* and *Lord* in Appendix 3.

[30] See the judgment of Lord Bridge in *Secretary of State for the Home Department* v. *Oxford Regional Mental Health Review Tribunal and another* [1987] 3 All ER 2 Oct 1987 8–14 at p. 10. This related to an appeal in *Campbell* above; see also Appendix 3.

basis for continuing detention even if they remained a risk to the public.[31] However, where in the Home Secretary's opinion, such a risk to the public existed, the view was repeatedly taken that the absence of the disorder had to be established *beyond all doubt* before patients would be discharged. Thus, Home Secretaries exercised their executive powers very cautiously. The conflict between individual and societal rights was resolved, in practice, by Home Secretaries adopting, on the one hand, a narrow view of individual rights and, on the other, a broad interpretation of what society should rightfully be protected from.[32]

(ii) Appointing judicial members to the tribunal Clearly the government was worried that the public would not have confidence in the tribunals as constituted under the 1959 Act, even though the legal members were appointed by the Lord Chancellor. Bearing in mind the substantial criticisms of the operation of these earlier tribunals and of the quality of their decision-making, this fear was perhaps justified (Peay 1981). But was this not an argument for removing the decision from the tribunals altogether and perhaps placing it instead in the Crown Courts? This was a solution which had been canvassed but rejected. Partly because of the existing pressure of work in the Crown Courts and the fact that extra judicial manpower would be required; and partly because it was recognized that the tribunals had built up considerable expertise in dealing with these cases. Their flexible procedures and inquisitorial stance were felt to be more appropriate for dealing with mentally abnormal offenders than Crown Courts schooled in the tradition of adversarial procedures.

Once the decision had been made to leave restricted cases with the tribunal, why were no additional changes proposed to improve the quality of their decision-making? The explanation for this may

[31] Of course, as it was clearly difficult to be sure that a mental disorder which was once present had become undeniably absent, it was exceedingly difficult for patients to establish to the satisfaction of the Home Secretary that their detention was no longer necessary or indeed justified.

[32] It is difficult to ascertain precisely what criteria the Home Secretary presently takes into account when exercising his concurrent power to release restricted patients. However, this research study will show that the advice offered to the tribunals in restricted cases continues to reflect underlying caution by the Home Secretary. It seems unlikely therefore that, when the power to release is exercised independently of the tribunals, the Home Secretary does not similarly take full account of criteria relating to the public's safety.

lie in the government's emphasis on the need to appoint those with criminal court experience. The likelihood of a tribunal so constituted making inappropriate decisions and releasing patients who could pose a risk to the public would, it was believed, be reduced. Therefore, the public's confidence in the system could be ensured. Furthermore, judicial confidence in the new system might be enhanced. This was considered an important factor since, if those who had the responsibility for imposing restriction orders were not happy about the system of release, they might be reluctant to impose such orders in the first instance. Judges in criminal cases, who might be considering making restriction orders, must not be able to regard them as a soft option; they had to be assured that the decision to release would be handled properly and doubts relating to the public's safety would be given due consideration. Giving the responsibility for the decision to tribunals presided over by lawyers with similar experience to Crown Court judges would thus, it was felt, satisfy both objectives at one and the same time. It was implicitly believed that an overall improvement in the quality of decisions to release would be achieved, thereby making further modifications to the tribunal redundant.

But, which lawyers with criminal court experience were deemed to be appropriate for this onerous role? Originally it was proposed that recorders from the Crown Court should undertake the tribunal work, but this solution was regarded as unsatisfactory once the number of likely hearings had been estimated. As recorders only sit part-time as judges, it was anticipated that about fifty appointments would have been necessary. This would have run the risk of introducing a considerable element of inconsistency into the decisions reached. Accordingly, it was decided that a smaller number of full-time circuit judges should undertake the work in addition to their Crown Court duties.[33]

Yet, in order to maintain some flexibility in the arrangements, the government decided that there should be no exclusive requirement that circuit judges should preside in restricted cases; indeed, there are no statutory limitations on the qualifications of presiding

---

[33] Judges were selected on the basis of their experience and willingness to adopt the new role, also taking into account their geographical location and accessibility to those hospitals where most of the restricted cases would be heard. Those circuit judges with the greatest experience were not requested to sit as tribunal judges largely because the circuit presiding judges showed some reluctance to lose these individuals from full-time circuit duties.

lawyers.[34] Other lawyers of suitable experience and standing may thus be designated for this role. A number of recorders who are Queen's Counsel have been duly appointed.

(iii) The role of the regional chairmen The appointment of circuit judges and recorders was not without its difficulties. The regional chairmen, who had built up considerable experience in dealing with restricted cases under the 1959 Act, if only in an advisory fashion, understandably felt ousted. Their role in the future was to be confined to civil admissions and hospital-order cases, where patients were not considered to pose a risk of serious harm to the public. Originally it had been proposed that where recorders were to sit, the regional chairmen might still preside over the tribunals and the former merely act as a fourth member. However, this suggestion was universally disliked. Furthermore, once circuit judges were nominated, the presence of another lawyer on the tribunal seemed to make even less sense—although no statutory bar to this exists. Finally, it was mooted that restricted cases might be divided into two categories, with easy cases going to the regional chairmen and the remaining cases going before a circuit judge, thereby creating a two-tier system. This proposal was also rejected; Parliament had been assured that restricted cases would be dealt with by lawyers with substantial judicial experience in the Crown Courts. The regional chairmen, although very experienced in tribunal work, did not have the necessary Crown Court experience.

There are a number of ironies arising out of the arrangements that were finally introduced. Many of the legal (but non-judicial) members believed that it was iniquitous that there should be two types of tribunal, for restricted and non-restricted cases; not all of the judicial members appointed have 'substantial judicial experience' in the criminal courts, although they may have substantial experience there as advocates; and the responsibility for pre-hearing procedures, including ensuring that cases are speedily and justly determined and resolving questions concerning disclosure, still lies with the regional chairmen.[35]

---

[34] S(1)(a) of Schedule 2 of the 1983 Act merely notes that legal members will be 'appointed by the Lord Chancellor' and have 'such legal experience as the Lord Chancellor considers suitable'. (see also rule 8(3) MHRT Rules). In this respect the regional chairman could have been designated as suitable to preside in restricted cases; however, the Lord Chancellor has declined to take that step.

[35] See Rules 5 and 13 of the MHRT Rules 1983.

Perhaps the greatest irony arises out of the way in which the new arrangements were presented to Parliament. Lord Belstead stated that, since there was no limitation on the numbers of members who could sit on panels, restricted tribunals would have available to them the 'experience and expertise ... of members of the existing legal panels'. He continued 'It appears to the government to be absolutely vital that tribunals carrying out such an important new role should have available to them the wisdom and knowledge of those who are already experienced in tribunal work.'[36] Yet, despite these laudable sentiments, the regional chairmen have not been involved on a day-to-day basis with restricted cases. Nor have they sat alongside circuit judges hearing such cases—arguably the arena in which their experience might most valuably have been brought to bear.

At this stage, one crucial question cannot be avoided. Will the new tribunals, with members of the judiciary presiding, be capable both of protecting the public, as the Home Secretary had striven to do, and of providing an effective safeguard for the liberty of detained patients, the traditional function of the tribunal? It has already been argued that protecting the public's safety is not an inappropriate objective in respect of the Home Secretary's exercise of discretion. However, given both the European Court's ruling and the statutory constraints discussed earlier, under which the tribunals exercise their powers (namely, that detention can only be justified in the continuing presence of disorder and not merely by a potential threat to the public's safety), are these two objectives compatible from the perspective of the tribunal? Or, is one to be achieved at the expense of the other? Verdun-Jones (1986: 111) has succinctly summarized this dilemma and predicted its likely outcome.'The inevitable conflict between the Janus-faced goals of protecting society on the one hand, and the mentally disordered individual on the other, has generally been resolved at the expense of the latter'. Whether the new restricted tribunals were to follow this path was one of the questions the research on which this book is based set out to investigate.

III. CONCLUSIONS

At the start of this chapter four main areas of conflict were identified as being likely to confront tribunals making decisions to

---

[36] Lord Belstead, *Parl. Debates*, HL, vol. 426, col. 762, 25 Jan. 1982.

release patients from hospital. First, there were those between a patient's rights and the interests of society as a whole; secondly, those between the rights of patients and those individual members of the society who might constitute their 'victims' were they to be discharged; third, conflicts between individual patients' therapeutic interests and their legal rights; and finally, those between the tribunals' formal role and that which they may strive to attain—namely, representing a safeguard for patients' rights and achieving a balance between this function and their wish either to protect the interests of the wider community or to act in what they perceived to be patients' best interests.

Aside from constraining the process whereby decisions are made in an attempt to achieve some form of procedural justice, it is clear from the statutory criteria governing tribunals' decisions that the 1983 Act is not principally concerned with achieving substantive justice. There is no exhaustive list of rules and principles designed to determine the outcome of decisions. Rather, the criteria, which are couched in the negative, merely concern themselves with what may not be done to individuals and represent the law's interest in achieving a form of 'negative substantive justice'.[37] The dual criteria, namely severity of the disorder combined with a justification for compulsory treatment, set some limits on the potential for erosion of individual rights in the name of societal goals. Hence, a patient's negative rights impose positive duties on the tribunal and these are enshrined within the statute.[38] But, the combination of procedural fairness with negative substantive justice none the less confers considerable discretion on decision-makers.

Moreover, it is clear that tribunal decisions are not made in a

[37] Andrew Ashworth has used the term 'negative substantive justice' to distinguish this approach in the law from that generally recognized as substantive justice: namely, a form of the law that is concerned to determine that certain outcomes do take place. Procedural justice, negative substantive justice, and substantive justice may be regarded as providing a range of legal strategies—from attempts to regulate process, through attempts to determine outcomes by regulating what may not be done to individuals, to the most stringent attempts to regulate what will be done to individuals. Between them they may cover both the form and the substance of legal decisions. For a discussion of negative rights see also Stone (1975, p.15).

[38] This is the reverse of the more usual position where positive rights are assumed to confer negative duties—for example, to refrain from obstructing action or interfering with choice. See Waldron (1984 at p. 11). See also Appendix 1 for the tribunal's full statutory criteria.

vacuum. Rather, they constitute one part of a dynamic system for release. Indeed, not all other decision-makers share the tribunals' perspective. The Secretary of State undoubtedly regards his principal client as the public; his decisions to release, although similarly bound by the Act, reflect a different emphasis on the interpretation of the facts of any individual case. Protecting the public by requiring an absolute guarantee of the absence of mental disorder shifts the balance from a consideration of the general probability of risk to a specific consideration of the perception of risk in an individual case. The two are clearly not one and the same.[39] Finally, there is another conflict arising out of that between patients' interests and their rights, which has been evident in the discussion: namely, the tension between consistency and flexibility. Consistency in the procedures adopted and between the decisions reached is a necessary prerequisite for achieving procedural justice. Yet, in any given case, the patient may be better served by sensitivity on the part of the tribunal to his or her individual circumstances and needs. What merit can there be in putting a severely disturbed patient, who has no obvious desire to leave hospital, through the trauma of a tribunal hearing? An answer can be provided if a rights-based perspective is adopted. But should the tribunal enjoy sufficient discretion to avoid the necessity for the question?

The themes which will recur repeatedly throughout this book will therefore be focused within three critical areas: the nature of the law, the objectives of the tribunal system, and the method of application of the criteria. The issues of rights versus rights, rights versus interests, consistency versus flexibility, and realistic versus idealistic goals will be played out within those areas and subjected to empirical examination.

[39] See Grisso (1988). Grisso notes that dangerousness judgments are relative risk attributions. By this he means that a judgment of dangerousness is not an absolute prediction that the individual will commit a violent act, but rather that this is a case in which the perceived degree of risk exceeds a level that the decision-maker is prepared to tolerate. See also Peay (1982b).

2. The Research Setting

The exercise of legal discretion is shrouded in mystique. What legal decision-makers do, and how they do it, has been the subject of considerable inquiry. But, as Hawkins noted in 1983, this work had resulted only in 'a very imperfect understanding of the ways in which legal discretion is exercised'. He substantially attributed this to 'the poverty of research in method and conception' (1983 a: 7). Yet, it is evident that there are real practical impediments which have constrained research efforts. Not only is the exercise of legal discretion frequently inaccessible, in the sense that decisions may be taken behind closed doors, but also, where decisions are made by single individuals, as in the exercise of judicial discretion, the decisions are essentially invisible. What goes on inside the heads of such individuals occurs behind the ultimate closed door. Routinely, researchers have had to resort to (i) defining what were the objective facts of a case for the decision-maker, (ii) noting the outcome as explained by the decision-maker, and (iii) intuiting the process occurring in between. Such an approach, given Gottfredson and Gottfredson's assertion that decisions are 'rarely ... rational' (1988: v), seemed hardly likely to produce convincing insights.

In this context, the present study of tribunal decision-making was exceptional in two respects. First, as tribunal decisions are made jointly by three people with divergent experience, it is necessary during their deliberations for members to explain and justify their own views to one another, if indeed they have formed any views. Hence, the visibility of the decision-making process is increased. Secondly, since I was given permission to observe many of these deliberations, it was not necessary for my understanding of the decision process to be solely reliant upon second-hand data.

This chapter starts with a brief description of the theoretical locus and objectives of the research, the methodology adopted, and the impetus for it. But, the bulk of the chapter is devoted to setting the scene—both statistically and contextually—for the subsequent empirical work.

I. THEORETICAL CONTEXT

The judicious use of legal discretion can serve to resolve, in a humane and sensitive manner, the conflict between two competing legal goals: first, the requirement for equality before the law, namely that individuals should be treated equally given violations of the same law; and secondly, the pursuit of equity. An equitable basis for decisions recognizes that the law cannot be applied fairly in individual cases without considering special mitigating circumstances. But, as Davis (1976: 52) notes 'Discretionary power can be either too broad or too narrow. When it is too broad, justice may suffer from arbitrariness or inequality. When it is too narrow, justice may suffer from insufficient individualizing.' Decision-making bodies, vested with discretionary powers, should strive both to avoid the inconsistency in their decisions that arises from treating similar cases differently, and to ensure that justice is achieved in individual cases. It is all too easy for research to demonstrate that decision-makers have failed in either respect.

Where a decision-making body is concerned principally with individualizing decisions, for example when a court has determined not to pass a tariff-based sentence or where therapeutic goals are pressing, as is frequently an issue for tribunals, there is arguably a greater adherence to the concept of equity. Although there may be both procedural constraints and formal and informal restraints in place to counterbalance equity with equality (for example peer pressure, *stare decisis*, and the threat of appellate review), these have been of variable effectiveness, and dependent partly upon the forum in which the decisions are made. For example, in individualized sentencing, strict legal regulation has tended to take second place to the attainment of full information.[1] Moreover, in tribunal decision-making, a body of case law is only slowly evolving to assist decision-makers, and the possibility of appeal remains remote in the vast majority of cases. Therefore, how tribunal members exercise their discretion, and whether all the recipients of its decisions have an equal opportunity to experience the benefits and injustices of these practices, are questions of considerable interest.

Moving on from the influence that decision-makers' goals can have on the exercise of discretion, it is evident that a number of

[1] Some change is evident in this arena in that the courts will not readily accommodate hearsay or entirely uncorroborated evidence even in mitigation.

other factors can affect how the law is applied in individual cases. The traditional legal view of decision-making assumed that only legally significant variables, such as the facts of the case, governed decisions, whilst the law could be viewed as a constant and the personality of the decision-maker an irrelevance. However, this view has been gradually replaced. 'It would be foolish to assert that when judges are engaged in solving problems all of their personal attitudes and values become dissipated in a bright glow of objectivity' (Fuller 1966: 1619). Indeed, there has been considerable research effort devoted to demonstrating that variables relating to the individual decision-maker could go a long way to explaining inconsistency in decisions reached.[2] Or, as Hogarth (1971: 350) asserted 'one can explain more about sentencing by knowing a few things about the judge than by knowing a great deal about the facts of the case'.

Tribunal decision-making has not been immune from this approach. That which tribunal members bring with them to the tribunal setting, namely preconceived attitudes and knowledge about the issues at hand, has been demonstrated to constitute a unique framework within which all new information about the case under consideration is assessed (Peay 1980).[3] Moreover, this frame of reference has been shown to have a powerful effect on the nature of the decisions reached by any individual member and indeed, to exert a significant impact on the nature of the decision made by the tribunal.

Although research has only just begun to chart the subjective complexity of decision-making as an individual process, numerous studies have illustrated that, given key information, predicting decision outcomes can be a surprisingly straightforward procedure (Simon 1971) particularly where there is some pre-existing knowledge of a decision-maker's prevailing philosophy towards the task faced (Hogarth 1971). These seemingly counterintuitive findings can be partly accounted for by the limited cognitive and processing abilities of human decision-makers. Thus, what appears inordinately complex is frequently transformed into a comparatively straightforward choice. This may occur, for example, through the

[2] See for example Hogarth (1971), and T. Palys and S. Divorski 'Judicial Decision-Making. An Examination of Sentencing Disparity among Canadian Provincial Court Judges', in Muller, Blackman, and Chapman, (eds.) (1984).

[3] In essence, members' attitudes and knowledge constitute one aspect of what Hawkins (1986) has coined the decision-makers' 'frame'.

processes of selective attention to and perception of the information presented. The cognitive limitations of decision-makers may also account for other aspects of the 'predictability' of decision outcomes. Crombag *et al.* (1975) noted that decision-makers tended to arrive at an early provisional decision for which they subsequently found supporting arguments. In an experimental situation, tribunal members were shown rarely to depart from a decision made on a limited amount of information, even where they were subsequently given conflicting information (Peay 1981). Thus, although decision-making may subjectively feel instinctive and inaccessible, the articulated outcome may be based on only a part of the information available; reaching it, therefore, may be less complex than taking part in the process would suggest. Moreover, the influence of 'conclusory' information, presented early in the evidential sequence, can be critical. This may be enhanced where there is deference to the views of those providing the information (particularly where those sources are attributed with considerable knowledge or status).[4]

Thus, it should come as no surprise that cases presented to the tribunal have been shown by research to be reinterpreted both against the background of the individual member's unique frame and against their early assessment of the case formed on an initial reading of the case papers.[5] Any further research would need to be sensitive both to these psychological findings, and to the legal and sociological contexts in which decisions are made. Once it is recognized that decision-making takes place in the real world and is subject to a series of influences which interact simultaneously, only a holistic research approach will suffice.

II. RESEARCH OBJECTIVES

Given the fact that changes had been wrought in virtually every important aspect of the tribunal system, comparative research over time, adopting either a quantitative decision-making approach or attempting to assess the effectiveness of the innovations, would have been problematic. As a consequence, the research was

[4] See Nuffield (1982, p. 11).
[5] In most instances (S2 cases aside) members will have been in possession of these case papers for at least a week before the hearing date.

planned with modest objectives: first, to describe the impact, if any, of some of the new provisions, particularly with respect to the application by tribunals of their powers in restricted cases and the operation of the new concepts of treatability and viability; secondly, to describe the way in which tribunals reached decisions. The intention was to diagnose, rather than remedy, potential problems.

However, even mere description in the field of decision-making is demanding. Tribunal review should be conceived of as a process. The decision ultimately taken will be constrained not only by the statutory criteria, but also by the prior structuring of information. Indeed, the choices made by those who provide the evidential bases for tribunal decisions, for example patients and their Responsible Medical Officers (RMOs), will be critical in influencing the final outcome. Similarly, their views about the tribunal's function, and the matters they will consider relevant, will structure the information these parties choose to present to the tribunal. This, in turn, can affect the tribunal's perceptions of what decision options are realistic. Clearly, the study needed to evaluate the tribunals' practices from a range of perspectives held by key participants in the process, whether they were formal or informal decision-makers. Equally it was logical that the study should take as its starting-point the initial decision by a patient to make an application, and progress chronologically thereafter. Yet assessing the applicability and suitability of the new criteria and procedures from the perspective of the tribunal and in the context of the kinds of patients appearing before tribunals was also of importance. Therefore, the research problem was to be addressed from the direction of both the providers and the assessors of information.

A. Methodology

(i) Procedures Since the objectives of the study were primarily descriptive, rather than prescriptive, extensive observation, supplemented by limited interviewing and documentary analysis, represented the most appropriate methodology. The formal aspects of the research were divided into three parts: (*a*) semi-structured interviewing with patients, RMOs, and judicial mem-

bers of the tribunal based in one Special Hospital region;[6] (b) observations of restricted and non-restricted tribunal hearings held in Special Hospitals, secure units, and local hospitals administered by two regional tribunal offices; (c) documentary analysis of case files held at these two offices.

(ii) Problems Even though the research objectives were modest, the procedures adopted were not without drawbacks. Interviewing decision-makers after the event constitutes a problematic strategy and one which was employed warily. Interviewing techniques are reliant upon individual phenomonology, which is, at best, notoriously ephemeral. As illustrated in the field of sentencing, there is a natural tendency for decision-makers to articulate the outcome of the decision without fully detailing the subjective processes that led to it. Indeed, those who make decisions are not necessarily the most accurate observers of their own reasoning and behaviour.[7] Or, as Hawkins (1986: 1175) has succinctly summarized, there may well be 'a disjunction between word and deed, and possibly one also between thought and deed'. Similarly, decision-makers may not even be aware of the numerous cognitive errors to which they are prone (Fitzmaurice and Pease 1986). In their review of research in legal decision-making, Konečni and Ebbesen (1984: 17) concluded that the available empirical findings represented 'a strong indictment of the use of interviews, questionnaires, rating-scales, and experimental situations'. Given all these cautionary tales interviewing techniques were used in this study primarily as a backdrop, to provide the context within which the observations of tribunal decisions were made and ensure a more balanced combination of methods.

Relying principally on ecologically valid research, namely the observations of tribunal hearings and deliberations, was thought likely to provide a better understanding of the tribunal's decision *process*. Observational techniques can certainly help to counteract

---

[6] Peay (1980) examined extensively the views of medical, legal, and lay members of the tribunal and empirically assessed their independent impact on tribunal decisions. Lay members, in particular, were found routinely to have a minimal impact on both the proceedings and decisions of tribunals. In the light of this research it was felt sufficient formally to interview only the new category of judicial members.

[7] See generally Ashworth *et al.* (1984).

the subjective perceptions, reflected in the interviews, of those involved in the tribunal system. But, wholesale reliance on observation has its own drawbacks. First, it gives prominence to the subjective, and arguably fallible, perceptions of the researcher. However, accounting for one set of semi-accessible prejudices, one's own, may be preferable to juggling with many. Secondly, the problems arising out of experimenter effects are writ large. And third, the difficulties of interpreting the data are enhanced when only one researcher is present at the event in question. Yet, even quantitative research requires interpretation of the data obtained. Or, as Claude Bernard's aphorism that 'One only needs statistics when one doesn't understand causation' implies, a quantitative approach should arguably be perceived as a method of last resort.

Some of the difficulties likely to result from the use of observational techniques may have been alleviated by the extensive informal contact I enjoyed throughout the study, and by my historical familiarity with the ethos of the tribunal system. Speculation may have evolved into informed speculation. At the very least, this close contact enabled me to enjoy a quality of feedback about the preliminary findings which is so frequently denied to professional decision-makers and is, incidentally, the root cause of so much criticism of the decision-making structures imposed on them.

(iii) Context In 1985 over 2,400 tribunal hearings were held, of which 30 per cent were restricted cases.[8] The bulk of these patients (in excess of 70 per cent) were detained in Special Hospitals. Yet, the statistics reveal that the probability of patients being discharged by the tribunal varied according to the Special Hospital in which they were detained.

One specific aspect of the study, namely matching cases dealt with in two different hospital regions (Regions A and B in Table 2.1), derived from understandable concern about these disparities in the discharge profiles of tribunals. If consistency in approach was considered an important objective for the tribunal system, then regional variations in discharge rates, particularly where they reached statistical significance, required some explanation.

---

[8] Figures compiled from DHSS statistics in DHSS (1985), supplemented by unpublished statistics for the period until 30 June 1986.

Table 2.1 Summary of restricted cases determined by tribunals in Special Hospitals in three regions for the period 1984–1986 (until 30 June)

	Absolute Discharge	Conditional Discharge	No Discharge	Total Cases Determined	% Discharges
Region A	2	17	354	376	6
Region B	5	64	371	440	16
Region C	11	27	330	368	10
TOTAL	18	108	1055	1184	11

A number of points should be noted from this table.

1. Absolute discharges make up only 14 per cent of all the patients discharged. Clearly, the opportunity which conditional discharge offers to monitor patients' progress and recall them to hospital (if there is any deterioration in their condition causing concern) creates an attractive option for tribunals.

2. There are statistically significant differences in the discharge rates (significant at greater than 0.001) between regions A and B. These statistical differences are sustained when a year-by-year comparison is undertaken.

3. Since the tribunals exercise their powers concurrently with the Secretary of State, the number of patients discharged on his authority on a region-by-region basis may influence the numbers of patients discharged by the tribunal. These figures are not complete but it is worth noting the following: (*a*) the majority of all restricted patients are discharged by the tribunal and not by the Secretary of State. In 1984 the tribunals were responsible for 67 per cent of discharges, whilst in 1985, the latest year for which figures are available, the Secretary of State made 59 conditional discharges and 6 absolute discharges whilst the figures for the tribunal were 83 and 18 respectively. Thus 61 per cent of cases were discharged by the tribunal. (*b*) For 1985, for which comparable figures are available, the regional breakdown from the Special Hospitals, with Secretary of State's discharges in brackets, was as follows: A 6 (6); B 17 (6); C 10 (1) (Home Office, *Mentally Disordered Offenders in England and Wales*, Table 8). On the basis of these figures it appears that the Secretary of State exercises his power to discharge as frequently in Region A, where the tribunal discharged comparatively infrequently, as in Region B, where

there were twice as many discharges by the tribunal. Thus, it is not immediately apparent that the Secretary of State's decisions explain the regional differences in discharge rates from the Special Hospitals: (c) Like the tribunal, the Secretary of State predominantly discharges conditionally rather than absolutely.

There are a number of potential explanations for these differences. First, they may be attributed to real differences between the nature of the cases heard by the tribunals in regions A and B. Secondly, they may be due to similar cases being treated differently because of the way in which the statutory criteria are interpreted and applied by the tribunals in the two regions. Third, there may be differences in the way in which similar patients are perceived by the two panels. Finally, there may be other contributory factors, as yet unknown. Without controlling for differences between the patient populations it would be impossible to draw any conclusions—even of the most tentative nature.

In order to address these difficulties, two chapters, 6 and 7, deal respectively with the cases of forty patients with principal diagnoses of psychopathic disorder and forty patients with diagnoses of mental illness.[9] The patients were detained in Special Hospitals in the two tribunal regions A and B above. The hospitals are hereinafter known as Acheland and Bendene, with the patients being identifiable only in terms of the location of their detention by the suffixes A or B.

Patients in the samples were matched in pairs on the basis of five factors: their psychiatric diagnoses, age, gender, period in confinement, and nature of the offence committed prior to their current admission to hospital. The matching was not exact in every case, but where differences were apparent in, for example, the numbers of years in confinement, the cases were paired because of other overriding qualitative similarities. Data relating to a number of other criteria were also recorded.[10]

---

[9] Although a majority of the tribunal hearings were observed live, in order to obtain two matched samples of patients detained in Acheland and Bendene whose cases were reviewed during the period Feb. 1985 to Nov. 1986, it was necessary to draw a proportion of the cases on a retrospective basis from the files kept at the tribunal offices.

[10] For example, Mental Health Act section; application or reference; represented or unrepresented (solicitor or barrister); independent psychiatric report (written or oral testimony); presence of exceptional witnesses (social worker, probation officer, family, etc.); views of RMO; views of Home Office.

Both Chapters 6 and 7 start by presenting the breakdown of the outcomes of the matched cases. This illustrates the predictability of the tribunals' decisions. Following this, there is a lengthier analysis which sets out, why, in individual cases, the tribunal seemingly felt constrained to reach the decision they did. The cases are not presented rigorously in their pairs, but rather, a thematic approach is adopted. Although the analysis is none the less occasionally repetitive, it is necessary to present the cases in this detailed manner in order to do justice to the nature of the data collected and the fine distinctions drawn by the tribunals in their reasoning. The presentation further substantiates the argument, made earlier, that whilst it may be comparatively easy to determine what the outcome of a decision will be, understanding the process by which the tribunal arrived at that decision remains shrouded in qualifications.

The impetus for initially matching cases was not merely to illustrate the commonplace finding that apparently similar cases will be treated in very different ways by different decision-makers. Rather, the approach attempted to illustrate *how* seemingly similar cases may be perceived in different ways (namely, the variables of diagnosis, nature of offence, etc. on which patients were objectively matched, may not be the criteria which the tribunals perceive as most relevant in their decisions and therefore the cases are not similar *to them*) and *why* this should have led tribunals to feel impelled to reach the decisions they did. Thus, the intention was to illustrate the distinction between objective comparability and the subjective complexity with which decision-makers perceive the cases presented to them.

B. The Working Context of the Research

Two observations must be made at this stage. First, during the period of the research the tribunal system operated under stress. Admittedly the system was still in its comparative infancy following the changes introduced by the 1983 Act. But the shortcomings could not be readily ignored. Administrators battled with shortages of staff and resources; tribunal members were frequently frustrated both by the consequences of these shortages and by the general problems arising out of organizing hearings where many parties' interests had to be juggled. Delays and adjournments were common, either because the relevant material or personnel were not available on the day of the hearing, or because some parties had not had access to all of the information to be presented. Not infrequently independent psychiatric reports were produced on the morning of the hearing. This would necessitate last-minute telephone calls to the Secretary of State (such calls were made to the division of the Home Office dealing with these matters for the Home Secretary) and occasionally even adjournments to allow the Home Office to comment at length. Similar frustrations arose out of the lack of information about potential placements either in the community or in other hospitals to which patients might progress. More frequently such frustrations arose because no one was apparently prepared to offer patients facilities outside secure hospitals (despite the best efforts of all involved) and yet the tribunal felt that the patient no longer needed the degree of security offered by the Special Hospitals. Finally, tribunals were often frustrated by their own limited powers.

Secondly, the extensive informal contact enjoyed during the research did not lead me to change the assessment of the tribunal members and those who work behind the scenes that I had formed during my previous research: namely, that their approach to their respective roles was that of 'thoughtful, dedicated and caring individuals' (Peay 1981: 168). It could, of course, be argued that this assessment is double-edged. These qualities may be desirable, but in themselves they are insufficient to satisfy what might reasonably be expected of a decision-making body charged with protecting individual liberties. However the source of real insufficiency arguably lay primarily with the inadequate tools which were brought to bear on the problems to be solved and with the absence of relevant resources in the community to provide tribunals and patients with realistic options.

(i) Informal Contact As noted above, extensive informal contact was enjoyed with numerous parties involved in the operation of the tribunal system. Such contact varied from immersion in administrative contexts—long periods were spent in two of the major regional tribunal offices undertaking studies of case files—to informal contact with tribunal members, most commonly over lunch, during those days spent observing tribunal hearings. These extended contacts also permitted the research to be informed by the views of, for example, nursing staff and psychologists at the hospitals visited, patients' legal representatives, and those inde-

pendent psychiatrists who attended the tribunals. Finally, there was more limited contact with patients' families and friends.

Similarly, meetings took place with those involved 'behind the scenes'; the Lord Chancellor's Department were most helpful in providing background information, as were both the administrative division at the Home Office dealing with restricted cases (C3) and the DHSS. Finally, as the research progressed there were a number of opportunities to present the preliminary findings of the research at conferences, seminars, and training exercises (meetings of the tribunal members to discuss matters of policy and keep abreast of developments in, for example, legal judgments) at which members of the tribunal panels or others involved in an administrative capacity were present. All of these meetings were invaluable, not only because they contextualized the specific research findings, but also because they created an opportunity to check out the wider validity of those preliminary findings.

(ii) Formal contact   The findings from the formal aspects of the research are presented in two groups of three chapters. The first three discuss the interviews with patients, responsible medical officers, and judicial members of the tribunal (Chapters 3, 4, and 5), and attempt to present the perspectives of these parties on the role and functioning of the tribunal within one Special Hospital, namely Acheland.

They also provide a partial backdrop to the subsequent chapters, which set out the observational findings. Two of the chapters (6 and 7) deal specifically with eighty hearings in Acheland and Bendene; whilst the final empirical chapter reviews the hearings of twenty patients detained outside the Special Hospital system, and deals primarily, but not solely, with non-restricted cases.[11]

The second half of Chapter 8 is based on a retrospective analysis of some 391 non-restricted cases in an attempt to explore the use of S72(2)—which required the tribunal to consider questions of treatability and viability (see Appendix 1). Technically, these criteria should only come into operation *after* the tribunal has decided that it is not obliged to discharge a non-restricted case under the statutory criteria laid out in S72(1)(*b*). They are thus designed to structure the tribunals' discretionary powers to dis-

[11] The cases in Ch. 8 are separately numbered from those in Chs. 6 and 7.

charge. However, in practice, such considerations may be found to have either little or no impact on members' decisions. Alternatively, they might generally underpin decision-making, and exert their influence by effectively stretching or shrinking the statutory criteria.

C. Locative Context

(i) Acheland's patient population To gain access to a Special Hospital patients are likely to have satisfied dual legal criteria: first, that they have been thought to require treatment 'under conditions of special security on account of their dangerous, violent or criminal propensities';[12] secondly, as the majority have had restriction orders imposed, that they have, of necessity, been thought to pose a risk of 'serious harm' to the public.[13] By definition therefore, patients admitted to the Special Hospitals will be treated with considerable caution.

It would be unwise to make generalizations about Acheland's patient population (then totalling approximately 520 patients); they could be characterized principally by their diversity. However, two points are worth stressing. First, there were no easy cases within the Special Hospitals. When interviewed, all of the RMOs were at pains to emphasize the complicated nature of their patients' problems, whether they derived from the inherent nature of the patient's disorder or from the systemic problems of finding patients appropriate placements. Amongst the difficult to manage group were those who had proved too disturbed or disruptive for other institutions to cope with. The Special Hospitals acted as the end of the line; a kind of final repository which could not refuse admission.[14] These patients frequently had massively disturbed backgrounds, sometimes with numerous previous admissions to psychiatric hospitals, prisons, and hostels; other forms of contact with welfare agencies were common. Their family and work

---

[12] S4, National Health Service Act 1977. Admission to the Special Hospitals is, in practice, controlled by the DHSS, who employ the criterion that the patient constitutes 'a grave and immediate danger' to others: DHSS (1983, paras 267–71) and DHSS (1987*b*).

[13] S41, Mental Health Act 1983 (or 'harm' under the 1959 Act).

[14] Even in cases where the RMOs might not have wished to admit patients, perhaps on the grounds that they were unlikely to respond to treatment, the DHSS, as hospital managers, could override their objections. Such occurrences were, however, rare.

relationships had also suffered, which in some instances exacerbated the difficulties of treating them. Other patients had come direct from the courts having committed one seemingly incomprehensible and horrific offence—often out of character. Treatment for these patients, who might neither accept their guilt, nor recognize that they were ill, nor demonstrate any insight into their condition if they did accept their need for help, was challenging. Or, as the medical director of one Special Hospital has stated,

It is sometimes hard to reject the suspicion that some patients are recommended for Special Hospitals more because they are considered dangerous, unusual and in need of containment than because of their supposed responsiveness to treatment, their motivation to receive it or their probable compliance with it . . . .

(Mawson 1983: 180).

Other categories of patients were more clearly difficult to place. Perhaps they should not have been sent to Acheland in the first instance; for example, patients who offended seriously, but during a comparatively short-lived bout of depression, or those who needed only medium security, but whom the appropriate unit would not accept because they were thought to require longer-term care. Some patients should have left the hospital years earlier, but hadn't; with their motivation to move on eroded and regarding Acheland as their home, they became even more difficult to place elsewhere. Thus, Acheland had to both care for and contain this range of patients—but often in different proportions.

Secondly, the hospital undoubtedly had a stigma attached to it, and certain expectations were generated of patients detained there. At the point of admission, patients had markedly abnormal backgrounds; indeed, at the time at which their offences were committed, many of the patients could have enjoyed some notoriety. Their Acheland and tribunal files fully record these aspects; similarly, incidents within the hospital environment were recorded, sometimes in meticulous detail. However, it was clearly more difficult to substantiate the non-eventful nature of the progress which most patients made within Acheland. The medical treatment patients received supressed their more worrying symptoms and the secure environment undoubtedly had a stabilizing and controlling influence. As in all institutions, patients were cushioned from the major stresses of life outside—admittedly they had to learn to cope with the special frustrations that enforced institutional life created—but the rapidity with which normality could be restored was astonishing.[15]

The net result was a surprisingly wide gap between how the patients appeared according to their files and how they presented in person within the institution. Patients invariably failed to match up to the expectations generated by their files. Yet it was this written information upon which many of those responsible for making decisions about patients, for example the Home Office, reached their initial (and often final) decisions. Similarly, it was this information, in conjunction with their pre-report clinical assessment of the patient, to which RMOs turned when writing their recommendations. RMOs frequently described patients initially, if not principally, in terms of their index offence—which may have occurred many years previously—and not primarily in terms of their histories within Acheland. One RMO put this succinctly when he remarked of the often competing interests of society and the patient—'society may loom larger because of past events'.

(ii) Patient subsample: Characteristics The patients interviewed were a random sample of patients who had tribunals pending on a given day. It was probable that there would be some differences between this sample and Acheland's total population, because the former, having exercised their rights to apply for a hearing, were in comparison likely to be somewhat better. However, a proportion of the sample had been referred automatically for a review of their case under the three-year rule.[16] As such, these patients were likely to be an exception to the rule.

Of the 26 patients interviewed there were 5 women and 21 men. They were distributed throughout Acheland's wards and in the care of 9 separate RMOs. Three patients were serving life sentences, having been first given life imprisonment and subsequently transferred under S47; 17 were on restriction orders (S37/41); 3 on hospital orders without restrictions (S37); and 3 on

---

[15] Yet it is also understandable that patients remained in Acheland for many years. Often there was no easy alternative for a patient—few local hospitals wished to expedite the return of patients they knew to be difficult; families were often reluctant or unable to offer accommodation; those with the authority to discharge were similarly cautious about exercising their powers where patients had a history of violence; some patients simply did not wish to leave the hospital.

[16] Automatic referrals occur under S68 for unrestricted patients and S71 for restricted patients (Mental Health Act 1983).

admission for treatment orders (S3). In total, 40 per cent of the women and 19 per cent of the men did not have restrictions attached to their detention orders; this can be explained on the grounds that many more of the male patients were admitted directly to Acheland from the courts with restriction orders attached, whilst on the female side of the hospital, more patients were admitted from local hospitals as unmanageable or disruptive.

Their principal Mental Health Act diagnostic classifications were as follows; mental illness 13 (mainly different forms of schizophrenia, but three were diagnosed as suffering from illnesses with major depressive components); psychopathic disorder 9; and 4 a combination of mental illness and psychopathic disorder (3 of these were women).[17] The association between their principal classification and whether or not they were receiving any medication was notable. Of the 13 mentally ill patients, 11 were, at the time of interview, receiving medication whilst of the 9 suffering with psychopathic disorder there was only one. All of the women, regardless of diagnosis, were on medication.

The offences which had caused them first to be admitted to Acheland varied from the most serious (2 murders, 4 manslaughters, 6 grievous bodily harm and 4 arsons) to the comparatively minor (5 criminal damage, assault, theft, etc.). Four of the offences had an explicit sexual element; 6 of the victims had close relationships with the patients (wives, sons, lovers, etc.), and 5 of the victims came to harm because of their professional relationship with the patients (psychiatrists, solicitors, clergy, etc.); 2 of the latter offences were categorized by the patients as 'cries for help'. Four of the victims had been incorporated into the patients' delusional systems (for example, they had experienced voices urging them to kill specific individuals).

There was no clear association between diagnosis and offence categories. With such a small sample it would be unwise to read too much into the figures; nevertheless two tendencies emerged. First, the least serious offences seem to have been committed by those suffering from mental illness rather than psychopathic disorder.[18] Secondly, those who had committed sexual offences

---

[17] Carlen (1983) has argued that female offenders are more likely to attract the label of 'psychopathic' than male offenders with similar histories. Coid (1987) also reports a greater preponderance of mixed diagnoses amongst female mentally disordered offenders.

[18] More extensive support for this proposition can be found in Dell and Robertson (1988).

were more likely to be diagnosed as suffering from psychopathic disorder than mental illness.

Of the 26 patients, 3 had been transferred from prison; and for 4 others it was their second period in Acheland—either because of recall or because of readmission. The average length of stay at the point of interview for the men was 8.5 years (range 18 months to 33 years) and for the women 4.5 years (range 19 months to 8 years). Virtually all of the patients knew their date of admission and all could tell me how long they had been in Acheland—even to the number of weeks. Some portrayed their plight in terms reminiscent of a scene from *The Count of Monte Cristo*. Despite all of the various benefits patients said they had received as a result of their stay in hospital, their subjective assessment of the experience of confinement undoubtedly was that it was punishing.

(iii) Acheland Hospital: Conflicting images of an institution's population Being a patient at Acheland aroused certain expectations not helped by the undoubted stigma associated with the hospital. Amongst the sample interviewed there were murderers, arsonists, and child sex offenders—society's bogey men and women. Even the files of those who had committed the least serious offences did not make pleasant reading.

Their psychiatric histories were similarly disturbing. Medical reports largely led me to expect a group of individuals who were either semi-literate, inarticulate, insightless, selfish, self-oriented, uncaring, deteriorated, or grossly psychotic. Even the staff, whom I saw briefly before and after the interviews, warned me of tendencies to lie; of violent unpredictability; of wily, devious individuals who were not to be trusted; and of patients with whom it was simply impossible to hold a conversation.[19]

Although some of the patients interviewed were clearly ill or suffering from the effects of medication or prolonged detention, none of them lived up to the expectations generated for them. They were surprisingly pleasant, co-operative, polite, thoughtful, articulate, well-orientated, and insightful about their own position and those of their fellow patients. Many left in my mind the question: 'Why was it they were still detained in Acheland?' It was

[19] One such remark illustrates the negative views staff frequently held about the patients. Following an interview with one patient I remarked casually in the nurses' office that he had seemed 'like a nice bloke'; with a questioning tone that implied 'how can that possibly be so?' the nurse replied 'he's in here' (or, he's nice because he's in here).

not difficult to understand why patients might experience anger and frustration in these circumstances.

Although the interviews with the patients and their RMOs concurred with regard to a number of factual matters, their perspective on, and interpretation of, events to which they were both party contrasted markedly. Similar disjunctions have already been noted between the image of the patients constructed by the staff and in medical reports, and the impression they created in face-to-face interactions.

Some of these disparities will have been inevitable. The RMOs, for example, may have been basing their views on the entire population of patients at Acheland, whilst those interviewed constituted what was arguably an 'improved' subsample. The fact that the interviewed patients largely had exercised their rights also set them somewhat apart. It might, of course, also be maintained that patients are on their best behaviour when being interviewed by researchers or, for that matter, appearing before the tribunal. There are however, a number of other factors which may contribute to the differing perceptions held by patients and RMOs, not the least amongst which is the arguable disincentive for patients to be wholly honest with their RMOs given the latter's custodial function.

In the empirical chapters which follow the patients' views are presented first, as their actions largely initiate the tribunal process. The strategy employed has been to allow these interviews to speak for themselves, relying heavily upon direct quotation, mainly without comment or analysis at these preliminary stages. Although only a small sample of RMOs and judicial members were interviewed, their responses are also dealt with at length. These two groups principally determine the likely length of stay of a significant proportion of the total population of restricted patients, and of some of those regarded as the most dangerous and disturbed in secure provisions; their decision-making skills are therefore critical.

Since Chapters 3, 4 and 5 are derived from individuals associated with Acheland Hospital, taken together they chronicle the complexity of the interactions between these three groups and their perceptions of one another. Finally, although these interactions may differ in their nature and extent at other hospitals, they none the less serve to chart the potential dynamics and resultant effects of the various parties' dealings on the proper functioning of the tribunal at one institution.

3. Praying Patience: The Patients' Perspectives

> The mere deprivation of liberty, however benign the administration of the place of confinement, is undeniably punishment.
>
> Raefelle Garofalo (1914 ed.)

Interviewing detained patients raises difficulties over and above those ordinarily entailed in conducting interviews. First, patients may be ill; or they may have been ill; or they may be on medication. Any of these factors can affect their ability (not necessarily their willingness) to give full and truthful answers. Secondly, although care was taken to explain to potential interviewees that as a researcher I could have no influence on their length of stay in Acheland, I was none the less a figure associated with authority.[1] As a 'captive' population, even if they recognized that co-operation would do them no good, patients may none the less have felt that non-co-operation might do them some harm. Verification of their replies therefore took on especial importance.[2] After checking, I found no indication that patients had deliberately lied to me and little indication that they were particularly confused about their own personal histories.

This chapter is based on the resultant often lengthy interviews

---

[1] I was ushered into a patient's presence by members of the nursing staff. Patients were told that the DHSS funded the research and that it was being undertaken with the agreement of their RMOs and the Acheland Ethics Committee. Following an explanation of the purpose of the interview, a patient's written consent was obtained. But it was almost unavoidable that they would have felt under some pressure. None the less, care was taken to guarantee patients' anonymity and to ensure that their comments were not passed on to any member of the hospital staff. Moreover, it was stressed that taking part would have no bearing on a patient's tribunal hearing (and, indeed, could have no bearing for those interviewed after the hearing had taken place).

[2] Prior to the interviews, any written information concerning patients' applications kept at the tribunal offices was reviewed, and in some cases ward notes were inspected. This information provided a factual basis concerning the patient's history, diagnosis, problems, and progress.

with twenty-six patients. In obtaining their consent, it was explained to patients that details of their individual cases were not of particular concern. Rather, the research was to focus on the general problems which they may have experienced with the tribunal process. In this respect they would be acting as spokespersons for other patients detained in Acheland.

The sample of patients interviewed was drawn randomly from all of those who had tribunal hearings pending on 20 February 1985. It included both restricted and non-restricted patients and those who had made applications or been referred automatically for hearings. Of the original sample of thirty patients four refused to be interviewed.[3]

On the date on which the sample was drawn, some of the patients' applications were well advanced and others had only just been made. It was a matter of concern to those involved in the tribunal system that it could take up to six months to make all the necessary arrangements for a hearing—the delays were particularly acute in restricted cases.[4] For the purposes of the research this was some consolation, since it enabled a proportion of the patients to be interviewed before, and the rest after their hearings took place.[5] This permitted some control over any bias in the patients' responses attributable to the outcome of their applications.

I. PATIENTS' RELATIONSHIPS WITH THEIR RESPONSIBLE MEDICAL OFFICERS

A. The Quantity and Quality of the Relationship

Patients' relationships with their RMOs could be characterized principally by the infrequency of the doctor–patient contact. That

[3] Two were actively psychotic. The third patient who refused was notorious within the hospital, as a 'non-co-operator'. The final patient refused before I could see him. I was informed by the charge nurse that the patient had recently received a recommendation for transfer from the tribunal. He was said to feel that since he had 'one foot out of the door' he didn't want to do anything that might disturb the plans for his transfer.

[4] This situation has somewhat improved. Delays for restricted cases do not usually extend beyond four months.

[5] Twelve patients were interviewed before their hearings and 14 after. A small number of patients were able to be interviewed who had no prior experience of the tribunal process.

patients reported having seen their RMOs for interview 'twice in three and a half years' and '40 minutes in two and a half years' would to the casual observer be incredible, except that most of the patients expressed similar dissatisfaction. On average, contact was not more than once every four months. Although one patient put the lack of contact down to the numbers of patients the RMOs had to deal with, the majority felt that their RMOs just weren't bothered with them.

A typical response, when asked to assess the quality of their relationship with their RMO, was to retort 'What relationship?'. Two remarked that they were 'terrified' and 'nervous' of their consultants and two others felt that their relationship had so deteriorated that they had accepted being left alone. Admittedly the comments were not all negative; some talked of getting on reasonably well. But only one offered real praise, noting that his RMO was a 'smashing chap', and that he had a 'good, superficial knowledge' of him. Mainly, the observations were about the absence of any communication, 'failure to communicate' when contact did occur, and of the RMOs not really knowing the patients in the way that the latter felt that they should. One patient remarked tellingly, 'I don't think he knows me well at all. I think I upset him. I don't think I give him the right answers.' The dilemma is clear. Patients had traditional expectations of the doctor–patient relationship. They would remark 'he has no bedside manner—he's stern and abrupt' (Patient 20). Yet, as the next chapter shows, the RMOs did not necessarily believe that this kind of contact was a vital element in their therapeutic relationships. As patients saw their RMOs infrequently they failed both to appreciate this or to acquire information about their own progress. As a result they felt frustrated.

There was a highly significant correlation between the frequency of contact and the extent to which patients believed their RMOs knew them.[6] Thus, Patient 13, who said his doctor 'knows me as much as any doctor can know my problems and what makes me tick', saw him once a month. In contrast, a patient who said that his RMO had told him that he was not mentally ill, but 'he

---

[6] A Spearman rank correlation co-efficient was calculated on frequency of contact and quality of patient–doctor relationship as defined by the patient. It produced an R of 0.87 which is significant at 0.0005 (Siegel 1956, pp. 204–12 and 248).

could not trust me and that was that', had been seen much less frequently.

There is, of course, an alternative explanation. When patients are first admitted to Acheland the acute nature of their disorders may inhibit any meaningful contact with their RMOs, and it is only as they begin to recover that the relationship develops—as one patient put it 'the passage of time has improved my opinion of him'. However, is this an index of recovery? Or an indication that, with time, patients inevitably build up some relationship (whether good or bad) with their RMOs, merely as a result of having seen them intermittently over a period of years? As one patient noted of his RMO, 'I make a point of seeing him every time he's on the ward, just to let him know I'm still here'. Patients also reported that the RMOs gained their impressions of them from the staff; whether this was perceived as advantageous or not, depended in turn upon the quality of these relationships. For example, 'he just rubber stamps the views of the staff' (Patient 17); 'the staff are the eyes of the RMO—they are in the best position to know the patient' (Patient 19); and 'he goes on what the nurses say and they think I'm crazy' (Patient 10). However, another (Patient 15), felt that his RMO did not even consult the staff; 'if he'd talked to the charge nurse his report would have been very different'.

B. Implications

The lack of frequent direct contact between the patients and their RMOs led to a number of consequences. First, it was believed that if the RMO did not know the patient, there would be no recommendation for transfer or discharge. One patient said that his RMO had told him to delay his application to the tribunal until he knew him better since he did not 'know me well enough to let me go'. Secondly, without the support of the RMO at a tribunal hearing, patients believed (rightly) that they had very little chance of moving on through this route. Hence, 'it doesn't matter what you say, if Dr. [X] says you should be here, the tribunal will agree'. Similarly, another said that his RMO had told him 'the law, the tribunal and the Home Office are all irrelevant, what I say goes'. Virtually all of the patients thought that if their RMO was against them they stood no chance; succinctly put by one patient 'you're impotent without your RMO'. There was no doubt in the minds of patients that the RMOs 'held the key to the door'.

In order to improve their relationships, patients recognized that they needed more contact with their RMOs, but their ability to achieve this was limited. Some RMOs operated a policy of seeing patients when they were in trouble or having problems—but this was clearly not the kind of contact that those who were keen to leave Acheland wished to have. Others would see patients if formally requested—but one patient claimed to have written three times to his RMO for an interview without success (a claim endorsed by another patient of the same RMO). The only strategy that was guaranteed to result in a formal interview and review of their case was an application to a tribunal.

Some patients applied to the tribunal for precisely this reason—to find out information from their RMOs—information which should arguably have been readily available to them. For example, Patient 13, who was diagnosed as suffering from psychopathic disorder, said, 'I applied because I had been told many times that I was not suffering from mental illness, so I wanted to find out why I was being detained. It was a quest for information. To get everybody to sit down round a table and discuss my case in front of me.' This patient did not wish for, nor anticipate, release for some years—so his application to the tribunal was a means to an end. Another said 'I asked to see him twice, but he never answered. He never discussed my treatment with me', and yet another that his RMO, with reference to his recommendation for transfer, was 'dragging his feet'.

Patients reported feeling that they had been 'messed around' by their RMOs. Patient 9, for example, related a history wherein he had withdrawn a tribunal application because his RMO had told him that he would get him out. According to the patient, the RMO took no further action. The patient reapplied to the tribunal. At the hearing, the RMO did support his application. The patient felt that his departure from Acheland had been unnecessarily and unjustly delayed.

1. PATIENTS' VIEWS ABOUT THE TRIBUNALS

A. *New and Improved?*

Nineteen of the patients had experienced tribunal review before and had a reasonable idea of what to expect. Some had had as many as ten previous hearings, although two or three was the more common figure. The time period over which these had taken place meant that a number of patients had experiences under both the 1959 and the 1983 Acts.

Virtually all the patients able to make the comparison said that the new tribunals were an improvement. Only one cynically remarked, 'the Act is the same as before, they've just changed the numbers of the sections'. Patients noted that tribunals were less formal and they believed that more care was taken in reviewing their cases. Also mentioned as positive features were the opportunity to see the reports and attend throughout the hearing, as well as being able to question the RMO. Finally, patients noted the rapidity with which they received the decision after the tribunal and the more frequent opportunities to reapply.

Curiously, the patients did not speak of these procedural improvements merely as basic rights, which they might reasonably have expected to be fulfilled. Rather, they expressed considerable gratitude. Moreover, patients especially welcomed the tribunal clerks' reassurances before their hearing and the tribunals' efforts to make them feel at ease.

As patients knew that tribunals did not readily make discharge decisions, most of them pitched their requests at a comparatively low level or, as Patient 9 remarked of those who didn't, 'they put it out of their reach and ask for too much'. Sometimes they would only seek a recommendation for transfer to another secure hospital (even Bendene was regarded as a 'way out'). Of the sample, eighteen patients were seeking transfer, usually to their catchment area hospital. Understandably, some expressed their desires simply in terms of going out—either on trial leave (one patient remarked 'going five miles up the road and back would suit me'), or, frequently unrealistically, to be back with their families. Two patients were trying for conditional discharge; one because he knew his RMO was opposed even to his transfer; as a last resort, he felt he had to persuade the tribunal to reach a decision they could put into effect. The other patient contested his guilt; from his perspective, transfer to another hospital would be inappropriate. If he had not committed the offence he was not ill. The RMO shared this view—provided the patient could establish his innocence.[7]

---

[7] This case (Patient 12) was a classic illustration of the difficulties which arise when a diagnosis, that of psychopathic disorder, is based on evidence of a single offence or series of similar offences. If the patient is innocent, there is no need for

Thus, patients were both reasonably attuned to and realistic about their positions. They accepted that an application to a tribunal could help to change a RMO's mind, or might act as a catalyst and spur along plans that had been verbally agreed with the patient but not put into effect. But they also recognized that a tribunal recommendation for transfer was meaningless without the support of their RMOs, since they might frustrate or merely ignore those recommendations with which they disagreed. Some patients therefore argued that tribunals should ensure that their recommendations were implemented.

In eleven of the cases which went to a tribunal the RMOs were opposed to any change in a patient's status. In nine cases the RMOs were reasonably supportive. Undoubtedly the best way to achieve a positive result from the tribunal was for the patient and the RMO to present a mutual package for action; but this occurred only infrequently. Where patients had their RMOs' active support and yet still nothing changed, alternative barriers were identified. Often the Home Office or receiving hospitals would be criticized for blocking a deserved move.

Patients were aware that the RMOs were capable of influencing the tribunals' decisions in ways more subtle than simply opposing discharge. Patient 4 noted that where the RMO had an untried treatment, the tribunal would delay making any decision to discharge or transfer until its outcome could be assessed. This viewpoint is amply illustrated in Chapters 6 and 7.

The decisions did not surprise them. Patients were grateful for the feedback even where the decision was not to discharge or recommend transfer. As one, Patient 25, remarked 'It did not set me back at all. It made me think what I've got to do.' Indeed, they said they prepared themselves for turn-downs and that it was only the 'really mad' who expected to get out. Some mentioned that they would have preferred fuller reasons—'where you are in the dark, how can you work through your problems?' (Patient 11)— but the following reflection on a decision not to discharge from Patient 8 was not atypical: 'I got the result. I wasn't disappointed. But then I've been a bit disappointed since I came back [to Acheland].'

---

treatment; if he is guilty, but continues to protest his innocence, this is a symptom of his disorder demonstrating a lack of insight and no motivation to co-operate in therapy to promote change. If he is guilty and disordered and not treated, he is too great a risk to release.

B. Why Patients Apply

In essence, patients did not apply to the tribunal because they expected the hearing to result in their release. The outcome was not the crucial criterion for assessing whether the process was worthwhile: 'having a tribunal is a good thing, even if you get a turndown'. Tribunals gave you a chance to discuss your case, to say that you disagreed with your RMO and to vent your feelings and frustrations.[8]

Even those exceptional patients who believed that they had a good relationship with their RMO did not necessarily fully understand his viewpoint. Patient 13 said he learnt things from his doctor at the hearing; in his view, the tribunal was an invaluable mechanism for improving communication—notoriously problematic even within general medicine. For those patients who found it difficult to talk to their RMOs, receiving their medical reports provided a necessary source of information.

However, one unexpected explanation was volunteered for applying—namely, that to have on your record that you had not exercised your rights 'made you look like a real screw-ball'. This reflected a general anxiety amongst the patients that they, as individuals, should be distinguished from those in Acheland who were 'really crazy'.

Finally, patients had more confidence that a tribunal hearing would facilitate an independent assessment of their circumstances. Under the 1959 Act it was believed that in 99 per cent of the cases the tribunal went with the RMO; patients had had few expectations. But by and large they believed that the tribunals were prepared to use their new powers, even if they did so infrequently. Many of the patients knew of others who had received conditional discharges (presumably the same handful of cases) and this gave them some confidence.

Admittedly, dissatisfaction was still expressed when the tribunal's decision merely 'repeated word for word what the RMO had said'. Or, as Patient 8 put it: 'very few get out on tribunals; unless the psychiatrist agrees to back you, you don't stand a chance; if the doctor is going to disagree with you why waste the time of the tribunal'. Tribunals, he believed, were only 'a straw to clutch at'. Others claimed that it was only the more disturbed patients who

---

[8] In this respect patients' views concurred with those of the RMO who described the tribunal as a safety-valve.

saw tribunals as a 'toothless formality, with no willingness to go against the doctors'. Patient 11, for example, believed that the approach of the tribunal depended upon its constituent members. He said that his first tribunal under the new Act had been probing towards absolute discharge (they had in fact recommended that he should be moved on from Acheland as he would not benefit from any further treatment there and that he was no longer a danger to himself or the public). His second tribunal, on virtually the same information, found him to be 'ill and dangerous'. He felt that this decision was attributable to the impact of the views of a 'hard-line judge' on the other two members. He described this particular tribunal as being like 'a puppeteer and two marionettes'.[9]

C. *Preparing for the Tribunal: The Role of the Representative*

How did patients set about preparing themselves for a tribunal hearing? An obvious, though not necessarily reliable source of information, would have been to discuss the matter with fellow patients. However, virtually all of those questioned said that their tribunal experiences were not a topic of conversation. The reason was simple; those who had 'failed' did not want to talk about it and those who had 'passed' refrained for fear of 'rubbing it in'. Tribunal applications were nobody's business but their own.

Most patients found out about the tribunal system by obtaining a representative. Which representative they chose to instruct varied: some did follow a recommendation by a fellow patient; some were advised by members of staff; and some chose a legal representative from the lists of solicitors posted on the ward notice-boards.[10] Others simply returned to the solicitors who had dealt with their case at court. But this was less usual, since a proportion blamed these solicitors for their original confinement in Acheland.[11]

[9] Certainly the two decisions make an interesting contrast. It should also be noted that patients frequently remembered their tribunals mainly in terms of the judge sitting and not by the other two members. But then, as the president of the tribunal, the judicial member invariably dominates the proceedings.

[10] The local solicitors benefited from this because patients believed that being close to the hospital they would receive more preparatory visits. Similarly, once a solicitor had an interest in a patient, he or she could often be prevailed upon to undertake other legal work, for example writing letters, for which the patient would otherwise have had to pay directly.

[11] Patients occasionally felt that they had been badly advised or misled about the merits of a hospital order rather than arguing for a sentence of imprisonment.

Of the 26 patients, 19 were legally represented at their current hearing.[12] Six of these had kept the same solicitor from their previous tribunal hearing, 3 had changed their solicitors and 10 had not been previously represented. By and large, patients were impressed by the efforts their solicitors made; and, despite remaining in Acheland, they believed they benefited from the continuity of retaining the same representative. Or, as one patient who had been referred automatically and had an approved solicitor from the Law Society's list remarked, 'he did not know me well enough to do a good job'.[13]

Of the 6 patients who had chosen not to be represented, 4 had never been represented. One of these claimed she had never thought of having a solicitor, but, if this application was not successful (and it was not), she would get one for the next. Another said that he wanted to speak for himself and was confident that he would be able to do so.

It is difficult to assess how many benefits representation brings. Clearly, cases are better prepared, independent psychiatric reports sought, and inconsistencies in the medical evidence and other reports explored. Also as a result of this contact, patients do gain some insight into the operation of the tribunal system and the law. However, it must be noted that even represented patients could be surprisingly vague about the tribunal's powers and practices.

As important as the quality of preparation is the proper presentation of the case at the hearing.[14] One of the most articulate patients, who had long experience of the tribunal process, said that even he 'felt inhibited, and didn't speak well' at his most recent hearing. Other patients felt that they had been rushed at the tribunal and didn't remember to say all they wanted to. No matter how hard the tribunal try to put them at their ease, patients understandably remain apprehensive. Challenging the RMO, so obviously a figure of authority, was not undertaken lightly. As one

---

[12] One of these had instructed a solicitor who did not turn up at the hearing.

[13] The Law Society maintains a list of approved representatives from whom patients may seek assistance. These are solicitors who have met certain minimum requirements, namely (i) they have represented 5 patients or attended 3 hearings as an observer; (ii) they have attended a MIND training course; (iii) they pass a Law Society interview.

[14] Patient 13 said 'my representative put my case so much better than I ever could have, everyone should be represented'. Another said that 'representatives help you to know what you are up against—you need all the information that you can get'.

remarked, since 'I'm only a patient, whose word will be taken?'

Several patients were disturbed about the financial barrier for those patients who did not qualify for legal aid because they had some savings.[15] The question was asked, 'Should you have to buy your way out of Acheland?' Patients who were both ineligible for legal aid and not confident of getting a recommendation for discharge or transfer were doubly reluctant to pay for legal assistance—regarding it as a 'waste of money'.[16] Patients were saving money for when they *left* Acheland, not to enable them to leave; those who did save were doubly penalized.

One further inequity emerged. One patient who had only been in Acheland for a short period (two years) following a serious offence was denied legal aid because, he was informed, he stood no chance of getting out. These limited expectations about both the outcome and the purpose of tribunal review were, it was claimed, shared by some other patients. Where it was believed that there was no chance of getting out, patients might refrain from exercising their rights to apply.

One final point to which patients brought attention should be stressed. Acheland, like many institutions, has a significant ethnic minority population, which fluctuates around 15 per cent. Although only a tiny proportion of patients (approximately 3 per cent) fail to cite English as their mother tongue, where language difficulties did arise, patients could be particularly disadvantaged. Not only might they have problems in relieving their stresses by talking to the staff or other patients, but also their limited resources could hinder them finding out how to set about applying to a tribunal. Thus, even this safety-valve might be denied to them.

D. *Patients and their Reports: Is Seeing Believing?*

Under rule 12(1) of the Tribunal Rules 1983, the tribunal is obliged to send 'a copy of every document it receives which is relevant to the application to the applicant, and (where he is not

---

[15] This previously stood at £750, but has now been raised to £3,000 so virtually all patients would qualify for legal aid.

[16] If it could be established that representation made a *real* difference to the tribunal's decisions, these patients may have been denying themselves the route out of Acheland. For those patients who chose to pay regardless, tribunals' decisions to defer for further information (often a prerequisite to a conditional discharge) result in more cost being incurred by the patient.

the applicant) the patient'. Although rule 10(5) obviates the need to send documents to a patient where these have been provided to his or her representative, in practice chairmen in some regions require papers to go to patients in *all* cases. Whichever of these procedures is adopted, the outcome is that patients who apply for a tribunal hearing will have the opportunity, for probably the first time, to read or be made familiar with the contents of all the reports written about them—including the RMOs' reports. Although subsection 2 of rule 12 can prevent the disclosure of documents that would 'adversely affect the health or welfare of the patient or others', this is no longer routinely invoked by the RMOs.

Where a patient is represented, the documents would normally be sent to the representative. Representatives may convey the information contained in the report either orally to the patient or by showing or sending him or her copies of the reports. For patients who are unrepresented, the reports will be sent to them direct. A potential difficulty may thereby arise. It is not unusual for unrepresented patients to be among the more inadequate and vulnerable; indeed, they are often the illest. It is these patients about whom the greatest concern arises when reports are disclosed. Yet, it is this very group who may not enjoy the protection which representation can bring. They will not necessarily have anyone with whom to discuss the content of the reports; whatever damaging effects these may have could be enhanced.

A number of patients were surprised by the contents of their reports. They were also upset that there were, in their view, so many inaccuracies. These could either be factual, for example, about personal details or incidents which had occurred in Acheland; or matters of interpretation, for example, describing a man as a 'habitual alcoholic' when he claimed to have drunk only two pints a night; or matters which were, according to the patients, opinions dressed up as facts.

The RMOs cannot be blamed for all of these. Patients were very retentive about things that had been said to them, possibly only in casual conversation, which the RMOs' reports may have subsequently contradicted. Any inconsistencies in the reports were quickly identified by the patients. They, in turn, cannot be blamed for adopting this attitude. Patients believed that these comparatively minor matters could be very influential in the tribunal's decision-making.

Perhaps the most hurtful criticisms were those maligning their characters. For this they blamed the RMOs for not knowing them better. For example, one patient, who had both visitors and contact with the outside world through letters, was disturbed when his RMO described him as solitary and not wanting to see anyone. Clearly the RMO was misinformed; yet this was the information which the tribunal would initially receive. Another patient resented being described as paranoid when at his previous tribunal his RMO had admitted that he had been the subject of false allegations. One patient confronted his RMO about the factual inaccuracies *before* the tribunal and the report was amended, but this happened rarely. Thus, the RMOs were right to say that it sometimes upset patients to see their reports, but the patients would assert that they were appropriately upset. Finally, some patients accepted that, even if the reports made uncomfortable reading, they did consider them fair appraisals and frequently found them 'helpful'. No patient said that they would have preferred not to have seen their reports.

Patients were also concerned about the disparity between their admittedly unfavourable histories prior to coming to Acheland and their subsequent behaviour in hospital. The written reports, which could be 'deadly', made great play of their early history, whilst patients claimed that little attention was paid to the ways in which they felt they had made progress. For example, 'My records are twenty years old but they talk as if it were yesterday' (Patient 17). Since a number of patients had experienced tribunals of quite short duration—under half an hour—they did not believe there was much scope for 'getting at the truth'. Furthermore, at the tribunal, the RMOs, according to Patient 17, relied on their credibility as doctors—the quality of their reports was necessarily assumed to be good.

To redress any possible imbalance, one point is worth making. The failure to communicate did not lie solely with the RMOs. Patient 15 readily admitted that his feelings had been hurt by what he considered to be derogatory statements made about him by the RMO. He said, 'but I wouldn't let them see I was needled about it'. In the report his RMO had written: 'He is somewhat solitary in the ward setting and generally uncommunicative with nursing staff.' Or, as the charge nurse put it 'he hides his feelings'. [17]

[17] It was to emerge in another forum where patients discussed their detention that some patients believed that you couldn't afford to admit to being ill in Acheland or 'you'd never get out'. Patients' preoccupations with leaving hospital, and the fear of remaining indefinitely, could lead to some of them having a less than open relationship with those seen as detaining them.

III. PATIENTS, THEIR TREATMENT AND THE IMPACT OF ACHELAND

Three factors emerged with surprising consistency. First, the vast majority of the patients accepted that they had needed to be sent to Acheland. Secondly, almost all of them agreed that being there had done them good. Third, most, but not all of them, felt that they were ready to leave.

A. Coming to Acheland

With the exception of two patients, all of those interviewed recognized that it had been right to commit them to Acheland.[18] 'If I'd not come in, I'd have killed somebody by now' (Patient 23); 'I had to come, I was not a reasonable person' (Patient 9); and 'I can see now I was ill' (Patient 15) were typical responses. There were some dissenters, but these were the exceptional patients who demonstrated little insight: 'There is nothing wrong with me, I don't know what they think is wrong with me ... even in prison you know why you are there' (Patient 14, a deteriorated schizophrenic). Usually, their assessment was more balanced; for example Patient 8, who had been recalled to hospital, accepted his first admission, yet felt his recall was unjustified: 'I ended up back here through peoples' anxieties—not because I'd done anything.'

There was a similar level of consensus that being in Acheland was preferable to being in prison, even if you ultimately stayed longer and on an indefinite basis. The social aspects of life in Acheland, the privileges, the responsibilities you were given, and the ability to earn more money than in prison were all mentioned. Hospital was considered less institutionalizing than prison. But principally, it was the time spent there and the opportunity this provided to re-establish relationships with people, both inside and out, which was the most important. The comparatively frequent visiting allowed understandably facilitated this.[19]

---

[18] One (Patient 12) maintained he had been wrongly convicted, and another (Patient 21) had been transferred from prison when the Court of Appeal quashed his life sentence and replaced it with a S60/65 order under the 1959 Act. By this stage he believed that he had recovered sufficiently not to require further treatment.

[19] At Acheland, seven visits per month and unrestricted visiting at weekends were permitted.

B. Treatment

Although none of the patients used the term, it was clear that the majority felt that the main benefit they had derived came from milieu therapy - a form treatment in which the patient's total living experience contrives to be therapeutic. They described it in the following terms: 'the experience of being here is the best treatment' (Patient 18); 'meeting other crazy people who are worse than you, helps you to sort yourself out' (Patient 15); 'the time here has been beneficial' (Patient 11); 'it's the walls, I needed the walls' (Patient 26); 'the benefit you get from this place depends on what you put in' (Patient 10); 'I've mellowed, I've grown up here—I can control my mouth and my temper' (Patient 24). But some patients, more particularly those diagnosed as psychopaths, received no specific treatment beyond milieu therapy. For those who did not appreciate its benefits, their situations felt fraught: 'You can't leave a man to rot for five years receiving no treatment.' Others saw their time in Acheland principally as a matter of survival rather than healing.

The patients' opinions of drug therapy were fairly consistent: 'On the drugs I still felt miserable and depressed, but I was too tired to do anything about it' (Patient 9); 'the medication makes me calm—it stills the voices' (Patient 26); and most tellingly 'the drugs slow you down, they calm you, but they don't solve your problems' (Patient 19). Not all of the patients felt that they needed medication, but all acquiesced in its administration. As Patient 16 put it 'medication is my ticket out of here'. In this he was correct. Even his RMO did not feel his medication was necessary, but the local hospital to which he was to be transferred insisted upon it. Others accepted the treatment, but denied they required it: 'I'm not mentally ill, I just need company. I don't feel the need for any form of security now. I just suffer from mood swings. Is that being mentally ill?' (Patient 10).

Surprisingly, for those who had experienced it, group therapy rather than medication seemed to be the treatment most resented. Patients did not relish the necessary discussion either of their crimes or of their past. Moreover, they were concerned about the lack of confidentiality outside the groups.

A few patients alleged that there had been changes in their treatment programmes as a result of applying for review, or, as one said, 'your case stops'. This concurred with observations made by the RMOs, although they principally blamed patients for non-co-operation during this period. However, the patients' view was, to some extent, substantiated by those instances where RMOs attended hearings and gave evidence of planned, but as yet inoperative, treatment programmes (that is, they were also awaiting the tribunal's decision). Another patient said that his medication was increased before the hearing; the staff confirmed this saying that he had become unduly anxious. Perhaps the most worrying suggestion came from a patient who said that the drugs to control the side-effects of his anti-psychotic medication had been reduced after his pre-tribunal interview with his RMO, but before his hearing. The RMO's report noted, 'At interview he manifests evidence of drug side-effects (tremor of extremities and slight speech impediment).' In this context it was unclear why the RMO might have done this (if indeed he did), but it does lend partial support to the allegation made by some of the RMOs that one of their colleagues had a policy of taking patients off their medication prior to a hearing. Whatever the truth of the matter, the patient said that the reduction in his medication 'had made no difference' to him.

C. Leaving Acheland

Most of the patients felt that they were ready for a move, even if this was to be approached cautiously; they wanted periods of rehabilitation and resocialization before leaving hospital care entirely: 'I need a constructive transitional period' (Patient 11). But it was inevitable that some believed that they had been in Acheland for too long. It was argued that the beneficial effects peaked: 'After 5 or 6 years it's counter-productive' (Patient 17—detained for eighteen years). Moreover, patients feared that they had become institutionalized; Acheland could make you 'too comfortable'. Patient 20, for example, was 'reluctant to go' but had accepted it.

It was clear from their comments that some patients relied upon time for crime arguments to support their perceptions of injustice. 'Ten years is too long for an ABH—it's really a life sentence' (Patient 10); 'I don't think he can keep me here forever—it was not a serious crime' (Patient 14). Others were implicitly critical of the tribunal, as well as their RMOs, for the length of time they had been detained; Patient 24 said, 'Perhaps if they knew what it was like they wouldn't keep us here so long'; Patient 12 that 'no one wants to take the responsibility for giving me a chance'; similarly, 'just because I'm mentally ill is not a sufficient reason to keep me indefinitely in a maximum security hospital' (Patient 11). The tension between detention for treatment, detention for safety, and detention *per se* was evident in their views, even if rarely articulated as such.

Patients also believed that the likelihood of being discharged depended upon a number of factors concerning their situation within Acheland; a planned course of therapy has already been identified by patients as one capable of reducing their prospects of getting a favourable result. Two patients noted that if detained on the special care unit ('punishment block') they stood no chance of leaving the hospital—because it implied 'you are amongst the worst in Acheland'. One even withdrew his application (he claimed on the advice of his RMO) when he was transferred to the special unit. He reported that his RMO was pleased 'because they take a lot of time'. Patient 6 noted that the timing of the hearing was all important; there was no point applying if you had just had some form of set-back, in his case a period of hyperactivity. Similarly, it was clear that incidents which occurred in hospital—not necessarily of a patient's own making—could make their situation worse; as Patient 12 said, 'I had a squabble over a snooker ball and now they are calling me a psychopath.'

Whether some of these incidents arose because of patients' powerlessness to do anything about their situation is a matter for speculation. Some patients were clearly frustrated: 'I feel ready now for a transfer, but I can't do anything about it' (Patient 25); 'I don't think I could do any better—I'm ready for a move to greener pastures' (Patient 24); 'I'm just fed up waiting' (Patient 22).

Further frustration arose because of the lack of channels through which patients felt they could complain. Although some invested considerable hope in the new Mental Health Act Commission, others said that if you complained to the Commission 'the staff will only get back at you' (Patient 18) and that 'any complaint is interpreted as a sign of being anti-authority; being anti-authority means being anti-social' (Patient 17), a label that could also set you back.

Similarly, lack of exercise meant patients couldn't work out their frustrations. Patient 26 asked for a gym: the response by her RMO when I raised this with him was 'If we let them have a gym they'd only become strong and more able to attack the staff.' If this comment was made seriously it can only reflect a disturbing gap in the perspectives of 'keepers and kept', and indeed highlights the differing therapeutic approaches at other hospitals: Bendene had a purpose-built and well-used gym.

With one exception, the patients were remarkably phlegmatic about their situations; indeed, patients expressed more anger about other patients who they felt had been badly treated or who had apparently been forgotten by the authorities. Others mentioned the penalties their families underwent as a result of their detention in Acheland. These observations, along with many others, contradicted the views of some of the staff about patients being selfish and self-orientated.

Finally, four patients related stories of others they had known who had been faced with the prospect of an automatic tribunal. These referrals were introduced under the 1983 Act as a safeguard for those patients without the ability or initiative to apply for a hearing. Yet some patients fail to exercise their rights simply because they wish to stay in hospital. Distressingly, the patients had allegedly become deliberately disruptive or had made threats or had self-mutilated, in the expectation that the tribunal would then consider them unfit for discharge. The patients in the sample who related these incidents felt sorry for the predicament of this small group of reluctant leavers; their RMOs received considerable criticism for this.

Some of the patients were aware of what it could feel like to be faced with the prospect of a move from Acheland, having experienced or watched others experience 'gate fever'. This change in behaviour, characterized by over-activity and over-excitement, might come about when patients had a date fixed to leave. Possibly it derived from a natural anxiety about going out. If this coincided with a tribunal hearing, designed to consolidate a proposal for a transfer, it could unduly affect a patient's behaviour during the hearing. The tribunal need to be aware of the consequences for some patients of both the threat of automatic hearings and the stress of actual hearings.

IV. CONCLUSIONS

There has already been some discussion about the likely validity of patients' responses. Although it has been argued that there was no evidence of patients being intentionally misleading, it remains possible that patients might have misinterpreted the significance of particular events. Patients were, after all, ready to impute madness both to some of their fellow patients and, in the past, to themselves. One such misinterpretation might be where patients argued that their RMOs could not know them because they did not have regular formal interviews with them; yet the RMOs might maintain an informed knowledge of patients through the reports of other members of staff with whom both they and the patients have contact. These individuals could include nurses, psychologists, occupational therapists, social workers, and the patient's families and friends.

However, precisely where the truth lies is immaterial. It is the patient's perception of events which will motivate his or her behaviour; dissatisfaction with their treatment, ignorance of the reasons for their continued detention in Acheland, or concern about the apparent lack of plans for their progress are all factors which may motivate patients to apply to the tribunal. Undoubtedly patients use the tribunal as a resource, both to increase their level of contact with their RMOs and, perhaps more importantly, to discover what their RMO thinks about them and their condition. Even if they don't describe the tribunal as 'rights-respecting', they do recognize that tribunals give them a fair hearing and, by and large, treat them well. Thus, even an 'unsuccessful' tribunal is regarded as a good thing because it secures information for them and is, in itself, therapeutic.

Yet, the act of application to a tribunal, even if motivated only by patients' desire for greater information about their cases, in turn has consequences for RMOs, solicitors, social workers, the tribunal, and patients' families. In particular the RMOs argued that preparing for a tribunal involved them in considerable additional work; some not only resented this, but also claimed that it interferred with more important clinical duties. Such a response suggests that the problem may well be a question of chicken and egg; if patients didn't apply to the tribunal, RMOs would be involved in less office review and report work, and would be able to see them more frequently. This may be true, but the resolution of the dilemma can only lie with the RMOs; the patients are in a comparatively powerless position. They can request to see their RMOs more frequently, but there is no guarantee that the RMOs will respond. Similarly, they have no right to insist that the RMO provides an up-to-date report about them, unless they apply for a tribunal hearing. Clearly the RMOs must take the initiative for improving the general quality of their relationships with patients.

It is, of course, worrying that so many patients considered these relationships to be poor, particularly since this assessment correlated significantly with the perceived level of direct contact with the RMO. The ramifications of this permeate the discussion. For example, where the relationship was poor or 'non-existent', it could significantly impair the likelihood of patients leaving Acheland. Patients recognized that this problem was acute with specific RMOs (many of the patients had come within the care of several different RMOs). A solution was proposed: each patient should have two medical officers responsible for his or her care. Although this is unlikely to find favour with the doctors, a greater circulation of patients between the RMOs might obviate the effects of problematic doctor–patient relationships.

Although the conclusion cannot be avoided that if RMOs were to see their patients on a regular one-to-one basis there would be a far greater interchange of information and patients would feel happier, this would not be a complete solution. In some cases, RMOs would still wish to withold information from patients on the grounds that it is important for them to reach an understanding of their problems through the therapeutic process, rather than having the solutions presented, as it were, 'on a plate'. In other instances, the fault lies rather with the patients, where, for example, they might perceive the RMOs as the only or critical source of information.

A number of other beneficial consequences may derive from an improved relationship between patients and RMOs. First, although the majority of the patients in Acheland are quiescent and phlegmatic about their situations, patients' frustrations do intermittently boil over and dangerous levels of antagonism can be displayed. RMOs are aware that these flashpoints can occur.[20] They should also be aware that such occurrences may sometimes be predicted and frequently could be defused if not avoided, if they had greater contact with their patients. For example, Patient 25, who reported infrequent contact with her RMO, only expressed real hostility towards him when she remarked that it was bad that he did not come to see her after she'd had a tribunal turn-down. The RMOs are aware of a potential for danger; should they not take it into their own hands to reduce it?

[20] One of the Acheland RMOs had a list on his wall of all the patients in Acheland who had, in the past, attacked psychiatrists.

Secondly, it is unfortunate that a measure introduced into the 1983 Act to protect some of the least able amongst the detained patients, namely automatic tribunals, may have had detrimental consequences for a proportion of that group. Those patients who lack neither the ability nor the initiative to make a tribunal application, but who may lack the willingness to do so, may suffer as a result of automatic tribunals. Perhaps if RMOs were better aware of, or made efforts to alleviate, some of their patients' fears, the desire to self-mutilate or create other disruption prior to a tribunal hearing might be avoided. Tribunals do not have a reputation for discharging patients who clearly do not wish to be moved, nor are they necessarily unsympathetic about patients' worries; for example anxiety about the need to go over, yet again, the details of their offences.[21] But patients are not necessarily to know this; their RMOs may well be able to act as a conduit for this type of information.

The interviews have indicated that patients could be better informed of their rights and of the benefits of both legal representation and tribunal review. As Patient 13 put it 'I had to find out by word of mouth and that clearly is not the best way.' He made the valuable suggestion that 'an easy reading booklet should be available to all patients'.

Finally, according to the patients, tribunals routinely follow the RMO's opinion in reaching decisions. The analysis of tribunal decisions by and large confirms this. Patients are understandably resentful that the tribunals follow the view of someone whom they believe does not really know them. Whether the tribunals would be more ready to oppose the RMOs if they were aware of the variable levels of doctor–patient contact is an open question. However, if the RMOs were to see their patients more regularly, patients might feel less thwarted, less unjustly treated, and have more confidence in the tribunal when their decision concurred with the RMO's view. Alternatively, RMOs who saw their patients more regularly might be more readily persuaded of their suitability for transfer. This might arise out of an improvement in the quality of their information—an improvement attributable to first-hand as opposed to received information.

---

[21] It should perhaps be noted that some tribunals do insist on seeing reluctant patients to confirm their unwillingness to attend the tribunal or whether their wish to withdraw is genuine. This can be upsetting for patients and should be exercised with caution.

4. The Responsible Medical Officers

> Besides purely clinical work in assessment and treatment of patients, consultants have much other work, including providing annual reports on patients, mental health review tribunal reports and appearances, preparation of reports for conditional discharge and transfer, reports recommending or advising against admission, court reports and appearances, as well as time needed to see patients outside, conducting follow-ups, for research, teaching and training others, continuing medical education, attending conferences and courses and administrative meetings.
>
> John Hamilton (1985:96–7)

This chapter draws on the views of eight out of the nine RMOs at Acheland, and addresses both the nature of the RMOs' interactions with their patients and the tribunal, and the consequences of one on the other. Since the remaining RMO had only a small clinical caseload, the interviews conducted can be seen as a reasonable reflection, at that time, of the perspectives of those with the major responsibility for the continuing care and treatment of detained patients in one Special Hospital.

1. THE ROLE OF THE RMO: THERAPIST AND CUSTODIAN

It will be apparent from the nature of the patient population that RMOs have to fulfil two, often conflicting, roles: first as therapists and secondly as custodians. In their first role, psychiatrists act as members of a profession with an essentially caring outlook. Although the desire to treat, to alleviate, and to cure may be held in common by psychiatrists, their individual perceptions of whom they are able so to assist can be at variance. Yet, because of the psychiatrist's role in admission decisions, these divergent perceptions of therapeutic prognoses can result in a range of patients entering hospital. These patients, with differing needs and often a variable responsiveness to treatment, will be taken into the compulsory care of the RMOs.

Thus, therapeutic assessments interact with the fulfilment of RMOs second and subsequent role of custodian or 'keeper of the keys'. In essence, RMOs act as a fulcrum within the hospital, since they not only influence the choice of which individuals are admitted (from the courts, other hospitals, and the prisons) but also exert considerable control over discharges. Indeed, for non-restricted patients they have the statutory authority to discharge and are obliged to *renew* patients' detention orders at regular intervals to prevent the authority for detention lapsing. And, when so doing, they are obliged to take account of the criteria of treatability and viability.[1]

Since the vast majority of patients in Acheland are on restriction orders, RMOs do not have this ultimate responsibility for the continuation of their orders. Yet their recommendations to the tribunal and the Home Office, the two bodies which do determine a restricted patient's length of stay, are highly influential.[2] Without some impetus from the RMO neither are likely to initiate change. Moreover, the two most realistic routes out of the Special Hospitals for restricted patients are either by means of a transfer or, for some psychopathic patients, where local hospital care may be inappropriate, by trial leave followed by conditional discharge. Both of these amount to a staged removal. Such changes in a patient's status are unlikely to be effected, even where tribunals recommend them, without the RMO's explicit support.[3] Thus, the combination of the RMOs' statutory responsibilities with their fulcral position places them in a position of considerable power over patients. It is they who, in reality, determine the likely minimum length of stay within Acheland.

The 1983 Act, described by one RMO as 'a coarse adjuster of justice', does little to resolve the dynamics of the interaction between RMOs' therapeutic and custodial roles. Clearly, it could not readily provide a blueprint for the essentially caring approach which psychiatrists employ when making decisions about their

[1] See Appendix 1.
[2] Under S41(6) of the 1983 Act RMOs are obliged at intervals (not exceeding one year) to examine and report to the Secretary of State on every restricted patient in their care.
[3] Even with it the DHSS or, more likely, the Home Office, may block or delay a transfer or deny trial leave. In this respect the empirical research suggests that the situation has changed somewhat from that noted in 1976, see Parker (1980).

patients. Here medical not legal criteria are seen to be paramount. Indeed, relationships with their patients were regarded as falling into the traditional doctor–patient model. The Mental Health Act was viewed as something of an intrusion into their clinical function. Their statutory responsibilities and consequent custodial role were seen as a necessary, but unrelished function.

This was put in its bleakest form by one RMO who remarked that, since he did not take any notice of the old Act, the introduction of a new one had made no difference to his practices. Another noted that the wording of the Act did not 'pay enough attention to clinical issues'. Not all of the RMOs were dismissive of the Act. Some adopted the pragmatic view that it was not possible to make the fine distinctions in human behaviour which the law required. But the implication was clear; they rarely 'took cognizance of the criteria of the Act', and their 'contact with them [patients] is as a doctor'. Legal restrictions were simply not at the forefront of their minds.

One RMO asserted that some aspects of the Act had deliberately been left vague and cited the definition of treatability. He argued that this constituted both a strength and a weakness of the Act. He illustrated the way in which disputes between psychiatrists would inevitably arise about patients' suitability for treatment. Amongst his colleagues, one RMO believed that those suffering from psychopathic disorder/personality disorder should receive custodial sentences and then be transferred under S47 of the 1983 Act, as and when their condition merited treatment. The alternative position, the humanitarian or compassionate view, stemmed from the belief that psychopaths were treatable (even if their responsiveness took many years), or may be treatable—the state of the art being unrefined. Even if they ultimately proved untreatable, this RMO believed that psychiatrists should take responsibility for that small group of patients who were dangerous, but who would be worse off elsewhere; he claimed he could at least prevent deterioration. In that sense, he had no objection to the 'medical underwriting' of indeterminate detention, since the alternative—a long and potentially damaging prison sentence—was wholly unattractive.[4] Others took the view that admitting these

---

[4] There was general agreement that this category of patient was unsuitable for medium security or interim units. As the length of their treatment would inevitably be protracted, they would block beds for other more deserving or more essentially mobile patients, creating a log-jam in the Special Hospitals.

patients to Acheland occupied valuable beds and created a damaging impact on patients and staff alike (Mawson 1983).[5] Disagreements over questions of treatability were compounded in the cases of those suffering from psychopathic disorder, where some psychiatrists experienced real difficulties in equating the statutory definition with their clinical experience; diametrically opposed views in this context were not uncommon. Did these markedly differing perspectives result in some RMOs resenting the need to treat (or try to treat) those whom they felt should be located elsewhere?

The shying away from fine legal distinctions and tolerance over their interpretation arguably resulted in some misunderstandings by the RMOs about the nature of the legal criteria they and the tribunal were expected to operate. Differing perspectives might, of course, be reconciled not on the grounds of differing interpretations of the Act, but by different medical assessments of their patients. However, there was also a basic unfamiliarity with the Act. None of the RMOs interviewed were familiar with the distinction drawn in the Act between the behavioural criteria necessary to satisfy a definition of psychopathic disorder and those necessary for mental impairment. Moreover, none of them could offer a distinction when the wording was put to them (although one RMO did state that he would prefer the term 'associated with' to be used in both definitions). The assumption that it would be necessary for the RMOs to stretch the criteria to keep within the constraints imposed by the Act was, therefore, not verified. RMOs felt they were already working within these constraints; quite how widely they were presuming them to be drawn was not clear.

For many patients the RMOs' combined role of carer-treater and custodian is an unfortunate one. In determining the length of time a patient may spend in hospital the RMOs say they frequently consider not only what is in the best interests of their patients, but also what is in the best interests of society. This would suggest that in some instances RMOs are prepared to exploit their custodial responsibilities to the possible detriment of their patient's immediate clinical interests. For example, the transfer process may not be commenced until the RMO is completely satisfied that this course is appropriate, even though it

[5] It is notable that the numbers of psychopathic patients on the admission wards had dropped significantly, suggesting that this latter view was beginning to have an impact on the selection process (see A. Grounds 1987b).

is accepted that an overlong stay in Acheland can be detrimental to the patient. Furthermore, this stance is defended even though it is well established that, given Home Office approval for transfer, there can be lengthy delays before a move is effected (Dell 1982).[6]

In order to do justice to those both inside and outside hospital, the RMOs wished to be more than sure. As one put it, '25 per cent of the patients are ready to go—they stay because we don't know enough about dangerousness—we are more cautious than the actual circumstances merit because we don't know what factors will make them dangerous.' Thus, patients who continued to experience sadistic fantasies, no matter how long they had been otherwise stable, would continue to represent unacceptable risks to the RMOs. If the original behaviour was associated with such fantasies how could the RMO be sure? Indeed, how could they even be sure that a patient who no longer reported fantasies had not simply learnt the inadvisability of expressing them?

Other categories of patient posed similar dilemmas, for example, the medication-stabilized paranoid schizophrenic who killed in response to 'voices'. Was his stabilized state a sign of remission or recovery? The view was expressed that people who had suffered from mental illness would remain vulnerable; and being vulnerable they remained susceptible to recurrences. The logic continued; if their illnesses had been associated with violence might the scenario not recur with a recurrence of the illness? Just because a patient was well-behaved in the hospital did not mean that he was not ill.

The conflict in role was most graphically put by one RMO who said that he could 'convince another psychiatrist of a patient's need to be in [Acheland] even if he couldn't convince a Mental Health Review Tribunal'. Within the confines of Acheland the RMOs remained supreme as arbiters of treatability and potential dangerousness—patients could fall at either hurdle. Or as one RMO put it, 'When they are untreatable I say they are dangerous.'

Another manifestation of conflict occurred in respect of interviewing patients (as opposed to reviewing their cases) in the traditional doctor–patient manner. This would happen spasmodically. One RMO revealingly remarked: 'why should patients have

[6] One RMO said his tactic was to get agreement in principle from the Home Office, then to find a suitable alternative hospital bed and *then* inform the Home Office of his recommendation for transfer. This both prevented him having patients on a 'transfer list' and expedited the Home Office's decision by exerting pressure, namely an available bed, on them.

the right to see me whenever they want—after all, in an ordinary hospital a patient would rarely if ever see his consultant.' The pre-eminence of the medical approach and a surprising lack of recognition of the statutory custodial role was apparent. Only after further discussion did this RMO accept that his influence over matters such as the compulsory treatment and detention of patients distinguished his role from that of other medical consultants.

The conflict between caring and custody is crystallized in the dealings between the RMOs and the Home Office in the case of life-sentenced prisoners transferred to the Special Hospitals. A policy appeared to be be in operation at the Home Office that, once considered fit to leave by the RMO, lifers had to be returned to prison to progress through the normal parole procedures. For those patients who had fulfilled the retributive element of their sentence, this was arguably a case of double jeopardy. The RMOs considered it intolerable that a patient should be in danger of being returned to a non-therapeutic (and possibly damaging) environment simply because he no longer needed the particular kind of help offered by Acheland, but may have benefited from the traditional staged-release route.

Although the RMOs recognized the need to be cautious, and took into account both therapeutic considerations and the safety of the public, virtually all of them expressed some resentment about what they perceived to be delays in 'merited' transfers. The major obstacles to transferring patients were identified as (i) the reluctance of local hospitals, medium/interim/regional secure units to take patients recognized as having been difficult (mainly female) or as likely to be difficult (mainly male); [7] and (ii) obstruction by the Home Office—for example, by making a 'late' reference to the Advisory Board (see Appendix 2). Where 'political' considerations were thought to be protracting a discharge date or blocking a transfer which the RMOs considered warranted, strong reactions were engendered. After the 'crescendo of effort' necessary *before* RMOs would recommend to the Home Office a change in a patient's status, such delaying tactics were seen as 'unfair'. In such

---

[7] One of the RMOs remarked that it was always the same hospitals which requested that their patients be transferred to Acheland. He attributed this to levels of incompetence and fear among the staff at these hospitals not found at other local hospitals. Thus, it was not patient needs which resulted in transfers, but staff needs.

cases the RMOs regarded recommendations for transfer by the tribunal (or even, on occasions, decisions to discharge with conditions) as putting useful pressure on the Home Office. This pressure was reciprocal. As both the tribunals and the Home Secretary had the power to discharge restricted patients, it was suggested that as the Home Secretary became even more cautious in his decision-making, the tribunal became ever more open-minded.

A. RMOs and the Tribunals

Given these somewhat reserved attitudes to the 1983 Act, the RMOs' assessments of the tribunals are understandable. They were regarded as at best a mixed blessing, and at worst an intrusion and distraction to their medical responsibilities. At the time the research was conducted Acheland was in a state of some disarray, and this may have exacerbated these negative appraisals. The recent death of one of the RMOs and an extensive rebuilding programme had resulted in disorganization and reorganization within the hospital. One house had been closed entirely; many patients had been transferred to Bendene; a new RMO had recently been appointed and another, semi-retired, RMO brought back part-time. The consequence was some reallocation of patients. But overall, there was a substantial reduction of the numbers of patients in each RMO's care. The RMOs' patient allocation was approximately 70 for those working full-time and 35 for those part-time, making a total in-patient population of approximately 520 patients.[8] Previous work-loads had varied—between 100 and 200 patients per RMO—as did attitudes to the appropriate work-load. Or, as the director of one Special Hospital has noted

All patients in special hospitals deserve the best of medical attention with regular review of their cases, and this cannot be provided properly when each consultant has over 100 patients to treat. One full-time consultant for sixty-five patients should prove a maximum case-load (Hamilton 1985: 97).

[8] Only one RMO had a mixture of male and female wards; the other RMOs confined their responsibilities primarily to one house. In addition to the RMOs there were eleven associate specialists, senior registrars, and psychotherapists variously involved with the patients and numerous other qualified individuals—for example, psychologists, social workers, and occupational therapists.

One RMO interviewed felt there should be a maximum case-load of 30—yet another felt that he provided better individual care when responsible for nearing 200 patients. How can these views be reconciled?

B. Tribunals: Administrative Burden or Therapeutic Tool?

(i) Contact Despite the assorted benefits which tribunals could bring, these were not considered to outweigh what were seen as numerous disadvantages. Some of the RMOs resented the amount of extra work placed upon them by the demands of the tribunals under the new Mental Health Act.[9] This was regarded as divisive both of their time ('more spent in office writing reports') and of a proper therapeutic relationship with and treatment programme for their patients. Indeed, one RMO forcibly maintained that the 'pressures and demands' generated by the tribunals were 'destroying [any] therapeutic relationship', and that he was no longer seeing patients on a treatment basis, but only on a review basis. Another argued that where patients believed that their 'way out' of the hospital would come via the law, rather than through treatment and change, they were not motivated to co-operate with therapy; where a tribunal was pending planned psychotherapy might be stopped.[10] Since patients had the right to apply every year and tribunals could take many months to arrange, it was sometimes the case that patients were only available for treatment for about a third of the year. The process was regarded as a vicious roundabout; patients would only 'come round' after two or three turn-downs by the tribunal, but up until that point they would not be co-operative. Thus, tribunals 'interrupt beneficial progress'.[11]

The frequency of tribunal review could also disrupt the RMOs' independent plans for patients. First, the Home Secretary might delay transfer on the grounds that a tribunal hearing was pending and the Home Office would like the benefit of the tribunal's advice. Secondly, the tribunal might not favour the transfer or conditional discharge of a patient which the RMO sought; hence, the tribunal could act as a stumbling-block rather than a stepping-

---

[9] One RMO was an exception—he said that there was no extra work because patients were regularly under review anyway.

[10] On the grounds that where resources were scarce it was better to direct them to those patients not seeking immediate discharge.

[11] This impelled one RMO to recommend a return to two-yearly applications to tribunals and not, as at present, annual.

stone. Third, one RMO, again pursuing the distracting impact of tribunal hearings, noted that at least three of his patients would have been moved on 'long ago' had he had the time to write recommendations for the Home Secretary, but with all the tribunal work and tribunal reports he had not even had time to get their files out.

Not all the RMOs regarded the redistribution of their time as retrograde, since it forced them both to review patients' cases and to muster their arguments cogently for the tribunal (as opposed to knowing that the Home Secretary would simply adhere to any recommendation they made for *no* change under the 1959 Act). Secondly, the opportunity for face-to-face explanations was particularly welcome. For example, one RMO said he went to the tribunal as the patient's ally; making it clear that *he* was not their custodian improved his future relationship with them. Third, some of the RMOs valued the opportunity to observe patients at hearings, under stress, in novel situations, and with their families. Others took the opposite view that they would be very surprised (and disappointed in themselves as RMOs) if anything new emerged at the tribunal hearing—'whatever is learnt is at great cost'. If their patients needed to be placed in stressful situations (a dubious proposition in itself) they, as RMOs, should already be doing it. Curiously, they also emphasized that the doctor–patient relationship needed to continue *after* the tribunal. A presumption that patients would not be discharged was evident.

Finally, one group of patients were identifed as benefiting specifically from tribunal turn-downs, namely the recently admitted patients. In those instances where patients claimed to have been unjustly sent to Acheland, this independent review of the necessity for their detention could help to settle them into a treatment programme.

(ii) Disclosure The RMOs were also split over the question of whether they should object to psychiatric reports being shown to patients. Initially, the tribunal staff had experienced real problems with the Acheland RMOs as they would routinely object to patients seeing reports. Rule 6(4) of the Tribunal Rules allows RMOs to recommend to the tribunal that patients should not see parts, or indeed all, of their reports—usually on the grounds that it would be harmful to the doctor–patient relationship. Clearly, there always are patients whose particular circumstances make such

provisions necessary.[12] The question becomes how much information and of what nature is it harmful for patients to know? Furthermore, does this include their present medical state, their progress or lack of it within hospital, and the psychiatrists' opinions as to what is the most appropriate course for them?

After some early rancour the Acheland RMOs had mostly decided not to pursue their objections to disclosure. Indeed, one of the most vocal opponents ultimately came to value disclosure. Another, although he remained unpersuaded, ceased objecting on pragmatic grounds. One or two RMOs objected more frequently than others, regarding specific patients as more vulnerable or less able to handle the *content* of the reports. Yet others believed that it was the *format* of the information which was most damaging; written reports could be handed around, reanalysed, misinterpreted, and brooded upon—their impact could thus be long-standing.[13] The remaining RMOs almost never objected, taking the view that it was preferable to have an open relationship with patients where information was freely exchanged; in this context the tribunal hearing was regarded as a 'tremendous bonus' for the doctor–patient relationship.

One point of likely consensus emerged; none of the RMOs had control over the content of the social-work report, which would also be disclosed to patients. Yet this information was often the most potentially damaging (since it might include, for example, families' attitudes to a patient's possible return home). Although social workers could object to disclosure, there was concern about whether they would necessarily know which parts of their reports the RMOs considered the most sensitive. This concern was heightened when administrative errors, described by one RMO as 'careless not malevolent procedures', at the tribunal office (or alternatively by representatives) led to patients seeing information where the tribunal had not advised disclosure. Such slip-ups were felt to make the RMOs' role significantly harder.

---

[12] For example, where patients confide in the staff and not the RMO, but that information is none the less passed on by the staff to the RMO, problems can arise over its inclusion in reports. Since the need for patients to continue to confide in someone, for example about sadistic fantasies, is considered paramount, it may be thought inadvisable that patients should learn that both their RMOs and the tribunal are, in fact, fully informed of these matters.

[13] One RMO made a similar point about *written* tribunal decisions.

(iii) Professional relationships There was also some dispute amongst the RMOs about whether other members of staff should present their views about the patient directly to the tribunal. They may well have had much greater contact than the RMO with the patient in question. None the less, such an approach was widely considered divisive, almost to the point of being regarded as disloyal to the RMO; one RMO firmly believed that he should represent the views of the staff and that a consensus would emerge *before* the tribunal. An increasing reliance on multi-disciplinary case conferences is, of course, likely to facilitate this. However, where members of staff had reached alternative views and submitted a separate report to the tribunal, considerable hostility had arisen between them and individual RMOs.

(iv) Decision-making with responsibility Although some of the RMOs criticized the tribunals for not being prepared to recommend for transfer those patients who remained ill, but did not require Special Hospital care,[14] they also feared that the tribunals made recommendations where the RMOs were opposed to any change in a patient's status. Thus, in cases where patients' illnesses had stabilized or receded, but where the RMOs believed they remained dangerous (or not *yet* ready to be moved on), the tribunals, being guided by their supposedly civil libertarian instincts, might recommend transfer or order a discharge. The empirical research suggests that these fears are groundless, vindicating the view of one RMO who noted 'all the tribunal is really concerned about is whether the patient is safe' and who further asserted that 'the judges were appointed simply to block the discharge of patients'. Whether these generalizations about the tribunal resulted from a lack of familiarity with the tribunal's criteria[15] or from having observed tribunal decisions is unclear. Alternatively, perhaps the tribunal merely reflected the advice they received from the RMOs; as one RMO stated 'for the very dangerous I don't mind bending the law'.

RMOs had all experienced decisions or recommendations by the tribunal with which they disagreed—usually in respect of the

[14] Although the RMOs said *they* would be prepared to make such recommendations in the presence of illness, implying the tribunals were intimidated by psychiatric illness.

[15] S72(*b*)(iii) and associated sections. The preceding subsections give pre-eminence to illness criteria—'dangerousness' appears rarely in the Act; its use in *b*(iii) above almost never applies in the Special Hospitals.

latter, because there was only a handful of cases where the tribunal had discharged against the RMO's advice. Further difficulties had arisen where the tribunal had given short notice of their intentions and there was little time for the RMOs to make the necessary supervisory arrangements. The RMOs were sensitive to the possibility that the tribunal might have assumed that they had tried actively to frustrate the decision. But they did accept that in the vast majority of cases the tribunal did not go against their advice. In this respect tribunals were characterized as 'a shop window [for the public] and a safety-valve [for the patient]'. Although the *process* of tribunal review had altered with the 1983 Act, the *outcome* was not much different from that under the 1959 Act. The RMOs seemed to regard this as for their patients' benefit and not to their benefit.

Clearly locating the responsibility for decisions, particularly those to which they were opposed, was identified by the RMOs as a matter of some importance; if things subsequently went wrong they did not want the accusatorial finger pointed at them. Decisions contrary to their advice might be made, for example, where an independent psychiatrist's advice was preferred by the tribunal. Their approach was to distance themselves: 'where tribunals discharge against my advice it's not my concern'.

The dilemma which arose when the tribunal made a recommendation for transfer with which the RMO disagreed was comparatively easily resolved. The view was put that it was no part of the tribunal's function to consider whether a (restricted) patient was well enough to be recommended for transfer. Some RMOs therefore said they would do nothing (although they accepted that the judges were increasingly alive to this tactic and were making further inquiries about the responses to their recommendations). Others said they would make an approach to the appropriate receiving hospital, but make their view clear—thus, 'going through the motions'. Only one said, 'I am happy to look for an alternative placement.'

Preferably, RMOs would try to bring the tribunal round to their point of view and ensure that inappropriate decisions were not made in the first instance. Two less reputable strategies emerged, employed by two different RMOs. One claimed that he told the tribunal directly that he would not comply with their recommendations. Another, it was suggested, would withdraw a patient's medication prior to the hearing so that the tribunal would be convinced that the patient was ill and in need of treatment and/or detention.

Similarly, the RMOs objected to 'independent' (or 'private' as some preferred them to be known) psychiatrists making recommendations about a patient's suitability for transfer without offering a bed in their hospital. Discussing the case with the RMOs or the staff was seen as a prerequisite to ensuring that these 'independent' reports were not written 'in ignorance of the facts'. Those who failed to engage in these preliminary inquiries were considered, at the very least, discourteous. Only one RMO said this discussion should not occur outside the open setting of tribunal. Finally, representatives were considered irresponsible when an independent psychiatric report which did not favour any change in the patient's status, was withheld from the tribunal. This was felt to epitomize the adversarial approach so denigrated by the RMOs, rather than an investigatorial approach which tried to cope with real problems in the light of all the evidence. Where independent reports had been prepared, but not presented to the tribunal, the RMOs had, on occasions, felt it necessary to inform the tribunal of the existence of this 'alternative' view.[16]

(v) Reflective v. reflexive decision-making Tribunal decisions were characterized by the RMOs, as essentially precipitative (alternatively, provocative). They viewed their own decisions as being made in the context of a longitudinal knowledge of the patient and a planned programme for moving a patient on. Conflict was inevitable.

This conflict arises first in the apparent gap between RMOs' recommendations in their reports to the tribunal (see Schedule 1 MHRT Rules) and those made to the Home Secretary in their annual reports, as required under S41(6) of the 1983 Act. As one RMO remarked, it was because tribunal decisions were black and white—and there was no black and white way out of Acheland— that the conclusions you were forced to draw at a given point in response to the tribunal would not necessarily tally with those you might simultaneously be sending to the Home Office in a report geared to urging transfer. Another, not dissimilar, perspective was advanced by the RMO who noted that the same information need

---

[16] The empirical research clearly indicates that 'negative' reports or reports concurring with the views of the RMO are routinely submitted to the tribunal. See also *W.* v. *Egdell and others* Times Law Report 14 Dec. 1988.

not necessarily impel one inevitably to the same conclusion. He explained that under pressure he had changed the conclusion to one of his reports (in this instance originally being *against* admission to a Special Hospital) without changing any of the preceding content. Having the opportunity to reflect on a decision may produce a rather different outcome to that of the tribunal where a decision is required at a specific point in time.

Most of the RMOs agreed that it was appropriate for patients to have the right to have the necessity for their continued detention reviewed by an independent body. But, at the same time, they felt that it was not essentially their business. One RMO expressed the view that it was right that a patient should be able to question the authority for his detention, but wrong that he (as RMO) should be cross-examined. His report represented his view, so why was it also necessary to 'put him on trial'? And if it was, shouldn't he also be legally represented? He felt that he should not have to sacrifice his clinical time to argue with lawyers about psychiatry.

The majority of RMOs neither encouraged nor discouraged patients in their applications (one exceptionally said he did encourage patients to apply). Another said that he liked to share his difficult decisions with the tribunal, whilst others agreed that a tribunal application could act as a catalyst in formulating their own views. One even accepted that the tribunal could alter his point of view. Finally, it was implied that the tribunal might have discouraged RMOs from actively pursuing their statutory role since, as one RMO put it, he 'allowed the tribunal to push where previously he pushed'. Although sometimes in conflict, the relationship between the RMOs and the tribunals was more complex; clearly, it was dynamic and occasionally symbiotic.

C. Time for Crime: The Moral Threshold

Under the 1959 Act, where the discharge of restricted patients lay solely within the discretion of the Home Secretary, it was generally held that patients would not be moved from Special Hospitals until they had been detained for a period of time commensurate with the gravity of the offence they had committed. This was known as doing 'time for crime'.

Since the 1983 Act specified that detention in a hospital is only justified where a patient requires medical treatment, it prohibits 'time for crime'.[17] Tribunals are obliged to discharge patients if they are not suffering from a specified mental disorder to the requisite degree *even if* detention would be justified in the interests of the patient's health or safety, or with a view to the protection of other persons.

If the statutory criteria are applied literally, problems can arise. Patients whose illnesses recede or stabilize under the Special Hospital regime, but who, in the view of their RMOs, the tribunal, and the Home Office remain dangerous, pose obvious difficulties. A flexible interpretation of the need for medical treatment (which the 1983 Act permits, for example, as habilitation under medical supervision) and a presumption that the underlying disorder continues despite lack of symptoms (a particular problem for psychopathic disorder where the definition depends upon the patient's *behaviour*) can get around the difficulty. But this may be open to allegations that the responsible parties have colluded in criteria-stretching. Thus, 'even if we cure a guy of his paranoid symptoms we don't necessarily cure him in the sense that he needs help with his grief' for what he may have done. And 'paranoid disorders reflect a personality trait—unless you've good reason to assume otherwise you have to assume that his interest in killing persists—just that his opportunities have been limited'.

In terms of time for crime two categories of problem arise: first, the 'potential understayers', patients who commit serious offences but make rapid recoveries; and secondly, the 'potential overstayers', those who commit comparatively non-serious offences, but whose disorders persist.

The latter group are not a problem in terms of the 1983 Act (but did worry those RMOs with a greater respect for the civil liberties arguments).[18] Although the RMOs were all painfully aware of the consequences of a wrong decision to discharge or transfer, the opposite conundrum, of a wrong decision *not* to move a patient on, was considered less pressing. As one RMO questioned, 'When a mentally ill patient has had his symptoms controlled is it necessarily morally wrong for him to continue to be detained—is it necessarily ill-treating him?' Although they recognised tendencies to overcaution in each other, they were largely reluctant to admit it in themselves. Moreover, as caution could result merely from a

[17] One exception to the requirement for medical treatment is admission for assessment S2(2)(*a*) 1983 Act.

[18] See, for example, Grounds (1987*a*).

failure to pursue their statutory responsibilities and the obligations arising therefrom with vigour, it was seen as an attractive failing.

Potential understayers clearly were a problem. Although the RMOs denied that a time for crime policy operated under the 1983 Act, they accepted that, in the final analysis, patients often remained for a period commensurate with their offences. In this respect the 1983 Act had merely changed the process of tribunal review, but decisions in restricted cases remained much the same as those previously made by the Home Secretary.[19] A number of explanations were offered. Some of the RMOs believed that, since risk was the tribunal's principal decision criterion, the potentially dangerous (but not actively ill) patient would remain in Acheland. Others alleged that the Home Secretary had recently begun to operate a time for crime approach. This meant that recommendations for transfer to local hospitals would be blocked, as these hospitals were in no position to detain patients for long periods when they were not ill. Once out of the clutches of the Special Hospital, where a longer time scale for recovery existed, the Home Secretary would have some difficulty in delaying the eventual discharge of recovered patients. Hence, lifers would be returned to prison for parole, and transfer would generally be opposed until the appropriate time-period had elapsed.

One RMO recognized that this policy might have an impact on his decisions to submit recommendations to the Home Office. If he knew they would be rejected on covert tariff criteria, there seemed no point forwarding a report in the first instance. But he also recognized the danger of second-guessing the Home Office. His personal judgment as to the tariff sentence—what the likely punishment would have been in years of imprisonment—influenced when he would submit his first report with a recommendation for change. Or, as Parker (1980: 468) notes

The apparent absence of conflict over discharge of restricted patients does not mean that such patients are not detained for purely custodial purposes, in some cases long after the cessation of any therapeutic reason for in-patient care. It is likely that doctors who are prepared to accept restricted patients learn to propose for discharge only those whom they know from past experience will tend to be acceptable to the Home Office.

---

[19] See Dell and Robertson (1988). Length of stay correlated with the gravity of the offence for those with non-psychotic disorders (the psychopaths), but not for those with mental-illness classifications.

Should this be so, then in some instances hospitals are being used in lieu of prisons.

This is obviously time for crime operating at second-hand, with no control over whether the RMO's judgments about the appropriateness of the length of time he delayed a report were correct. Since no change was likely (with the rare exception of tribunal discharge) without this impetus from the RMO, the impact on patients remained the same as under the 1959 Act, even if the process was covert rather than overt.

Another RMO refuted this position and blamed the ambiguity in some of his colleagues' reports for the fact that the Home Office were able to flex time for crime arguments. An authoritative conclusion, he believed, would overcome this problem; 'time for crime' was 'erroneous, fallacious and unacceptable except', he added, 'at the very serious end of the scale.' He did not specify where this 'very serious end' started.

Another potential source for time for crime judgments derived from the staff, who were alleged to 'cling to time for crime'. Since institutionalization was recognized to be as big a problem amongst some of the staff as amongst the patients, it was not assumed that staff's attitudes had changed in line with the legislation. However, none of the RMOs identified this as causing them problems. This was a little unexpected; the readiness to accept a problem with the Home Office, but not to realize that much of the information about their patients came to them filtered through the eyes of staff who, in turn, were likely to base their assessments on some questionable value-judgments, was ironic. The irony was heightened when one RMO blamed the Home Office's time for crime judgments, not on political considerations (which may or may not be the true source), but on the fact that the Home Office were likely to come to a bleak view about patients because all their information came to them in report form—second-hand at least. The same handicap applies, if a little less forcibly, to the RMOs, but their filter was identified as unreliable, whereas presumably the Home Office's assessment of the RMOs was that they were reliable. Thus, one group of decision-makers, the RMOs, gave credence to a source they considered questionable (the staff) whilst another group, at the Home Office, were prepared to reject the recommendations of a source presumably valued (the RMOs).

II. CONCLUSIONS

The role of the RMOs in Acheland is undoubtedly challenging. They have to cope with a range of difficult and disturbed patients, some of whom would be better located elsewhere. Whatever view one has of the practice of psychiatry, RMOs are in the unenviable position of having to wear two hats—and hats arguably only properly donned by magicians. First, they are charged with 'curing', or, at the least, caring for the mentally disordered. Secondly, RMOs have the legal responsibility for ensuring that these individuals 'disappear' from public view for only so long as is medically justified. But, what is justified has a legal definition, as, for example, in the case of psychopathic disorder, and not a purely medical one; conflict is immediately apparent.

Wearing their two hats, as therapist and custodian, RMOs come into further conflict with almost all of those with whom they have contact: patients, staff, the tribunals, the Home Office, and independent psychiatrists. There may be disagreements even with their colleagues over which patients to admit or whether it is possible to treat them; as therapists, they may not consider amenable to treatment those in respect of whom they are required to fulfil custodial roles. Difficulties arise both out of their conflicting roles in respect of different categories of patients and over the appropriate time-scale to be employed.[20] It has already been noted that some RMOs characterize tribunals as an unfortunate interruption, disturbing continuity of care; yet the tribunal can be equally critical, regarding some RMOs as dragging their feet, wishing to hang on to their patients, and being uncooperative and overprotective.

Despite these accepted difficulties there are a number of areas where RMOs might improve their practices or, indeed, minimize some of the inevitable conflicts. The first is in respect of their dealings with patients. It has already been argued that RMOs must take responsibility for resolving the problems which arise when patients apply for hearings with the principal intention of discovering information about their own cases. On the basis of

---

[20] One RMO readily accepted that the time scale within Acheland was much longer than outside. Therefore, independent psychiatrists and tribunal doctors who may view a period of twelve months' stability as sufficient evidence to move a patient on, were likely to be at odds with an Acheland time-scale seeking, in some cases, three or more years stability.

these interviews it might be suggested that some RMOs are relying upon the Act and the extra work entailed in hearings, as a justification for obviating some of their therapeutic responsibilities. Certainly, their limited view of patients' motivations in applying (that of litigious patients keen to be discharged) is inaccurate. However, it has a number of unfortunate consequences. The most worrying concerns a tendency to interpret an application as a sign of non-cooperation, and consequently to put treatment temporarily 'on ice'. Moreover, the interviews with the patients have suggested that contact between patients and their RMOs can be infrequent—and certainly is less than most of the patients would have wished. The RMOs' interviews confirmed this low level of direct contact. Some of the RMOs clearly blamed tribunal work for this; others adopted a policy of seeing patients on request (although some patients denied that this facility worked), or at crisis points. As a result, patients who neither created management problems, nor presented clinical crises, nor regularly exercised their rights to apply for a tribunal, were likely to experience greater difficulties achieving a satisfactory level of contact with their RMOs than their less quiescent peers.

It is also notable that the RMOs readily accepted that their relationships with some patients were difficult. This was, in some respects, inevitable. Often the patients regarded their RMOs as the principal stumbling-block to their moving on; their custodial role did not enhance the doctor–patient relationship. Although two of the RMOs recognized this difficulty (one attempting to combat it by using the tribunal to take partial responsibility for decisions about patients) the majority did not identify it as a major hurdle in their role of 'treaters'. But, from the patients' perspective, RMOs determined not only what treatment was appropriate, and when or whether it had been successful, but also how long patients would be detained in terms of their potential dangerousness. It might be argued that their therapeutic role would be improved by divesting RMOs of this custodial function—probably an attractive option to RMOs resistant, if not hostile, to the aims of the Act. Some still retain the 'doctor knows best' approach; the resentment shown to other staff members expressing independent views testifies to this.[21] But there would be drawbacks. For example, because of their central position, when properly fulfilling both roles, the RMOs can ensure that patients do not stay in

[21] See Peay (1988b).

compulsory treatment any longer than is justified. Therefore, the dual hat system may be a necessary evil.

Perhaps the solution lies in educating the RMOs about their roles, and ensuring that they give credence to their legal responsibilities. This constitutes the second major area where the RMOs might succeed in reducing conflict. The research has shown the RMOs to be ready to criticize independent psychiatrists for making what they perceive to be irresponsible recommendations (even though RMOs know that there is no point in an IP offering a bed unless it also happens to be in the patient's catchment area). Yet the RMOs do not fully accept the responsibilities that come with their custodial role. They are critical in initiating change. They may argue that they are only one part of a dynamic system, but nevertheless their role is central, both in providing information and as guardians of patients' day-to-day well-being; they rest on the top of the credibility hierarchy.[22] To give precedence to their therapeutic hat or even to employ it as a means of avoiding these responsibilities may be understandable, but is it justified? To allege that the tribunals have overdeveloped civil libertarian instincts is not merited; that is their function. Indeed, the research findings suggest that it is a function which they do not fully pursue. Perhaps the RMOs would benefit from having such instincts more acutely developed? It is ironic that the research should show some of the RMOs attempting to retain power and sustain their previous working practices by working around the Act. Properly applied, the Act puts them in a position of considerable power.

Finally, there is the area of conflict between the RMOs and the tribunals. Clearly, patients who pose dilemmas for the RMOs in terms of their statutory role within the 1983 Act (e.g., the stabilized chronic schizophrenic, the sexual deviant) should also pose dilemmas for the tribunal. Yet, in practice, the tribunals follow the RMOs' 'non'-decisions, illustrating the real influence of the RMOs. Even where decisions were made to transfer patients, the legal bind continued; the 'Gordian knot' was not untied, but simply passed on. Or, as one RMO put it, 'the tribunal see themselves as the last protective barrier'.

In order to exert this powerful influence, the RMOs have to be present at hearings. In this respect their attendance is not a 'waste of time'. Since there is frequently considerable delay before

[22] See Becker (1967) at p. 239.

hearings take place, RMOs have to be present, if only to update their reports. In addition, they may wish to expand on what may be a comparatively short report, when a different perspective is placed on the facts by patients or their representatives. But perhaps the most important reason for the RMOs' attendance concerns the gap, discussed in Chapter 2, between how patients appear on paper and how they present in person. At tribunals, many patients seem quite well—intelligent, articulate, charming, and not at all the image of their reports. Yet, from the RMOs' perspective, this is inevitable. The RMOs readily accept that they would wish to keep patients for a year or more within the secure environment *once* they are stabilized. With the frequency of reviews patients will naturally have hearings during this stabilized period; there will therefore be conflict between the tribunal and the RMO. As RMOs recognize, tribunals deal with the 'here and now', psychiatrists with the past and the future. When a precipitative decision-making body comes into contact with the caring, but careful and cautious approach of the RMOs, something will have to give. With RMOs present at hearings, it seems that it is not their views, but ultimately the integrity of the tribunals' decision criteria which have to be compromised. If the RMOs were not present, would the tribunal's decisions so frequently concur with theirs?

5. The Influence of the Judicial Approach

The era of judicial openness ushered in with the appointment of Lord Mackay of Clashfern as Lord Chancellor in October 1987 post-dated the conduct of this research. The Kilmuir rules, which counselled that 'So long as a judge keeps silent, his reputation for impartiality remains unassailable', were hence in full force, making access to the judiciary problematic.[1] The judicial interviews on which this chapter is based thus represent one of the few attempts to question judges directly. Indeed, it was the first study to pass successfully through the monitoring process set up by the judiciary after the demise of an earlier inquiry into sentencing practices.[2]

This chapter draws on extended semi-structured interviews conducted with all of the judicial members of one regional panel, consisting of eight judges and three recorders.[3] In the light of the difficulties of gaining access to the judiciary, even these small numbers constitute a minor coup. Although the interviews ranged widely over matters concerning both the 1983 Act and the Tribunal Rules, they focused specifically on issues relating to the tribunal's function, questions of procedure, the quality of the information submitted to the tribunal, and the interpretation of the tribunal's decision criteria.

---

[1] The Kilmuir rules emanated in 1955 from the then Lord Chancellor, to provide serving judges with guidance about their 'non-judicial' public pronouncements (see Judge James Pickles. Kilmuir rules—OK? *'Guardian'* 14 Feb. 1986). Overcoming the resultant impenetrability of the judiciary required a draft interview schedule to be submitted in the first instance to the Lord Chancellor's Department. With their advice and support this document was further submitted to the office of the Lord Chief Justice, where permission was granted for the judicial interviews to proceed. A High Court judge was subsequently nominated to oversee this aspect of the research.

[2] These special arrangements were introduced after an inquiry into sentencing practices carried out by the Centre for Criminological Research was blocked by members of the senior judiciary. See Ashworth *et al.* (1984).

[3] Undoubtedly the support of the senior judiciary was influential in obtaining excellent co-operation and a 100 per cent response rate from the judicial members.

Interpreting and reporting interviews with judges also raises problems. By the very nature of their experience—working primarily in isolation from one another—judges' views are unlikely to be cloned. Their opinions are frequently strongly held and expressed with colourful force. In the context of the undoubtedly demanding role judges have undertaken in dealing with restricted cases, where there are rarely right answers, it would have been easy, but unfair, to compare and contrast divergent views at the expense of judicial soundness. Moreover, the small sample size makes it divisive to discuss the absolute numbers endorsing particular positions. As a consequence, the judges' views are presented primarily as tendencies towards differing approaches.

1. THE RATIONALE FOR JUDICIAL APPOINTMENTS

It was readily evident that there was some confusion and uncertainty amongst the judicial members about the impetus behind the strengthening of restricted tribunals and, indeed, for their own appointment. In essence, there were three principal reasons. First, concern for public safety. Individuals with judicial experience in the *criminal* courts might be expected to be more aware of factors of risk to the public and the probability of repetition of criminal behaviour and hence to give more prominence to questions of public safety.[4]

The second major consideration is not easily distinguished from the first. It could crudely, and controversially, be characterized as providing an appropriate retributive element in the decision to discharge. In principle, once the decision has been made in the Crown Court to make a hospital order, there should be no scope for retributive considerations. The 1983 Act is quite clear on this one point. If a person no longer suffers to the requisite degree, detention cannot be prolonged in spite of any risk to the public that might be predicted, let alone any consideration of desert.[5]

However, what was meant by the announcement that the new tribunals would have to 'command the confidence' of those Crown

[4] The emergent judicial interest in the details of patients' previous convictions, their confession statements, and details of the index offence support this.

[5] It could, of course, be maintained that this creates a false dichotomy at the point of sentence, into the bad and the mad—particularly inappropriate because it does not need to be established that there is any connection between the offending behaviour and the mental disorder—only that the individual is mentally disordered at the point of sentence.

Court judges making the initial orders? The implication was that unless the decision to release was handled properly, restriction orders might not be imposed in the first instance.[6] But what kind of errors might be made? First, 'letting people out too soon' might imply either making wrong decisions (in terms of letting out those who were still ill and potentially a risk to the public) or making risky, but legally correct decisions (in terms of letting out those who were not ill, but were a risk to the public). Alternatively, tribunals might be thought to be in error by some sentencers if they released those who may be neither a risk nor ill, but who had not spent a period in detention commensurate with the gravity of their offence—in common parlance, they had not 'done enough time for the crime'.

There are some circumstances where retributive and/or protective considerations may properly be taken into account when dealing with the cases of mentally disordered offenders. For example, where offenders receive life sentences and are then transferred to hospital for treatment, the executive retains control over their ultimate return to the community.[7] Although these patients are entitled to have their cases reviewed by the tribunal, the tribunal only has advisory powers. Where they advise that discharge would be appropriate, the Secretary of State has the option under the Act to order the return of the patient to prison and/or instruct the parole board to review the case. Thus, retributive and protective considerations can be used to overrule the tribunal's treatment-based recommendation. It is therefore arguable that the decision to appoint those with criminal rather than civil court experience may have reflected a desire to take some account of broader considerations than those strictly permitted under the Act. After all, why was it that confidence could only be guaranteed if those reviewing cases shared the sentencers' experience of criminal cases?[8]

---

[6] It would be fair to say that there always has been concern about the tribunal making 'wrong decisions', but this was recently re-expressed in DHSS and Home Office (1986).

[7] See S47 of the 1983 Act. Moreover, as changes in the parole rules for life-sentenced prisoners now require the judge to make an early statement of the retributive element in their sentence, the minimum period of custody, regardless of other factors, is established in each case.

[8] Particularly since the experience of civil court judges, who both weigh the evidence and make judicial (binding) decisions, might have been considered more appropriate to the task of presiding at a tribunal, when matters of evidence have to be weighed.

The third possible impetus for the selection of judicial members might have been to enhance procedural correctness. Tribunals under the 1959 Act had been criticized as being inconsistent in respect of both the procedures they adopted and the decisions they reached. Since, under the new arrangements, the notion of appointing solely recorders had been rejected because of potential inconsistency in their decision-making, this third explanation bears some weight.

Thus, it might have been anticipated that revisions to the tribunals' membership would both improve the way in which decisions were taken, and potentially alter the nature of those decisions.

A. *The Judicial View: Caution and Constraint*

How judges perceived their role when sitting on a tribunal was an area of some importance in the light of two of the findings of previous research. First, there was the fact that members' views about the fundamental purpose of the tribunal correlated with the number of discharge decisions they had made.[9] Secondly, the relationship between a member's attitude towards discharge and his or her discharge rate was most marked in the case of legal members. This was in itself not surprising; as the president of the tribunal, there was greater scope for the attitudes of a legal member to exert an influence than was likely to have been possible for either of the non-legal groups. Given that the tribunal's new powers in restricted cases make the nature and consequences of their decisions considerably more onerous, attitudinal factors, whatever their role, could be of some importance. As many judges observed, responsibility for the impact of one's recommendations could be a key factor in determining the nature of those recommendations.

The majority of judicial members believed that their appointments reflected considerations of public safety and that this should

[9] Peay (1980) found that, under the 1959 Act, tribunal members who selected an option which stressed the necessity of reaching a balance between the safety of the public and the liberty of the individual (56 per cent of the sample) were *less* likely to have been involved in discharge decisions than members who emphasized the protection which the review tribunal afforded the patient against unjustified detention (35 per cent of the sample). This conceptual division in respect of the tribunal's fundamental purpose is replicated in the judicial responses.

be their role. The view was also expressed that this task was regarded as so important that it had originally been intended that High Court judges should undertake the work; only public expense had resulted in the responsibility being given to those of Crown Court status. Another view expressed was that the decision had to be made by judges in order for it to be 'judicial'; judges, it was claimed, stood back from the adversary system, and were therefore better qualified to weigh public-interest considerations than those lawyers who from time to time represented one side or the other.[10]

Although most of the judges broadly endorsed the reasons already advanced for their appointment, with the question being posed 'who would impose a hospital order if the decision to release were denigrated by placing it into the hands of a lawyer with no judicial status?', one interpretation contrary to the public safety rationale was advanced. This was predicated on the belief that their job, as judicial members of the tribunal, was 'to ensure tribunals have the courage to let people out'.

Ambivalence also emerged in respect of the tribunal's role. One judge expressed the view that its primary purpose was to ensure that people 'were not deprived of their liberty when they shouldn't be'. Others took a not dissimilar view, regarding the tribunals as a means of 'placing critical pressure or encouragement where others are reluctant to take the decision alone', or as 'no more than a long stop—to rectify injustice, misunderstanding and cussedness'. However, the majority more clearly saw the tribunal's role as a balancing act: 'we're not only concerned with the individual liberty of the patient but with the safety of other people as well', and 'our decision is wider ... we have to take into account public dangers and risks'.

Perhaps the most revealing divergence emerged in response to one specific question. This concerned the well-known lacuna in the Act relating to patients who do not satisfy the statutory criteria for continued detention, but are considered to remain a danger to the public. There were in essence two approaches. The first can be loosely characterized; namely, that these patients posed unwelcome, but unavoidable, risks. Where the evidence represented an overwhelming case for discharge, the tribunals were obliged to release—albeit under stringent conditions. It was typified by one

---

[10] This would seem to constitute an argument against the appointment of recorders.

judge who stated, 'Where patients have reached the criteria I've had to release them, even if I personally feel that they will do it again. It would be dishonest to say that on the evidence we must release him, but won't.' This was endorsed by another who took the view that if patients were not ill 'but merely criminal and dangerous I would favour discharge so that they would be in the same position as in prison'. However, such comments were not typical.

The more common approach reflected the judges' primary disposition to be cautious. The statutory criteria facilitate caution; not only do the tribunal have to satisfy a stringent 'belief' criterion, but a flexible approach to the boundaries of uncertainty allows judges to give weight to public-safety considerations. These factors are discussed at length below. However, a majority of the judges were inclined to be cautious, over and above any impact the statutory criteria might have. It was clear that protective considerations were manifest in their thinking; concepts of proportionality were raised and there was widespread endorsement of the approach that permitted the 'potentially dangerous' to continue to be detained. Hence, patients who were regarded as posing unavoidable risks under the first line of reasoning advanced above, were redefined by the majority of the judges as posing unacceptable risks; these patients would not be discharged under the statutory criteria. As one judge succinctly remarked, 'The scales are heavily weighted against the mentally ill who have offended.'

Five interrelated and interdependent factors emerged which facilitated the tribunal's adoption of this fundamentally conservative approach. These factors, a combination of pragmatic and conceptual rationales, also illustrate how tribunals were able to resolve the legal difficulties which they perceived; they clarify the *why* and the *how* of tribunal decision-making.

(i) Criteria It is implicit in the criteria which tribunals should apply under S72 and S73 of the Act that in cases of uncertainty the patient should continue to be detained. This is because the wording of the statute is couched in the negative. In order to reach a decision to discharge, the tribunal has to be satisfied that the patient is not then suffering from a specified mental disorder of a sufficient nature or degree, or that it is not necessary in the interests of the patient's health or safety or for the protection of others that the patient should receive treatment. They thus have to

satisfy a belief criterion known as the 'double negative', i.e., where the tribunal is not satisfied that the patient is not suffering, they are not obliged to discharge—although they may of course still exercise (in non-restricted cases only) their discretionary powers to discharge. Hence, the criteria enable the tribunal to make cautious decisions—and indeed positively encourage them so to do.

It should also be noted that the burden of these criteria is almost the inverted image of the manner in which they appear at other sections of the Act, for example on admission to hospital.[11] Any uncertainty there will result in the patient remaining free from compulsory provisions—the balance technically favours the patient. Yet at the point of discharge, uncertainty will result in patients continuing in confinement. In this respect the Mental Health Act is 'out of keeping' with many other provisions dealing with the liberty of the individual, for example, in child-care legislation; normally it is the detaining authority who would have to make out the case for continued deprivation of liberty; at tribunals, the burden seemingly falls on the patient.

It is interesting that many judicial members did not like having to employ the double negative—they considered it grammatically 'inelegant' and conceptually difficult.[12] However, it gained in favour as members came to realize that, in cases of uncertainty, it captured well the position in which tribunals found themselves. Therefore, some tribunals employed the tactic of phrasing their decision in the positive when they were confident that the patient required further treatment (hence, 'the tribunal is satisfied that further detention is necessary', etc.) and in the negative in borderline cases where they were uncertain about the possible benefits of, or further necessity for, continued treatment (hence, 'the tribunal is not satisfied that the patient is not suffering', etc.).

(ii) Powers In restricted cases the tribunal's powers are constrained; they may reach a decision to discharge, either conditionally or absolutely, and they may defer the direction for a conditional discharge, but they enjoy no explicit powers beyond these. There is little scope for manœuvrability. In essence,

---

[11] At the points of admission or renewal of compulsory orders (S3 and 20), those applying the criteria have to be satisfied in the positive, i.e., that patients are suffering to the requisite degree.

[12] Indeed, one judge went so far as to say he found it 'incomprehensible' and that his rule of thumb was that he needed to be 'satisfied that it was safe'.

tribunals are bound to take high-risk options, or not to discharge at all, since the easing strategies that they might employ to test out whether a patient is ready to be moved away from conditions of special security are not available to them. They can, of course, invest their hopes in the decisions of the Home Secretary and recommend that patients be transferred or given trial leave, but there is no guarantee that he will follow this option. The frustration arising out of these narrow precipitate powers had caused one judicial member not to seek reappointment to the tribunal after completing his first three-year period. The view he expressed—quite widely endorsed—was that the tribunal's work was not judicial. Tribunals invariably either made advisory recommendations to the executive or they merely rubber-stamped the authority for detention. As one judge put it: 'In 90 per cent of cases the patients do not meet the criteria and they cannot be released—therefore our function is a formality.'[13]

Furthermore, a considerable number of the judicial members believed that their advice about the future management of patients was not in practice likely to be followed by the Home Secretary. Their logic was quite straightforward. As a matter of practice the Home Secretary refers recommendations of the tribunal to the patient's RMO, for his comments.[14] The Home Secretary takes the view that the RMO's longitudinal knowledge of the patient places him in the best position to assess the immediate wisdom of the tribunal's recommendation. Unless the process of tribunal review radically changes the RMO's opinion it is inevitable that the RMO will advise the Home Secretary against the tribunal's recommendations. This is because, had he been in agreement to, say, a transfer or trial leave, he could independently have so informed the Home Secretary before the hearing even took place. Therefore, he will have been opposing change in the patient's circumstances at the tribunal and will continue to do so, through the Home Secretary, after the tribunal.

There is, of course, an alternative scenario which was more common at one of the Special Hospitals. There, RMOs had, in

---

[13] There was also some cynical resentment that the judicial appointments had been made to ensure that those release decisions which proved incorrect—in the sense that the patient 'publicly' re-offended—'would not be associated with career politicians, but that the tribunal would "carry the can"'.

[14] The administrative arrangements have now been clarified in a parliamentary answer, discussed in Ch. 9 below.

some cases, been urging the Home Secretary to transfer or, less commonly, discharge patients. Where the Home Secretary had chosen not to accept their advice, RMOs had supported the patient's application to the tribunal. In some of these cases tribunals were disposed not to accept the RMO's advice; after all, they would have received a report from the Home Secretary to the effect that the patient was not fit to be moved on. But in those rare cases where the RMO was recommending transfer and the tribunal endorsed this view, yet still the Home Secretary did not grant his permission, the tribunal found itself in a doubly frustrating position.

(iii) Evidence The occasions on which a tribunal would wish to go against the views of the RMO were infrequent; disagreements almost always concerned matters of timing rather than matters of substance. However, very occasionally the tribunal were faced with more than one independent psychiatric report (IPR), all firmly of the view that further detention for treatment was unnecessary. This evidence could outweigh that of the RMO. Similarly, in a few instances the tribunal took the view that the RMO had become stale on the case, and adopted a too rigid or unjustifiable view that the patient was not fit (and might never be fit) to move on. Moreover, the small number of judicial members sitting at the Special Hospitals had become aware of the different personalities and styles of the detaining consultants; intransigence in a RMO quickly gained him a reputation that was neither helpful to the tribunal nor productive in respect of his perceived relationships with individual patients.

In addition to his *assumed* quantity of knowledge, the views of the patient's RMO would, from the tribunal's perspective, almost inevitably prove to be more persuasive because he would always appear at the tribunal to give oral evidence and up to the minute progress reports on the patient. Any challenges to his views, coming from the patient's representative, could thus be answered or otherwise refuted. Independent Psychiatrists (IPs), when they had submitted a written report to the tribunal, would not usually come to the hearing in person to back up their reports. They could thus be criticized by the tribunal at a number of levels: namely, for their so-called superficial knowledge of the patient; for their failure to offer an alternative placement if they believed the patient should be transferred (an unfair criticism bearing in mind that representatives do not always select IPs from the catchment region to which the patient must be returned); and for not having the up-to-date information that the RMO had at his command (the observation can be made that an IP's view might have changed or might change in the light of recent evidence from the RMO). Thus, unless their authors attended the tribunal hearing, and allowed their evidence to be tested through cross-examination, questionable weight was attached to independent reports. Finally, some, but not all, judicial members adopted the view that since IPs were employed by patients' solicitors, they could not truly be regarded as independent. The judges claimed that they had been pressed by the RMOs to regard these as 'private' reports, on the grounds that 'he who pays the the piper calls the tune'. This view was strengthened where reports, once prepared, were not submitted by the representative. These largely negative appraisals were encapsulated by one judicial member, 'Without a personal knowledge of the patient, independent reports are not terribly helpful because of the level of knowledge about the patient. There is a danger of textbook generalized views if there is not enough practical knowledge of the patient.' This contrasts markedly with the judicial member who refuted the suggestion that independent reports should be regarded as 'partial'. He noted that, in medicine, it was accepted practice for a doctor giving a second opinion to base it on a single examination of a patient.

Bearing in mind the general preparedness of the judiciary to endorse psychiatric recommendations for treatment, particularly where treatment was being proposed in conditions of security, it was not surprising that tribunals routinely deferred to RMOs.[15] As one judicial member put it, 'It's a brave tribunal to say that a patient is fit for conditional discharge in the teeth of opposition from the RMO. I would hesitate long before doing it unless there was very strong outside evidence.' It was only where the medical member of the tribunal was strongly in favour of some form of change (and many medical members had questionable experience for making such authoritative recommendations) that the tribunal were prepared to grasp the nettle and cajole, coax, coerce, or, in exceptional circumstances, confront the RMO with an alternative view.

[15] There is a greater tendency to defer where hospital orders are recommended than when psychiatric orders are being proposed—see Mackay (1986).

However, the majority of the judicial members stated that they were most likely to be opposed to an RMO's views where they believed he wished to take an unjustifiable risk, for example, allowing the patient greater freedom. Therefore, it was *not* the case, as might intuitively have been expected, that disputes between tribunal and RMO occurred primarily when the RMO was being too cautious. Rather, according to the judges, they arose where the tribunal perceived the RMO, or for that matter the IP, as being insufficiently cautious.[16] In this respect the balanced view tribunal review seemingly afforded was, in practice, tilted in favour of public safety considerations.

(iv) Systemic Difficulties Unless the tribunal ordered some form of discharge, the Home Secretary enjoyed the last word in restricted cases. Where any doubt existed in the Home Secretary's mind he could defer to the cautious view of the RMO where medical expertise so advised, or he could defer to the tribunal where the RMO's medical 'in-expertise' was promoting an unjustifiably incautious approach.[17]

Similarly, the tribunal knew that, where the RMO was opposed to transfer, he could cause exploratory inquiries at other hospitals to fall on stony ground—merely by making it plain that, as the patient's RMO, he did not believe that the time for transfer had come. Or, as one judicial member put it: 'We are totally ineffective when the RMO doesn't agree to transfer; it's a major weakness in our jurisdiction.' Or, more simply put by another: 'we have no teeth'.

Whether the source of the judges' frustration stemmed from the cautious approach of the Home Secretary or from intransigence by RMOs, it was clear that the majority would have welcomed some power either to enforce their transfer recommendations or to be able conditionally to discharge patients to other hospitals. Some judges would have welcomed as an alternative strategy the power to lift a restriction order. However, it was also very clear that the judges were not prepared to act in a manner which they considered to be irresponsible, namely, by changing a recommendation for

---

[16] These claims were supported by the subsequent observations of tribunal hearings.

[17] This implied criticism of double standards can be equally applied to the tribunal—deferring to the RMO when he says illness is present, but overruling him where he says it is not present, or not present to the requisite degree.

transfer to one of conditional discharge. Or, as one member put it, 'even if I know my recommendations will not be followed, I'll go on making them rather than change my decision'. But, the possibility that some tribunals might act precipitately, or 'out of pique', when frustrated beyond forbearance, was recognized as a potential danger.

(v) Experience of members with release decisions One last major factor may have contributed to the cautious approach, namely the comparative inexperience of the judicial members with tribunal work.[18] A minority recognized this potential drawback and expressed the view that more information about medical matters would have been welcomed, as would more training—of the sitting by Nellie format—before presiding at tribunals. But the majority argued that their judicial backgrounds, and their experience of making hospital orders and listening to psychiatric evidence in court, either equipped them for the work or, at least, made it likely that they would pick it up quickly. Clearly, judges had to weigh risks when ordering a non-custodial disposal or allowing bail. However, decisions to place someone in a secure psychiatric disposal are of a fundamentally different nature from decisions to release someone from such an environment. The first entail almost no risk to the public—restriction orders are invariably made without limit of time and can only be made given a minimum of two medical recommendations. On the other hand, decisions to release entail some element of risk, since they are invariably made against the advice of at least one group experienced in such decisions, namely, either the Home Secretary or the detaining RMO. Moreover, in these circumstances, the tribunal can potentially encounter criticism from the public, or more likely, the press.

Previous research had demonstrated that decision-makers who lacked knowledge about matters relating to psychiatry and the treatment process were less likely to reach decisions to discharge patients from hospital than those who displayed more knowledge about medical matters.[19] It could be argued that those judicial members who considered themselves sufficiently well-informed

[18] It should be stressed that the inexperience of judicial members in the region where interviews took place was not necessarily typical. Certainly, of seven judges appointed in another region, five had had experience as presidents under the 1959 Act.

[19] Peay (1981, at p. 176).

felt they did not require further information or training before undertaking tribunal work; the minority view may simply have reflected genuine inexperience in this field. Yet, the fact that a few judges felt they would have benefited from a more comprehensive initiation process was, in itself, worthy of note. The question remains, does inexperience raise doubts which cannot be resolved and which, in turn, induce caution?

II. RULES AND PROCEDURES: INTERPRETATION AND APPLICATION

It has been argued that dissatisfaction with the degree of variation in the interpretation and application of the Tribunal Rules led to their revision and may have contributed to the impetus behind the appointment of judicial members. What impact did these combined changes have on tribunal hearings?

A. The Judicial Style

The comparatively diverse backgrounds of the judicial members appointed (they were not drawn exclusively from the Crown Courts) may have exaggerated a finding familiar to those who regularly observe judges at work—namely, that judicial styles differ noticeably. Indeed, judges often acquire reputations as much for the manner in which they conduct cases as for their sentencing practices. The judicial members of the tribunal had been variously described by patients, the RMOs, and the tribunal staff as 'authoritative', 'fair', 'bombastic', and in some cases 'bumbling'. However, these attributed characteristics had not led patients to seek an adjournment for their cases so as to avoid particular judges (as occasionally happens in the Crown Courts). Even where a judicial member had a reputation that resulted in patients preferring not to have him or her preside at their tribunals, this was invariably because the patient had direct personal experience of that particular tribunal member. Hence, judges' reputations did not precede them—rather, they followed after them.

Whether these differences in judicial styles were merely superficial or whether they could have a real impact on the inherent fairness of proceedings will be discussed with reference to four areas: prehearing reviews; the disclosure of medical evidence; the timing and content of the medical member's assessment; and the conduct of the hearing.

(i) Prehearing reviews More than one of the judges appointed had considerable County Court experience. Having dealt with civil matters, often with complex family interests involved, and having had the experience of sitting as 'judge and jury', they were inclined to run their tribunals as informally as possible. Some judges even held prehearing meetings at which the RMO and the patient's representative would come before the tribunal to clarify what were the main issues in the case. This procedure expedited matters at the hearing. Another tactic employed by judges with primarily civil experience was to curtail lengthy cross-examination or indeed 'examination-in-chief' once the crucial issues had been established.[20]

(ii) Disclosure of medical evidence Under rule 6(4) of the Tribunal Rules, the RMO can request that specified parts of his report should not be disclosed to the patient. This provision was widely used by RMOs in the early stages of the operation of the 1983 Act as a way of preventing patients seeing their reports at all. In the region in question the tribunal chairman (a 'legal' rather than 'judicial' member) routinely turned down such blanket requests and asked the RMOs to specify which parts were, in fact, sensitive. Following these early teething problems this provision in the rules had been more sparingly employed. As a consequence, requests for non-disclosure under rule 12, that went for their adjudication to the tribunal (where judicial members preside in restricted cases), were more likely to be treated sympathetically. Indeed, the predominant view was that, where medical reasons were advanced for non-disclosure, the tribunal would invariably accede. This accords with the previous discussion of deference to medical expertise.

It is clear that a process of negotiation had occurred. Whether the judicial members would have taken the same view as the legal

[20] Patients' assessments as to whether or not they'd had a fair hearing were to some extent time-assessed ('I was in and out in 20 minutes', etc.), but were primarily based on whether or not they had had an opportunity to say whatever they wanted. This was not time-constrained, but related to whether the judicial member returned to the patients at the end of the hearing to give them the last word.

('non-judicial') chairman cannot be known; deference in clearly defined circumstances cannot be taken to mean whole-hearted deference. The *legal* approach has made its mark; even if the effects of the *judicial* approach were less clear.

(iii) Timing of the medical member's report to the tribunal There has been a long-standing debate about whether the medical member's observations, arising out of his examination of the patient, should constitute part of the evidence or part of the deliberative process. Which view is preferred affects the stage of the hearing at which the tribunal's legal member will seek the views of the medical member. The situation in practice remains unclear.

It was the opinion of the committee which reviewed the Tribunal Rules that the medical member's views were not part of the evidence; they should accordingly not be open to challenge by the patient or his representative.[21] However, this assessment has shifted somewhat. The powerful influence of the medical member's views has now been recognized and hence the inherent 'unfairness' of them not being put to the patient—at least in summary form.

The reason why the medical member's opinion can be so influential is clear. In cases where there is a direct conflict of evidence between the RMO and an IPR, the medical member may give the third and decisive opinion. The tribunal is not necessarily equipped to test conflicting medical evidence. Many of the medical members of the tribunal are not versed in the art of cross-examination—even if they are willing to undertake that role. On the other hand, the judicial members, who will have experience of advocacy, may not necessarily have the appropriate technical knowledge to cross-examine effectively. So, in cases of doubt, the medical member's opinion will hold sway.

The position which the majority of judges had come to adopt was that they would not seek the medical member's assessment until all of the evidence had been heard, and the parties had left the tribunal room. This approach enabled the legal and lay members to hear the patient's evidence untainted by the potentially influential views of the medical member; it also permitted the medical member to put into his assessment any further information which may have emerged as a result of the patient's perform-

[21] DHSS (1978).

ance at the hearing. One judicial member also expressed the view that any approach which allowed the medical member to express his views early would be likely to make it very difficult for the *lay* member of the tribunal to approach the case impartially.

However, opinion was divided. A number of the judicial members considered it to be a gross breach of natural justice for the patient and his representative not to be aware of the medical member's views—particularly if the tribunal intended to act on them. Some of them relied upon the medical member to speak up at the appropriate moment. Others sought the medical member's general views early so that points of disagreement could be put by the chair to the parties—thereby maintaining the appearance of a tribunal and minimizing open disagreement and conflict between the assorted medical opinions. These divergent approaches result in an obvious difficulty. If the medical member is not clear about which approach the judge adopts, and not all judges clarify the position at the start of the hearing, he may not speak up at the appropriate moment.

The Tribunal Rules are unhelpful on the matter, save in so far as it is plain that any relevant *document* they receive should be shown to the applicant (under rule 12). Some medical members had previously prepared brief written reports of their examination of the patient for the tribunal's sole consumption. Rule 11 makes it clear that medical members may make 'such notes' as they require. However, since any written submission would have to be disclosed to the patient, this practice had almost completely fallen into disuse: medical members had come only to make oral reports to the tribunal.

Another interesting divergence in practice emerged in respect of the application of rule 12 to the patient's case notes. The view was expressed by one judicial member that if he chose to look at the case notes rather than to rely on the medical member's assessment, and report on these, they would then also have to be disclosed to the patient (and incidentally, in the case of a restricted patient, to the Secretary of State). Since this was arguably inadvisable, he had refrained from inspecting the notes himself. However, many of the other judges interviewed seemingly did not share his view; it was common practice for the judicial members to refer to the case notes in order to resolve ambiguities in the reports or evidence. The case notes were not necessarily always disclosed to either the patient or his representative.

(iv) The conduct of the hearing Observations of tribunal hearings in different regions supported the conclusion that stark differences existed in the format of hearings despite the appointment of members of the judiciary to the tribunals. Some judges adopted a procedure wherein the patient would give evidence first and then an opportunity would follow for both the RMO and the tribunal to ask the patient questions. A similar strategy would be employed if the patient's representative called an IP to give oral evidence, or if members of the patient's family were present. Only when the patient's case had been completed would the RMO be asked to give his views; an opportunity would then follow for the patient or his representative to ask questions, along with the tribunal. This might be characterized as standard criminal-court procedure. However, some judges heard evidence from the RMO at a much earlier stage; in some cases RMOs were not given an opportunity to ask the patient questions or indeed to raise matters with the IP. Similarly, there was no standard procedure in respect of whether a patient's family should be present throughout the hearing. Some judges, as a matter of routine, invited them to hear the entire case; others, equally as a routine procedure, excluded them. This procedural difference could make it difficult for representatives to prepare their cases and their clients for the hearings. It is also plain that not extending the opportunity for cross-examination could well lead to the tribunal receiving partial information.

B. Applying the Decision Criteria

One of the most damning criticisms to arise out of earlier research concerned the demonstrable lack of familiarity of members of the tribunal with the statutory criteria they were expected to apply. This criticism was applicable even to the legal members of the tribunal—less than half of those questioned were aware of the tribunal's discretionary power to discharge in S26 cases (Peay 1981). The concept of knowledge being pooled at a tribunal was felt to be somewhat illusory.

The appointment of judicial members, combined with judicial seminar days to familiarize members with procedural and legal problems, should arguably have rectified this situation. However, those questions in the interview schedules relating to fine points of interpretation and detail on the statutory criteria were not generally rewarded with explicit answers. In some areas this was not surprising, because the law itself was not clear. For example, in respect of the tribunal's power to alter psychiatric classifications in restricted cases, some judges believed that they could amend classifications: others believed that they could substitute classifications but not add them; and yet others that they could add but not substitute.[22]

In areas where their understanding of the statute was less diverse, it was evident that there was judicial resistance to enforcing finer points of law. Or, as one judge put it: 'I adopt a common sense not fine detail approach to the law. If it goes against common sense then it's almost inevitably wrong'. Others echoed this view. In respect of the psychiatric definitions within the Act one judge noted that he was 'here to make decisions on the evidence ... I've not concerned myself with definitions'. Matters of definition, despite the meanings set out in $S_1(2)$ of the 1983 Act, were seen to be for the psychiatrists. Thus, 'I go for the evidence; if one [psychiatrist] says he is [psychopathic] and one says he isn't then it is for me to decide.' The judicial task of making decisions was familiar; weighing evidence and reaching conclusions was something undertaken every day in court. This was their principal role. The finer points were, as one judge noted 'for the House of Lords'.

The tentative conclusion drawn, therefore, is that the judicial members do not consider interpretation of the precise detail of the Act to be of the utmost importance; some positively expressed the view that it was irrelevant to their task. The implications of this for the attainment of a consistent application of the statutory criteria are open to speculation.

C. *Additional Information*

By and large the judicial members took the view that the more information they had to go on, the better their decisions would be. Apart from one dissenting opinion that out-of-date psychiatric reports were irrelevant, the majority of judges wished for greater access to previous psychiatric reports—admission reports were

---

[22] A similar area of confusion in respect of the power to recommend transfer in restricted cases was clarified by the cases of *Grant* v. *Mental Health Review Tribunal* and *Regina* v. *Mersey Mental Health Review Tribunal, Ex Parte O'Hara* (*Times Law Report*, 28 Apr., 1986).

singled out as most important (possibly as a counter-balance to the RMO's longstanding knowledge of the patient). They also wished automatically to be given previous tribunal decisions (two dissenting opinions); and to have comprehensive lists of previous convictions (four dissenting opinions). The desirability of having nurses give evidence to the tribunal was less clear cut—although a majority felt that this day-to-day knowledge, or a brief report culled from recent nursing notes, would be useful. Some of the judges also mentioned that they would welcome more details about the offence and about the patient's responses to any previous exposure to trust.

That those with sentencing experience should seek such details was predictable—previous convictions are the best guide to reconviction; but, quite what purpose they would serve, as other judicial members pointed out, when patients had been detained for an extended period (and were thus conviction-free) was unclear. Similarly, the offender with one very serious offence to his name, with either no antecedents or only an adolescent history of minor theft or criminal damage, might argue that information on previous convictions was at best irrelevant, and at worst misleading.

It can, of course, be maintained that less information is required to be satisfied that someone is suffering from a psychiatric disorder, than to be satisfied that they are not suffering, or not suffering to the requisite degree. This was captured by the judge who stated that 'the fullest possible reports are required when considering letting someone out, in order to feel quite safe'.

Another question is whether tribunals would reach better decisions if they were given more information in the same haphazard form in which they currently receive it. Alternatively, would they merely selectively use the information to confirm decisions which they would have reached regardless? Hogarth's (1971) seminal study of decision-making demonstrated that information inconsistent with the preferred outcome was actively filtered out by sentencers. Thus, would more information just increase their level of confidence in the decisions they make, probably in itself a good thing, rather than changing the inherent nature of those decisions?

III. CONCLUSIONS

It has already been noted that it is harder to be satisfied that something which was present is now absent, than to be satisfied that something which was absent is now present. This difficulty is fundamental to the nature of the problem facing tribunals and goes some way to explaining some of the divergences of opinion and of practice outlined. Indeed, it is crucial to an understanding of why, on occasions, the tribunal, RMOs, and the Secretary of State may find themselves at odds with one another and yet all believe, perfectly justifiably, that their assessment is correct on the available evidence.

Making a decision to release inevitably involves some risk. Or, as one of those interviewed put it, 'judges are in the risk business—there is bound to be some risk, but otherwise you will go on being wholly cautious and no-one will ever be let out'. The difficulty lay principally in agreeing upon what was an unavoidable risk (when the statutory criteria seemingly obliged the tribunal to discharge) and what was an unacceptable risk (one which individual tribunals might or might not be prepared to take given their assessment of the evidence they have heard); and upon which categories of case fell into which bracket. More than one of the judges took the view that it was 'kindly, but wrong' to keep in hospital the medication-stabilized patient who was likely to refuse to continue with medication if discharged—this was therefore categorized as an unavoidable risk. But, many tribunals have regarded such cases as posing unacceptable risks—namely, ones which they were unwilling to take. Ultimately, such divergencies in practice are not unexpected, particularly where decision-makers strive to fulfil competing objectives. Grosman (1982: 174), discussing the dilemmas facing prosecutors noted, 'The dichotomy between the ideal and the practice is not so much a dissociation from the ideal as it is an accommodation to competing considerations.' Given the multiplicity of aims to which tribunal judges attempt to adhere, some innovative decision-making practices were bound to emerge.

Yet the tribunal's dilemmas are compounded by the conceptual and practical constraints on their decision-making. Unless tribunals are prepared to take what they may see to be high-risk options, the system will conspire against them to ensure that no half-way measures take their place. The need for certainty in decisions (satisfying the double negative) combined with the trade-off between high-risk options and making no change in a patient's circumstances, will insure that the probability of acting as an effective safeguard or, at the minimum, operating to effect change in the status quo, is small. The magnitude of these factors will tend to obscure any significant impact that the appointment of the judges may or may not have had on the outcome of tribunal decisions. The relative infrequency of discharge decisions in restricted cases, compared with the higher proportion of cases where some form of change is recommended, probably reflects the tribunal's comparative impotence—with or without the judges.

However, the existence of divergences in judges' views about fundamental issues relevant to their responsibilities is worrying. It is similarly a matter of some concern that the judges seemed ready to relegate, to a place of secondary importance, technical aspects of the law; common sense was trumps. This is, of course, not an untypical judicial response. But the fact that, by and large, the judges felt sufficiently well-qualified to take on the resolution of the very complex questions arising in the arena of mental health law without any further specific training, suggested a somewhat narrow approach. Indeed, it might be perceived as complacent.

There is also some disparity amongst the judges over the handling of cases where patients seemingly stand no chance of being discharged or are seeking only a recommendation that the tribunal have no power to enforce. Some judges took the view that they acted merely as a rubber-stamp and therefore dealt briefly with the cases; others were similarly prepared to 'shorten' cases where it was evident that the tribunal were being asked to pursue a course for which they had no statutory remit. In contrast, other judges recognized that the tribunal hearing fulfilled a variety of functions for patients who readily accepted their lack of real prospects of being discharged. These judges were prepared to hear evidence at length and thoroughly to explore the relevant issues in the presence of patients and their RMOs.

Whatever view one takes of the proper fuction of a tribunal hearing, there is clearly scope for some greater standardization in hearing procedures. Patients who apply with the intention of 'airing the issues' may be sorely disappointed if their cases come for review before a tribunal presided over by a judge who perceives this not to be its proper function.

Similarly, the appointment of judicial members has not served automatically to iron out crucial differences in procedure. As these can affect the information which is forthcoming to the tribunal they cannot be ignored merely as stylistic differences. For example, if the medical member's views are as influential as research has shown them to be, the point at which they are made apparent to the tribunal may be of fundamental importance. Furthermore, the fact that the medical member's views may not be made plain to the applicant, or may be made plain in an obtuse form, cannot be in keeping with the spirit of natural justice. Thus, depending on which judicial member sits on the tribunal, representatives and patients may neither know the full case against them (in the sense of knowing what the tribunal knows) nor know whether they are going to know it. It is clear that all of these matters would merit clarification and rationalization.

6. Patients with Classifications of Psychopathic Disorder

> The making of recommendations and decisions about discharge and continuing care of mentally disordered offenders entails, fundamentally, the assessment and prediction, by one group of human beings, of the probable future behaviour of another... The complete elimination of any risk to the public could only be achieved by continuing to detain these patients perhaps indefinitely, long after many of them had recovered from their mental disorder, and for periods in excess of any term of imprisonment they might have served as sentence for their offences. We are sure that in our society this would be seen as an inhumane avoidance of the responsibility for making a proper judgement in each case.
>
> Aarvold Report (1973, para. 57)

All of the difficulties and uncertainties associated with the discharge of mentally disordered offenders outlined in the Aarvold Report (1973) are writ large for tribunals reviewing the cases of patients diagnosed as suffering from psychopathic disorder. Indeed, there can be no doubt about the intractability of the problems posed by this group of, almost exclusively, offender-patients (Grounds et al. 1987). These have prompted some to argue (Dell and Robertson 1988; Grounds 1987a; Mawson 1983) with varying degrees of enthusiasm, that those suffering from psychopathic disorder should not, in the first instance, be dealt with under the provisions of the Mental Health Act. Rather, they have broadly advocated that such offenders should be sentenced first, and, if treatment were desirable, subsequently transferred to hospital. If this course were to be adopted, tribunals would not be faced with the difficulties associated with the prospect of releasing offender 'psychopaths' from hospital, since, if their conditions improved, 'psychopaths' could be returned to prison to complete their sentences.

A recent review of the problems specifically associated with offender 'psychopaths' (DHSS and Home Office 1986) also advanced a series of possible changes in the existing arrangements for their sentence and release. Yet, none of the statutory options the consultative document proposed were adopted. It seems likely, therefore, that the current system will remain in its present form for the foreseeable future (Peay 1988a).

This chapter examines the tribunal hearings of forty 'matched' patients suffering from psychopathic disorder detained in Acheland and Bendene Special Hospitals. It illustrates the specific problems posed by psychopaths and how tribunals attempt to resolve them. In this context, Dell and Robertson's (1988) findings that non-psychotic patients were likely to have been detained for a period commensurate, at a minimum, with the gravity of their offences, are of especial interest. If the length of detention of these 'psychopathic' patients is not determined by changes in their mental state, it is questionable whether tribunals can fully enforce 'illness' criteria when dealing with these patients.

1. PSYCHOPATHIC DISORDER: DEFINITIONS AND DIAGNOSIS

The concept of psychopathic disorder and its clinical diagnosis have a long and vexing history which has been well documented.[1] In 1970 Hare argued that although there was a problem of diagnostic reliability, in the sense that it was not always possible for psychiatrists to agree on which individual warranted the diagnosis, there was reasonable agreement about what the term meant in the abstract. More recently some progress has been made towards reconciling this apparent paradox.

The consensus view is that psychopathic disorder is not a description of a single clinical disorder but a convenient label to describe a severe personality disorder which may show itself in a variety of attitudinal, emotional and inter-personal behaviour problems. The core problem is impairment in the capacity to relate to others—to take account of their feelings and to act in ways consistent with their safety and convenience.[2]

---

[1] See Lewis (1974), Home Office and DHSS (1975), the 'Butler' Report, and Prins (1986).
[2] DHSS and Home Office (1986, para. 12).

Psychopathic disorder is thus a variant of personality disorder, but one whose diagnosis is peculiarly reliant upon the skills and assessment of the clinician. Although most psychiatrists would agree that its characteristics *should* be recognizable by the time of adolescence, the possibility that they either may prove elusive or may not have existed in the first instance, creates considerable grounds for diagnostic doubt.[3] Therefore, it is not surprising that in the cases analysed disputes emerged between psychiatrists both as to whether particular patients ever fell within the categorization and/or whether they could be presently so categorized.

In addition, the legal definition of psychopathic disorder raises special difficulties (in contrast with the non-defined category of mental illness) principally because it is a legal definition and not a clinical one. As set out in S1(2) of the 1983 Act, psychopathic disorder means 'a persistent disorder or disability of mind (whether or not including significant impairment of intelligence) which results in abnormally aggressive or seriously irresponsible conduct on the part of the person concerned'. Yet, many psychiatrists would prefer to use the generic term 'personality disorder'. This is because, although all of those who would qualify for the legal classification of psychopathic disorder could probably also be diagnosed as suffering from a personality disorder, not all of those meriting the latter clinical diagnosis, whom psychiatrists might wish to detain and treat, would necessarily qualify for the former legal classification. At a given point in time, for example, when reviewed by a tribunal, patients may fail to demonstrate 'abnormally aggressive or seriously irresponsible conduct' even if they had done so in the past. Yet, the diagnosis of personality disorder may be sustained in the presence of *less* behavioural evidence. Finally, further controversy arises in respect of the very existence of an underlying disorder of mind and whether this is identifiable in isolation from the behaviour it is assumed to cause. Whether the term psychopathic personality is intended to identify an individual with a disorder (the prevailing English approach) or to characterize those with certain persisting attributes (the American approach) has further implications for the treatments to be

---

[3] Blair (1975). Blair argues that the true psychopath has almost always exhibited severe disturbance in all areas of behaviour from a very early age. The presence of a persistent disturbance is, of course, implicit in the criteria for a diagnosis of psychopathic disorder under the 1983 Act.

adopted.[4] Thus, does the term describe what someone is or what he does?

The principal indication of psychopathic disorder in this 'matched' sample of forty cases usually concerned the nature, context, and repetition of offending behaviour, although psychometric testing and examinations of the patient's early history and school work were sometimes mentioned as serving to confirm (or count against) the diagnosis (Robins 1978). Little additional evidence was required to sustain the diagnosis. It was possible to argue that the underlying personality disorder persisted, and that the reason the patient did not continue to manifest 'abnormally aggressive or seriously irresponsible conduct' was because he or she was detained in a secure environment where the opportunities for such behaviour were limited. It was therefore very difficult to refute the diagnosis, once made, and comparatively easy for it to be sustained, even given model behaviour by the patient.

In stark contrast, the major mental illnesses are associated with positive symptoms which continue to manifest themselves even when patients are detained. The symptoms may be controlled by medication, but the underlying presence of the illness may be demonstrated by reducing or withdrawing medication. This may appear a simplistic distinction, but its implications are plain. Where some diagnostic ambivalence is present (for example, where behaviour may be attributed to a transient psychotic episode or to a persistent underlying personality disorder of which the behaviour is the first manifestation), one of the ways in which clarification may be achieved is through exploration of the patient's responsiveness to medication. Thus, where an inappropriate diagnosis of mental illness has been made, stable behaviour over time without medication will tend to favour a reclassification to psychopathic disorder (the more difficult diagnosis to refute). Although patients may be described as 'incubating' mental illnesses (a phrase sometimes used with reference to schizophrenia), such assertions become increasingly less convincing as time passes. Therefore, in the context of a long-term detained population, the tendency is for patients to be reclassified from mental illness to psychopathic disorder. Reclassification in the opposite direction did not occur in the sample of analysed cases.[5]

[4] See Blackburn (1982) and Blackburn (1983).

[5] In their survey of male patients detained in one Special Hospital Dell and Robertson (1988, p. 26) found three patients formally reclassified from psychopathic disorder to mental illness.

There is one further factor to stress, namely the certainty with which psychiatric diagnoses are made. Because of the progressive nature of the mental illnesses, diagnoses tend to become firmer with the passage of time. The presence of 'recovery' may also be more readily established, although there are particular difficulties with reference to episodic illnesses. With psychopathic disorder, the diagnosis, if anything, becomes less certain over time because the necessary behavioural evidence may not continue to be manifested, and the ability to ascertain the motivation and state of consciousness of the patient at the time at which the offence was committed may become more difficult. However, such growing uncertainty will rarely erode the diagnosis to a point where it can no longer be sustained—because of the difficulty of proving the absence of a disorder, which in itself, manifests few, if any, positive symptoms.[6]

II. THE TRIBUNALS' DECISIONS: OUTCOME MEASURES

The apparent discrepancies both in discharge rates and in the tribunals' 'advice for change' shown in Table 6.1 may be primarily accounted for by the nature of the advice tribunals received from the patients' RMOs. Tribunals in the two regions endorsed their recommendations in 85 per cent of the cases.

Where RMOs were recommending some change in a patient's status, those at Bendene were more likely to advise the tribunal that patients did not satisfy the statutory criteria necessary for

TABLE 6.1. *Tribunal outcomes in the cases of 40 patients with diagnoses of psychopathic disorder detained in Acheland and Bendene*

	Discharge (% in brackets)	Other advice[a] (% in brackets)	No discharge (% in brackets)
Acheland	1 (5)	7 (35)[b]	12 (60)
Bendene	6 (30)	3 (15)	11 (55)

[a]Transfer or trial leave recommended.
[b]Includes one case adjourned for trial leave.

[6] Therefore, the diagnosis which is most likely to stick over time, in the sense of being irrefutable, is psychopathic disorder. Diagnoses of mental illness are likely to be confidently confirmed or tentatively rejected—but a state of uncertainty is less likely.

continued detention and were entitled to be discharged. There were nine such recommendations as opposed to only four for transfer or trial leave. In contrast, the RMOs at Acheland were more likely to advise that patients did satisfy the criteria for continued detention, but no longer required the special security offered by Acheland. They were, therefore, ready to be transferred or given trial leave. Hence, at Acheland there was only one recommendation for discharge but nine for transfer or trial leave.

Why the nature of the recommendations by the RMOs at the two hospitals should differ in this respect is unclear. It may be partly attributable to their interpretations of the statutory criteria which impel them to give one type of advice or the other. It may also be a differential recognition by the RMOs of the tribunals' limited powers to enforce recommendations for transfer and trial leave. It was certainly felt by the RMOs at Bendene that their advice to the Home Secretary had frequently gone unheeded. Therefore, the only route for patients out of Bendene was tribunal discharge, which RMOs may ultimately have recommended. The RMOs at Acheland did not seem to have experienced a similar difficulty; whether they had advised fewer patients as being fit for transfer or trial leave to the Home Secretary (and therefore been turned down less frequently) or whether they made recommendations which the Home Secretary more frequently adopted, is not clear.

Another factor may be the differing approaches to rehabilitation within Acheland and Bendene hospitals. Rehabilitative facilities within Acheland were limited. Patients who had become institutionalized and required more gradual reintegration into the community were likely to be recommended for transfer to a hospital which specialized in rehabilitative programmes for psychopaths. One such unit, with minimal physical security but a high staff/patient ratio, was frequently recommended as just such a stepping-stone—hereafter known as the 'Retune Unit'. At Bendene, a more active rehabilitative programme was in place; patients not infrequently enjoyed escorted and, occasionally, even unescorted leave from the hospital. The RMOs accordingly felt that their patients did not necessarily require further specialized rehabilitation.

In both hospitals, self-care and social-skills problems were not as acute for the psychopathic patients as for those with long-term mental illnesses, where drug side-effects, personality deterioration, and more obvious institutionalization made such a stepped progression from hospital more necessary. Therefore, the term rehabilitation was often used to double for a progressive relaxation of security, providing an opportunity to test out patients' behaviour in less secure conditions. Again, this understandably cautious approach was more in evidence at Acheland than Bendene, where 'security in the community' was more commonly advised. Stringent conditions of supervision and residence were, of course, recommended when conditional discharge was advised. Bendene also recommended that supervision be undertaken by the Special Hospital because they knew the patient well. At Acheland, RMOs preferred to see their patients moving through regional or interim secure units, with the decision to discharge and offer supervision ultimately resting upon the recommendations of psychiatrists in these hospitals.[7] Which approach is preferable is arguable; but, the existence of contrasting approaches undoubtedly contributed to the nature of the advice offered by the RMOs to the tribunals in the two regions.

As noted above, the tribunals' decisions concurred overwhelmingly with the recommendations made by the RMOs. In all of the six cases in which the RMOs' advice was not adopted by the tribunal, the decision reflected a more cautious approach than that advocated by the RMOs. Although it was apparent that the tribunal might occasionally have wished to go beyond whatever was being proposed by the RMO, it must be emphasized that in no case did this occur. In this respect, the tribunal acted only to insure that incautious recommendations were not pursued, rather than reaching conclusions which would have indicated that the RMOs had been adopting a too cautious approach.

Independent psychiatric reports (IPRs) were submitted in 32 cases. Although the tribunals endorsed their views in 16 cases, in 15 of these the IPR supported the recommendations of the RMO. In the sole case where the tribunal followed the advice in an IPR and rejected the advice of the RMO, the independent psychiatrist (IP) was advocating a significantly more cautious approach than the RMO. Of the 16 cases where the tribunal rejected the advice offered in an IPR, in 12 they followed the RMO's advice for a

---

[7] Transfer via the catchment area hospital was least likely because psychopathic patients were rarely on drugs to control their behaviour. They were therefore considered less suitable for local hospital care where high staff/patient ratios are not usually enjoyed.

more cautious approach, while in the other 4 they rejected the advice of both the IP and the RMO.

Thus, of the 6 cases where the tribunal did not follow the RMO's advice, and reached a more cautious decision, in 1 case they were supported by an IPR, in 1 case there was no IPR, and in 4 cases they rejected the advice of both. In the 7 cases where the tribunal reached some form of discharge decision, 6 were cases where the advice of both the RMO and IP (sometimes multiple opinions) favoured discharge and 1 was a case where there was no IPR, but the RMO favoured discharge.

Given that the crucial source of information which determines whether a 'psychopathic' patient may leave the Special Hospital will be the evidence of the RMO, do IPRs make any difference to the tribunals' decisions? This preliminary analysis would suggest not. A favourable IPR will not assist a patient unless it is also supported by the RMO, and even where it is, the tribunal, in respect of the discharge/no discharge divide in this sample of cases, rejected both opinions (4 cases) with almost as great a frequency as they accepted them (6 cases). Moreover, where the IP offered less cautious advice than the RMO, this was rejected by the tribunal. It is likely that it will mainly be where IPs offer more cautious advice than the RMO that their opinions will be preferred by tribunals. Thus, an IP may serve to support an RMO's opinion, but they cannot ensure a favourable outcome for patients, even with a supporting RMO's opinion.

III. THE TRIBUNALS' DECISIONS: RATIONALE

For the purposes of discussion, the tribunals' reasoning in the forty cases is divided into four subgroups: (A) straightforward no discharge cases; (B) classic dilemmas; (C) dischargeable cases; (D) diagnostically difficult cases.

There were 32 male and 8 female patients. The female patients were particularly problematic for the tribunal. They were more likely to be detained without restrictions and were more frequently overtly disturbed. This was reflected in the unusually low number of independent reports submitted—only 3 in this group, all of which recommended no real change in the patients' circumstances. All but one of the women had been convicted of arson.[8]

The suffixes A and B to the case numbers denote the hospital at which the patients were detained. It should be stressed that instances of diagnostic ambivalence (cases where there had been or was an additional element of mental illness) extended beyond the confines of those dealt with in subgroup D. In all, 13 patients had mixed diagnostic histories; 5 were formally reclassified by the tribunal either as suffering from psychopathic disorder alone (when they had legally been detained as mentally ill), or as suffering from psychopathic disorder in addition to mental illness. Finally, in one case a patient had a classification of mental illness added to the pre-existing diagnosis of psychopathic disorder.

A. Straightforward No Discharge Decisions

This subgroup of six cases all represented uncomplicated decisions for the tribunal not to discharge—either because the fine detail of the statute readily permitted continued detention or because the patients' conditions clearly merited it. The first four had been convicted of serious offences (violence or arson) and were either seeking or being recommended for further treatment. Moreover, all four had been detained for comparatively short periods—under five years. None therefore satisfied an underlying 'time for crime' criterion. There was little impetus from any source for changes in these patients' circumstances.

In contrast, Patients 1A and 11B had committed comparatively minor offences, yet their psychiatric histories were more long-standing and worrying. The problem faced by the tribunal (a moral not a legal dilemma) concerned reconciling these patients' arguably inequitably lengthy detention, with the risk posed by discharging them with their psychiatric conditions unabated. In the first case the patient's barrister, supported by an IPR, argued that Patient 1A had never carried out his threats and that it was unnecessary to curtail his liberty in this way. Indeed, were he subsequently to be reconvicted, the patient could be dealt with in the penal system, with due regard paid to arguments about equity.

---

[8] Both Coid (1987) and Hamilton (1985) similarly note the prevalence of arson offences amongst female psychopaths.

'But' the tribunal asked themselves 'what will he have to be convicted of? What if it's murder?' In the second case an IP argued, without any enthusiasm, that there was some sense in discharging the patient before his time-limited restriction order expired, so that conditions might be imposed on him. In both cases a trade-off occurred between the course arguably most appropriately taken at that time and its interaction with the patient's likely future behaviour. In each instance, the attractions of not discharging and maintaining immediate control outweighed those associated with future flexible control.

B. Classic Dilemmas

This subgroup constitutes fourteen patients, whose offences had all involved a sexual element combined with violence—in six of the cases amounting to manslaughter. Apart from two patients, all of the group had been in hospital for very lengthy periods; ten of them for an average of fourteen years. Their lengthy detention inevitably caused problems for the tribunals in determining how these patients were likely to behave outside conditions of security. The fear for the tribunal of what might prove to be an unjustifiable risk was overpowering. It meant that even in a case where a patient had been detained for forty-five years and where concerted medical opinion favoured a move from conditions of special security, the tribunal could not bring themselves to discharge. Their reasons stated: 'We accept that in the final analysis the only way to discover whether he would still behave in a dangerous manner is to discharge him into the community. However, we consider that the risks involved are so great . . . that such a course cannot be justified at the present time.' Estimating risk was the key issue in these cases. Yet it was acutely difficult. Rarely did 'psychopaths' receive any medication and there was not, therefore, the potentially attractive option of chemical control. Moreover, these patients caused few, if any, management problems; frequently they were characterized as model patients. Their recent behaviour could not provide a justifiable basis for continuing to detain them. The tribunal therefore preoccupied themselves with the imponderable dilemmas of whether good behaviour in a secure environment was a valid index either of the continuing presence or absence of disorder, or of the nature of the patient's likely behaviour if released into the community?

(i) *Equity and treatability: The unequal exchange* Two patients were detained on notional S37 orders; their restriction orders had lapsed with the passage of time. The tribunal's powers in these cases were wider, and the criteria governing their decisions meant that questions of treatability should have been taken into consideration. Yet it was clear that the tribunal felt themselves disadvantaged. They could not discharge S37 patients with conditions attached, which, if breached, would lead to their recall to hospital. Hence, the possibilities of achieving control in the community, with the safety net of recall, were more limited.[9] Both patients had been transferred to hospital towards the end of comparatively short sentences of imprisonment; both had subsequently been detained for periods vastly in excess of their original sentences, which again raised a moral dilemma for those with finely attuned civil libertarian instincts. Patient 15A had never been a management problem and had co-operated with all the therapeutic programmes the hospital had offered. An IP who attended the hearing said that there was no evidence of psychopathic disorder and if the patient required any further treatment it was of a kind that could only be provided outside hospital—namely, contact with adult women. He recommended delayed discharge under S72(3) to enable the appropriate after-care arrangements to be made.[10] The RMO contested this view; he did not address the question of treatability, merely concluding that the patient continued 'to be an inadequate and immature person who is likely to encounter difficulties in relationships with females outside and hence to revert to his previous sexual behaviour of assaulting children'. He thus presented the patient in terms of an unquantifiable risk, a view endorsed by the tribunal judge who was demonstrably concerned about the risk to children. The question of risk echoed the observations of the medical member of the tribunal prior to the hearing; he had told his fellow members that the patient required indefinite care under conditions of security. He further asserted that the patient's long period of incarceration would, in itself, contribute to his dangerousness since 'any normal person after 17 years will have such a head of resentment that he will be a danger'. Since the tribunal could not satisfy themselves that the patient would be safe, they decided to leave his future in

---

[9] The power to recommend leave of absence does exist under S72(3).
[10] The tribunal characterized this advice as 'dangerous'.

the effective control of the RMO, who was given a watching brief to advise on the diminution of risk.

While it was clear that the tribunal had satisfied themselves that they could not be satisfied that the patient was not a risk, they had not overtly addressed their minds to the preceding question as to whether the patient indeed suffered from psychopathic disorder, and whether it was of a nature or degree to make medical treatment appropriate. Moreover, despite the fact that during the deliberation the judge had stated that he did not believe the patient to be treatable, there was no reference to the statutory criteria's requirement that the tribunal have regard to treatability—either in the tribunal's decision or in their deliberations.

In the case of Patient 46B the RMO adopted a similar approach, failing to address questions of treatability explicitly, but rather submitting reports to the tribunal dating back to 1969 which concerned his potential dangerousness. One of them stated: 'It is not putting it too high to describe him as a potential Ian Brady.' The RMO believed that the absence of evidence of psychological change, combined with continuing homosexual activity in the hospital (obviously with adults), meant there could be no certainty that, under stress outside, the patient would not resort to young children as partners. An IPR asked the tribunal to consider questions of treatability (in his view the patient was not treatable) and equity (the patient had been in confinement for eighteen years although his offences would only have warranted a prison sentence of some five years). The tribunal adopted the RMO's cautious approach; they argued that, even if treatment did not alleviate his condition, detention prevented deterioration. Again, the uncertain risk posed by the patient resulted in the tribunal leaving the case in the hands of the RMO, and justified so doing in terms of the lowest criterion available (preventing deterioration).

(ii) *True to form: Tribunals as regressive/passive decision-makers*
Tribunals are not infrequently swayed by the views of the medical member of the tribunal. These may have the impact either of overriding plans which the RMO has in train for the patient or swaying the other members of the tribunal away from a course which they intuitively believe to be correct, but for which hard evidence is unavailable or unpersuasive.

For example, in the case of Patient 18A the RMO favoured moving his patient into conditions of lesser security and had arranged a bed at the Retune Unit. Yet the tribunal ultimately rejected this plan and made no recommendation for discharge or transfer. Support for this course could have derived from the views of the Home Office, who were opposed to any change in the patient's circumstances, and employed the concept of the insufficiency of negative evidence to support their views. They had reservations about the 'lack of information on the patient's fantasy life', shared, they claimed, by the medical director of Acheland. In essence, the Home Office frequently sought 'some positive evidence' that patients would not present a danger if released. But, quite what would constitute this was rarely clear.

Although the views of the Home Secretary may have been influential, the tribunal's deliberations suggested that the real source of opposition to the RMO's plans lay with the medical member. He had been adamant in his belief that the patient should remain in conditions of special security. In the prehearing discussion he said that the patient was a 'liar' and that he was 'quite certain that he would do anything to prevent being found out'. It subsequently emerged that this particular medical member thought homosexuality 'quite wrong' and readily admitted that he didn't 'understand it'. During the tribunal's deliberations, he made it plain that he believed that the patient posed a serious risk to younger persons. Despite skilful handling by the judge, it was impossible for the tribunal to ignore the medical member's opinion. Their decision, which failed to offer any positive recommendation—'transfer is a matter for the Home Secretary and the RMO'—reflected their dilemma.[11]

In the case of Patient 12A the impact of the medical member was also apparent. The patient had been convicted fourteen years earlier of three indecent assaults on adult women. He had cooperated in all the therapy the hospital had to offer. Two years previously at a case conference it had been decided that there was no real prospect of further improvement and that he should be transferred to Retune where he had been offered a bed. However, before this could be carried out the patient's RMO died and the plan went into abeyance. At the tribunal, the patient, supported by an IPR, was seeking to be transferred. His new RMO, who had formally interviewed the patient on only one occasion since taking

---

[11] Interestingly, the previous tribunal to review the patient's case, under the 1959 Act, had recommended that he be discharged directly into the care of his sister; but their powers had been merely advisory.

responsibility for him, opposed his transfer. He argued that the patient didn't deal competently and confidently with sexual pressures and that it was possible that there would be a repetition of the index offences. The patient was obviously ill at ease with his RMO, believing that he never recommended those with psycho-sexual disorders for release. There was an impasse.

Two factors swayed the tribunal in their deliberation. First, the RMO was offering the patient a new course of group psychotherapy for sex offenders (supposedly starting the following Monday). The tribunal were not sufficiently confident to deprive him of this option. Secondly, although both the legal and the lay member did not feel the patient to be dangerous, the medical member had raised the possibility of the patient becoming involved with small children. There was no history of this and no evidence given to that effect even by the RMO. However, since the IP had not come to the tribunal to back up his report, the legal member did not feel that he could allow his gut assessment (that the patient had changed, that twelve years was 'long enough' and that he should be making rapid steps) to outweigh the only medical evidence presented orally to the hearing, namely, that the patient was not fit for transfer. As he remarked, had the IP come 'things may have been different'. The patient's moving plea to the tribunal combined with his representative's persuasive presentation of the argument in favour of transfer (including 'the longer he stays, the harder rehabilitation becomes') was not sufficient to overcome the simple assertion by his present RMO that he was not fit to go.

(iii) *The tribunal as ratifiers* In the three cases below the tribunal followed the recommendations of the patients' respective RMOs; in one case to recommend transfer, in the second to continue to detain, and in the third to discharge. The cases illustrate that the critical factor in the tribunals' decisions was the nature of the advice they received from the RMOs and not any independent features of the case. In each three it was apparent that the tribunal could have reached a different decision.

In the case of Patient 14A the tribunal were asked to support the RMO's recommendation that the patient be transferred to the Retune Unit, where he had been offered a bed. The only stumbling-block to this plan came from the Home Office, whose assent was a prerequisite. They had referred the case to the Advisory Board and were not prepared to reach any decision until their advice was received. The tribunal seemingly had little choice. The entire hearing, including the deliberation, took no more than fourteen minutes.

Two features are interesting. First, looking back over the reports for the previous five years, it was plain that the clinical assessment of the patient had changed little. He was no management problem, was receiving no active therapy, and had good reports from all areas of the hospital. He was actively, but discretely, homosexual. However, the conclusions drawn in the medical reports had shifted. Initially the patient was represented as having a long-standing personality disorder with deviant sexual tendencies, constituting an unjustifiable risk. Subsequently he was characterized as posing a risk that, in recommending transfer, the RMO was prepared to take. Although the RMO regarded the patient as having achieved 'sufficient maturity', it was hard to ascertain what new evidence, other than the mere passage of time, supported this conclusion. His behaviour had been consistently good over a number of years. Secondly, the case shared many of the features of those already discussed, yet the tribunal took little time to agree with the RMO that this was a case fit for transfer. Why were not similar doubts raised about the possibility that the patient might transfer his affections from adult males to small boys (the subject of his index offence)? The tribunal characterized as 'glib' his assurances about his abilities to abstain or control his drinking, since he had spent the previous fourteen years in an alcohol-free environment. But even this did not dissuade them from endorsing the RMO's plans. Perhaps the neatly packaged option with which they were presented meant that they had little scope to reject the plan; indeed, they may have acquiesced in the knowledge that no progress could be made in this patient's case until the Home Office agreed to a transfer. It was, therefore, a comparatively low-risk decision.

The package approach in the case of Patient 1B was also evident, although there it favoured continued detention. The patient had made a significant improvement and had good insight. But the fact that he was part-way through a beneficial treatment programme, combined with his own view that discharge would be premature, meant that the tribunal were unlikely to reach any disruptive decision. They concurred with the RMO's plans that the patient should remain in the hospital for the time being. One interesting feature emerged. The patient had recently been transferred from Acheland where he had been regarded as 'sly, manipulative, arrogant and highly dangerous'. Yet, reassessed by his new RMO, none of these epithets were applied. Rather, he was regarded as 'an intense individual with problems' who required, and was responsive to, counselling. Admittedly these cases are problematic. But, such a radical reappraisal of a patient's character must cast some doubt upon the reliability of assorted RMO's assessments and make a matter for concern the tribunal's apparent ready acceptance of them.

In the case of Patient 13B the tribunal discharged, following the advice of the patient's RMO. He had been convicted of multiple offences of violent assault (against adult males) and had been detained for less than five years. For most of that period he had been regarded as posing a risk of serious violence. But, during the year prior to the hearing, there had been, according to his RMO, a profound and dramatic change in him. His RMO, the medical director of Bendene, an IPR, and the psychiatrist who had been identified as the most suitable to supervise the patient, all considered him fit for discharge. It was argued that since the patient did not require intensive rehabilitation he could be maintained in the community, live with his parents, and be dealt with on an out-patient basis. The only dissenting note came from the evidence of the Home Office (supported to some extent by the views of the DHSS), who were not convinced of the true extent of the patient's transformation. They were not, in this case, completely opposed to discharge, but argued that the patient needed to be monitored first on trial leave from Bendene. The tribunal rejected this view believing that supervision by the psychiatrist in the locality to which he was to be discharged was likely to be more effective than that offered by the Special Hospital RMO. Again, the tribunal had acted on the medical evidence before them, only in this instance it impelled them to release.

(iv) *Interactive issues* These four cases were unusually complex. In each, difficulties were encountered by the tribunal in reaching their decisions. The first two cases illustrate the problems patients experience where they wish to progress from secure conditions but do not have the support of their RMOs; in these circumstances tribunals are largely impotent. The second two cases illustrate the dramatic consequences that can stem from tribunals exercising, or failing to exercise, their statutory functions as the final arbiter.

First, the two cases where the tribunals merely flexed their powers. Patient 42A had had a long and frustrating experience with the tribunal system. He had been detained for eighteen years and, eleven years previously, had been recommended by a tribunal for a conditional discharge. However, having consulted the Advisory Board, this advice was rejected by the Home Secretary.[12]

The patient continued to seek a conditional discharge. His RMO was opposed to this. Although he accepted that the patient was not likely to change in Acheland, he considered him a 'high risk case' and entertained 'grave doubts' about him. His continued detention was primarily for protective purposes.

At the hearing the tribunal received written reports from two IPs to the effect that Patient 42A did not suffer from psychopathic disorder and should be conditionally discharged. The first noted that he had no underlying persistent disorder of mind. The second, from a consultant at the regional secure unit, asserted that the patient did not suffer from mental illness, that it was not clear that he had 'truly got a psychopathic personality', and that he had never shown any real violence in the hospital, only 'verbal assertiveness'. The IP was opposed to transferring the patient to his unit since this would 'merely lead to another long indecisive period of incarceration which would be as frustrating to him as it would be to the doctor looking after him without there being any specific psychiatric condition to treat'. He did, however, volunteer to supervise the patient on an out-patient basis.

Although at the hearing the weight of the evidence favoured conditional discharge, the RMO remained firmly opposed to such a course. He cited the patient's non co-operation with psychophysiological testing as a worrying feature. The patient justified this on the grounds that if the tests were negative this could not, in itself, establish that there was nothing wrong with him (a correct application of the difficulty which arises when trying to establish

---

[12] Another tribunal, which dealt with his case under the 1983 Act recommended that the need for transfer was 'urgent'. But they apparently had little confidence that their recommendation would have any effect because they recommended that the patient apply for a further review and hoped that 'we shall be invited to constitute the tribunal that hears the application'. Were they trying to regulate the impact of their recommendation? Whatever their purpose, the tribunal members were duly reappointed.

the absence of something). He further feared that Acheland might 'fix' the results of the tests—he thus had nothing to gain and everything to lose from co-operating.[13]

In the event, the potential dilemma posed by a situation in which the weight of the evidence favoured discharge, but discharge would have had to take place in the teeth of opposition from the RMO, was avoided. The report from the RSU had not been submitted to the Home Secretary. The tribunal therefore adjourned. In so doing, they wrote to the Home Secretary informing him that they were minded to make a deferred conditional discharge with stringent conditions and they requested that he be represented at the reconvened hearing. This was an unusual course, and may be taken to reflect the tribunal's hesitancy.

The Home Secretary's comments were predictable. His view was that the weight of the evidence had previously favoured a finding that the patient had a psychopathic disorder and that he was not satisfied that this had evaporated. Further, 'to allege that the positive is not apparent is not to prove the negative'. In order to be satisfied of this, the Home Secretary stated that he would 'expect to see a recent history consistent with the absence of disorder and some unanimity of medical opinion'. Finally, it could not be contemplated that the patient might leave hospital until there was a clearer understanding of the motivation for his index offence—and this could not be achieved until the patient co-operated with his RMO. The evidence of the RMO and the views of the Home Secretary were completely at odds with those of the RSU and the IPR.

At the reconvened hearing two factors were to make what looked like a potentially difficult decision for the tribunal comparatively straightforward. First, the social worker, despite considerable effort, had been unable to find a hostel prepared to take the patient direct from Acheland without 'a period of decompression' in a local hospital. Secondly, the consultant from the RSU had revised his opinion and, during testimony, it emerged that he believed the patient had 'stronger and more formed suspicions' than he had supposed. He wished to reappraise his previous views.

---

[13] Although this behaviour might suggest that the patient was abnormally suspicious, in this case his suspicions might have been merited. In fact, a number of allegations had previously been made against the patient and subsequently retracted by Acheland.

With this erosion of the medical case in favour of discharge, the tribunal stated that there was 'now no evidence to refute that of [the RMO]'. What they meant by this was that there was no oral evidence—the report of the other IP would still have been valid.

The tribunal felt obliged to make a decision not to discharge. Although they sympathized with the patient's predicament (no hostel place without transfer to a local hospital, no transfer without the RMO's and Home Secretary's permission, no permission without co-operation with psychophysiological testing), they could not satisfy themselves that he was ready for discharge. Their comment that 'the question of the patient's transfer to a less secure hospital should be kept under constant and urgent review' did not, in itself, constitute a firm recommendation for transfer. Hence, after a review process lasting over a year, the patient remained in exactly the same position, and was arguably worse-off.

The case of Patient 40A exemplified the rare circumstances where a tribunal might wish to go beyond the recommendations of the RMO; although in this case they ultimately agreed to follow his proposed course, at least for a limited period. In November 1984, they had made a deferred decision to order a conditional discharge to a hostel. This decision was 'in excess of the recommendations' of the RMO and the clinical team. Although attempts were made by Acheland to find a suitable hostel placement, these were unsuccessful.

At the reconvened hearing the clinical team recommended that the patient be given trial leave at the Retune Unit, though the RMO harboured reservations even about this. He believed the patient manifested 'residual impulsiveness' because he did not want to progress gradually from hospital but was still seeking a conditional discharge. The Home Office had been actively opposed to a conditional discharge; the patient, like Patient 42A, had refused to co-operate with some parts of the psychophysiological testing and this created concern at the Home Office that he might continue to have aggressive feelings towards women. Essentially, they were not satisfied that he was safe to release. However, in the light of the deferred conditional discharge, they were prepared to endorse trial leave at Retune.

The patient, supported unusually by an independent social-work report, wanted to be discharged directly to his sister's home. He believed, like Patient 42A, that since trial leave could not be guaranteed by the tribunal, such a recommendation might become a stumbling-block rather than a stepping-stone to his eventual discharge. The tribunal were sympathetic to this argument; the lay member went so far as to say that if this stepping-stone could not be arranged (the admittedly preferable course), the patient was entitled to go without one.

The tribunal felt that their wishes had been frustrated, but under the circumstances there was little they could do about it. They could not make a hostel place available, and to go against the advice of the RMO, the Home Office, and those hostels that had been approached, seemed too extreme. Their reasoning clearly placed a premium on expediency over the patient's legal entitlement to be discharged. Although keen to see the patient out of Acheland, they wished him to leave the hospital successfully. As the legal member put it: to ignore the advice they had received was to do so 'at our peril'.

There were arguments in favour of direct discharge: there was the firm offer of a job and the medical member noted that many people come straight out of prison after long periods of institutionalization. But these were not sufficient to enable the tribunal to make an obviously risky decision. They resolved to adjourn for four months, with the intention that if a decision about the patient's trial leave was not made rapidly, they would order a conditional discharge instead. Whether this would ultimately have been implemented is unclear; it is arguable, however, that their use of the adjournment procedures was questionable.[14] Moreover, the subsequent case of *Campbell* confirmed that they would have had no power to rescind the original deferred conditional discharge.

In the case of Patient 14B the much sought-after 'unanimity of medical opinion' was present. Indeed, no fewer than seven medical opinions advised conditional discharge.[15] This represented an overwhelming case not merely by psychiatrists whose knowledge of the patient might have been seen as questionable, but by those who knew the patient best and who had cared directly for him. Even a medical report commissioned by the Home Office found that there was 'no way in which [the patient] could benefit from

---

[14] See also the case of *Thomas* and *Crozier* (Appendix 3).

[15] A number of the medical opinions went so far as to say that the patient did not even suffer from a personality disorder (the more widely used clinical term). Four of the medical opinions were given orally to the tribunal, and were supported by the evidence of three nursing officers, a senior social worker, and the chief psychologist at Bendene—all of whom knew the patient well.

continued treatment in hospital'. There seemed no compelling reason not to take the risk that might have been associated with his discharge, and certainly no evidential grounds for so doing.

The tribunal concluded that they had heard:

a substantial body of evidence which subscribed to the view that the patient is not suffering from mental disorder. Such evidence was firmly expressed and unshaken by cross-examination on behalf of the Home Secretary. There was no evidence at all from any source that [the patient] was at present suffering from mental disorder.

They felt they had little choice but to make a conditional discharge; even the tribunal medical member did not dissent from this view. Yet, within six months of his release the patient was rearrested for, and subsequently convicted of, offences of violence not dissimilar to his previous convictions.

Although a mistake had arguably been made in releasing the patient (although not in terms of the tribunal's remit) it would be difficult to apportion responsibility. On the evidence, the tribunal felt they had no option. The terminology of constraint was evident in the baldness of their reasons: 'the abundance and quality of this evidence which stood uncontroverted'. Although the Home Secretary had questioned whether 'good behaviour in the artificial confines of a Special Hospital is necessarily sufficient evidence that a diagnosis of psychopathic disorder is no longer appropriate', no further evidence was presented on his behalf to the effect that the patient *did still suffer*. Although doubts were (with hindsight) sensibly expressed about the patient's motivation for his offence being little or unsatisfactorily understood, this was not regarded as being specifically relevant to the question of whether or not the patient was still suffering from the disorder. Indeed, even the IP employed by the Home Secretary had concluded: 'I doubt whether much further clarification of his motive for the index offence is possible.'

There was therefore no basis for any lingering doubts that the tribunal might otherwise have used to justify a decision not to discharge. Permission for unescorted day leave had been repeatedly refused by the Home Secretary. The only evidence therefore available to the tribunal concerning the patient's behaviour outside hospital came from escorted leave—which could not be regarded as truly testing him. Transfer to a secure unit was not considered as a real option—if the patient was not suffering there was no basis for continued detention.

The case of Patient 21B had a number of similarities with that of Patient 14B, although the outcome, not to discharge, was diametrically opposed. The case convincingly illustrates that uncertainty can always be generated if the tribunal are so minded. Seven medical opinions averred that the patient could no longer be described as suffering from psychopathic disorder within the meaning of the Act and recommended conditional discharge. On what might the tribunal have based their conclusion that the patient was not fit to be discharged?

First, the chronology of Patient 21B's case was complex.[16] This resulted in Patient 14B being released and recharged before Patient 21B had had his case resolved. Perhaps the knowledge that another tribunal had discharged in a similar case on the grounds of overwhelming medical evidence, but still 'got it wrong', prompted the tribunal for Patient 21B to examine the evidence with much greater stringency. Indeed, they may have been seeking reasons not to discharge.

Secondly, the Home Office made a lengthy submission backed up by presentation of the case at the hearing by counsel. They argued that there could be no certainty about the absence of disorder and that there were, anyway, significant inconsistencies between the various medical appraisals of the patient's motivation and his long history of prior offending. They argued that 'the number and nature of this patient's attacks on women, and particularly young girls, make his discharge into the community an exceedingly grave matter... In a case of this gravity, where such doubts remain... the question of the protection of the public is in the forefront of the Home Secretary's mind.' The familiar argument was used. The tribunal had to consider not how the patient had behaved in a secure environment, but the likelihood that he continued to suffer from a psychopathic disorder which could, if he were discharged, cause him to commit further offences of violence.

The RMO argued that it was logically impossible for him to prove that the patient's disorder was not now present. His was a

[16] Under the 1959 Act a tribunal had advised conditional discharge, but this was rejected by the Home Secretary. A subsequent tribunal under the 1983 Act decided against discharge, but their decision was overturned.

clinical judgment, based on lengthy interviews with the patient, psychometric testing, and observations of his behaviour both in Bendene and on numerous escorted trips from the hospital. He believed that there was a 'high probability of being correct' that the patient's personality had developed in such a way as to remove him from the appropriate diagnostic category, but he could not prove absolutely the absence of an abnormality of mind.

This inevitable shortcoming provided the necessary uncertainty for the tribunal to satisfy the first element of S72(1)(b)(i), but there was still the question of 'nature or degree'. The second line of reasoning employed by the Home Office thus became of crucial significance. They argued that given uncontradicted medical evidence in favour of discharge, the tribunal was still entitled to form a different view. This was for two reasons. First, tribunal proceedings are not strictly adversarial. Secondly, the medical member's views, formed from his examination of the patient, may enable the tribunal as a whole to disagree with the medical evidence presented. Provided all the interested parties were given an opportunity to deal with the medical member's view, the tribunal were not obliged to follow the consensus of the evidence submitted.

The events at the hearing were to lend further support to the theoretical case against discharge. The medical member of the tribunal did take a different view and thoroughly examined the evidence of those who attended the hearing. This emerged as more contradictory and less convincing than had appeared from the numerous reports submitted. Furthermore, the patient, in the tribunal's view, 'lied, became angry, didactic and oversensitive in turn'. Even taking into account the stresses of the hearing, the tribunal interpreted this behaviour as convincing evidence of the continuing presence of the relevant disorder. It outweighed that proffered as an index of his recovery, namely, years of behaviour with no evidence to substantiate the presence of the disorder. Although the tribunal were prepared to accept that the patient had changed, the quantum of change was insufficient to convince them of either S72(1)(b)(i) *or* (ii), given the deep-rooted and severe nature of the patient's original disorder.

Their views were clear. They were not satisfied that the clinical judgments relied upon for discharge were correct and they doubted the reliability of some of the evidence used in reaching the various clinical decisions.[17] Thus, despite a seemingly overwhelming case in favour of discharge, the tribunal found itself able to take a more cautious view than that advocated by the RMO, the Responsible Authority, and numerous independent opinions.

(v) *Against the grain* In the final two cases in this subgroup of classic dilemmas, the tribunal endorsed recommendations by the RMOs that the time had come for the patients to be moved on from conditions of special security. Yet, the tribunals' recommendations were both made in the context of evidence which could have prompted them to adopt a more cautious approach. For Patient 40B there was recent evidence that he had shown 'an institutional type reaction to the prospect of greater freedom'. Moreover, the tribunal expressed the belief that if the patient were to break down he would constitute a danger both to himself and others. Similarly, for Patient 6A the hospital gave the opinion that they could not be certain that he did not continue to nurture sadistic fantasies. Yet, in neither case was the uncertainty sufficient to deter them from making recommendations for change, given that the RMOs were advocating change. Finally, for Patient 6A the RMO notably argued that if his movement was delayed much longer he might become institutionalized and his problems entrenched. This line of reasoning was much more convincing, emanating as it did from the RMO, than had it been proffered by the patient's representative, the more usual source.

C. *Dischargeable Cases*

This subgroup of ten cases provide a marked contrast to those already discussed. In five, decisions to discharge were reached.

[17] The tribunal were careful to provide adequate reasons. An earlier decision in this case had been quashed because insufficient reasons had been given. That tribunal had concluded: 'We are not persuaded that because of the applicant's improved behaviour within the strict regime in hospital it necessarily follows that such behaviour would be maintained in the community.' Mr. Justice Forbes (QBD 12 July 1985) subsequently found that it was 'impossible, without some further indication, to come to a conclusion about whether that sentence was directed at the inquiry as to whether it was necessary for the protection of others or whether that insofar as medical opinion was based on his improved behaviour in hospital, the tribunal were not content to assume that that medical opinion was soundly based'. Thus, it had not been clear whether their reasons addressed the diagnostic issue (a medical question) or the more policy-oriented question of whether it was safe to discharge.

They illustrate the overriding influence that RMOs have in determining the outcome of tribunal decisions, but also highlight how RMOs' evidence is vulnerable if either the legal or the medical member of the tribunal takes a different view during the tribunal's deliberations. The medical member's influence is discussed in greater depth in the following chapters, but one case here will illustrate the irrefutability of opinions offered by the medical member.

Patient 17A was, in the view of his RMO, 'free from any sign of mental illness at present and has not shown any signs of mental illness for some years now'.[18] He was not a management problem, had no psychosexual problems, didn't lose his temper, and socialized well. The RMO recommended trial leave to a hostel.

The RMO had approached the Home Office with this plan and they were intending to consult the Advisory Board. The tribunal were merely being asked to support the RMO's recommendation. The case should have been comparatively straightforward, given that the patient had no legal representative to question the RMO's assessment that the patient could not be said to be 'mentally ill in the ordinary sense'. However, the case was to constitute another example of caution seemingly overriding the potential impact of the statutory criteria.

It emerged that the medical member of the tribunal was very worried about the prospect of the patient leaving hospital. He believed that there was a real risk that the patient would attack another women and be violent if rejected in his sexual advances. He made great play of the patient's emotional flatness as a negative symptom of his continuing illness. His concern was such that he said that he would wish to have his opposition formally recorded, if the tribunal decided to discharge. His views were readily apparent to the patient, who broke down during the hearing, made an emotional plea to the tribunal, and showed convincing remorse. However, this did not sway the medical member. During the deliberation, rather than restating his views about emotional

---

[18] A report from his catchment area RSU maintained that the patient had been reclassified to psychopathic disorder, but there was no mention of this in the RMO's report. There were some grounds for such a reclassification: the patient was described as 'a very controlled person'. Earlier reports had indicated 'overcontrol' and noted that he had 'sexual fantasies of a sadistic nature' and that there had been a lack of change in his personality. None the less, no reclassification was sought.

flatness, which were no longer sustainable, he suggested that the patient had stored up 'tremendous bitterness'. He asked the tribunal to speculate about how this bitterness might find expression if the patient were released. Indeed, he gratuitously raised the possibility that the patient might use a knife at the hostel. The legal and lay members rejected this. The legal member stating 'it's less than obvious that he's a major risk'. But, in the teeth of opposition from the medical member, and given that the patient was only asking for trial leave, they could do little else but endorse the RMO's plan. Their view, that further delay might be disastrous, did not find explicit expression in their recommendation. In seeking support from the tribunal for the RMO's plan for trial leave, there might equally have been a complete rejection of the recommendation. Patients and RMOs should recognize this possibility when considering using the tribunal as a lever on Home Office approval—it might as easily turn out to be a hatchet.

(i) *The impact of the RMO in facilitating change*

Undoubtedly RMOs can transform cases from being readily categorized as 'no discharges' to being regarded as suitable for transfer. Sometimes, the mere assessment by the RMO that a patient (104B) had 'reached a peak'—a phrase reminiscent of the terminology employed by those considering paroling prisoners—appeared sufficient to outweigh many other negative features. Moreover, the influence of the RMOs extended beyond the impact of their advice to the tribunal, to the actions they took and plans they initiated in respect of individual patients. For example, whether they chose to seek a second independent psychiatric opinion when the first did not concur with their view of a case, and whether they became actively involved in the search for a hostel placement for a patient could be critical. The actions of a RMO could transform a non-dischargeable case into one which was likely to be perceived by the tribunal as fit for discharge. Finally, and this is a theme already touched upon, the fact that for two of these patients there were multiple changes of RMO and multiple changes in the direction the cases were to take, illustrates that different RMOs may perceive the same case in quite contradictory ways. This, in turn, may have a profound affect upon a patient's prospects.

The cases of Patients 4A and 103B illustrate the differential impact RMOs can have. Both concerned older women who had been detained for over twelve years. For Patient 4A the tribunal endorsed transfer to an interim secure unit, where a bed was available. In the case of Patient 103B the RMO's recommendation was for conditional discharge to a hostel. The tribunal found the patient still to be suffering from psychopathic disorder, but decided that its nature and degree were not such as to warrant detention in hospital.

Little distinguished these two cases other than the packages with which the tribunals were presented. Even for Patient 4A the RMO accepted that only a short period was likely to elapse before she was moved from the secure unit to hostel care. Whilst for Patient 103B the RMO accepted that she might well behave antisocially in the future, but since 'no further treatment could be offered' at Bendene 'the normal course of events should be pursued'—namely, if reconvicted the patient should be sentenced within the penal system. Whether this equity-based argument would have found similar favour, if more than merely antisocial behaviour was envisaged, seems unlikely. Certainly, in the already explored context of male, potentially serious offending, it was given short shrift.

The cases of Patients 30A and 12B further illustrate this theme of RMOs packaging cases in different, but highly influential, ways to the tribunal. Both patients had been convicted of the manslaughter of women unknown to them. Both had been partially disinhibited through alcohol when the offences were committed. Both had previous convictions and not infrequent contact with the police and psychiatric services dating back to their teens. Both had been in hospital for substantial periods—eight and twelve years respectively. Both patients had IPs recommending conditional discharge present at their tribunal hearings.

Despite these many similarities the tribunals reached diametrically opposed decisions. For Patient 30A it was neither to discharge nor to recommend transfer, whilst for Patient 12B the tribunal made a deferred conditional discharge. The distinguishing features seem to be that for Patient 30A the RMO and the senior hospital social worker had wanted the patient to progress via a medium secure unit; whilst for Patient 12B the RMO, supported by a case conference assessment, was firmly advising conditional discharge. In the former case, the RMO had approached a forensic consultant at a regional secure unit whose view was that the patient did not fall within their catchment area, but none the less offered the opinion that the patient might be satisfactorily managed on an out-patient hostel basis. The RMO preferred to take a more cautious approach and requested *another* opinion in the alternative catchment area. The view of this psychiatrist was that the patient did not sufficiently appreciate 'his potential at times of frustration to become dangerously violent'. He recommended that a further period in Acheland 'would be a necessary salutary experience'. The RMO thus presented a somewhat uncertain line to the tribunal. Despite a firm recommendation from the first IP for conditional discharge, on the grounds that the patient no longer satisfied 72(1)(b)(ii), combined with an offer of out-patient supervision from him, the tribunal took the view that there would be a 'substantial risk to the public were he to be discharged'. Indeed, the tribunal judge had stated that 'the public does not like to be used as a guinea pig'. Thus, the RMO's opposition to conditional discharge, combined with the uncertain position relating to transfer, easily outweighed the IP's argument that the patient did not fall within the terms of the Act. The tribunal effectively decided to leave the case in the hands of the RMO, in the knowledge that no action was likely to be possible for some time to come. No additional active therapy was being offered within Acheland.[19]

Yet in the case of Patient 12B the hospital and the IP presented a united front in favour of conditional discharge on the grounds that the patient did not satisfy the criteria under 72(1)(b)(i) for continued detention. The only contrary view came from the Home Office, who were not represented at the hearing, but who stated that good behaviour was not 'sufficient evidence to indicate fitness for discharge'. They recommended that progress should be made gradually through conditions of lesser security and made it plain

---

[19] Interestingly, the IP had argued that since the patient's index offence had occurred following a long period of criminal and social deterioration, it would be readily apparent if the patient went into a similar decline whilst on conditional discharge. Furthermore, since the only continuing manifestation of his supposedly underlying psychopathic disorder was his verbal violence, he was uncertain whether this constituted an aspect merely of the patient's normal personality, i.e., that he had a temper and this was a sign of a strong resilient personality, as opposed to being a negative feature and indicative of a psychopathic personality. He was thus uncertain as to whether the patient satisfied 72(1)(b)(i), but was satisfied that he did not satisfy 72(1)(b)(ii). He therefore merited discharge on the grounds that his problems could be managed outside hospital.

that they intended to seek the advice of the Advisory Board. The tribunal were alive to this view, but none the less felt able to conclude, having heard the evidence of the RMO and the IP, that 'the burden of proving he no longer suffers from a mental disorder has been discharged'. They recommended that the patient be reintroduced to the community gradually (he eventually went to a hostel on a weekend's trial and then a month's trial leave) and that he be supervised by a named psychiatrist and named social worker for a period of five years.

It is clear that in the former case an element of doubt was introduced by the RMO and seized upon by the tribunal, providing them with grounds for their decision not to discharge or recommend transfer. In the latter case, there were no evidential grounds for such a cautious approach; the tribunal were merely invited by the Home Office to take a different view of the facts. In the light of the united medical evidence they felt able to reject this. The relative merits of a 'high risk, high gain' strategy (for Patient 12B) as opposed to the middle course stepped approach (for Patient 30A) are well illustrated.

The tribunal discharged in the cases of both Patients 25A and 43B, demurring to the patients' respective RMOs. For Patient 43B the decision was unproblematic. The RMO and an IP stated that the patient did not satisfy the criteria for continued detention. As a S37 patient, the Home Office played no part; there was therefore no impetus for continuing detention. Indeed, the RMO could himself have discharged the patient. For Patient 25A discharge occurred slowly over four hearings by the same tribunal and three changes of RMO. The patient was in the unfortunate position of being recommended for conditional discharge by his RMO, only to have his RMO die before he could be discharged. His new RMO took the view that he was not fit to leave hospital. Only with another change of RMO was this gradually reversed; the third RMO originally said merely that he would not oppose a conditional discharge, but finally actively recommended and offered to supervise the patient on an out-patient basis. After the third tribunal hearing, where deferred conditional discharge was recommended, a place became available in a suitable hostel and, at a fourth hearing, the tribunal ratified its earlier decision.[20] The case

[20] Throughout these adjournments and deferrals Patient 25A paid for his own legal representation (his savings of £2,000 made him ineligible for legal aid). Initially, he had been unrepresented. But the tribunal appointed a legal representative, under rule 10(3), following the second RMO's appointment.

is interesting because the tribunal took an *informal* role in referring what they considered to be inadequate reports by the second RMO to the medical director of Acheland. This seemed to act as a catalyst to the third change of RMO. Clearly, the RMO's views were crucial in either promoting or delaying progress in the case.

(ii) *Impact of the legal member of the tribunal*

Both Patients 33A and 22B had been convicted of manslaughter; A of his lover in a suicide pact and B of his wife. Both had histories of deviant sexual fantasies and there was some evidence of consenting sado-masochistic practices. In both cases serious doubts were raised as to whether the patients had ever been correctly diagnosed as suffering from psychopathic disorder.[21] In both cases medical evidence was submitted that they were not currently so suffering. Despite these numerous similarities, Patient 22B was conditionally discharged, yet the tribunal for Patient 33A only went so far as to recommend 'immediate' trial leave. The explanation for why such discrepant outcomes were reached lies in the impact of the legal member in the case of Patient 33A.

The RMO in the case was opposed to discharge and was recommending that the patient be transferred to a local hospital for rehabilitation. Two IPRs contested the diagnosis of psychopathic disorder. They argued that the patient's early history was 'wholly inconsistent' with the diagnosis and that there was little or no evidence presently to support it. One of the IPs was offering the patient a bed in a hostel he supervised; however, unlike the other IP, he was unable to give oral testimony to the tribunal—an application for adjournment was turned down.

The legal member's views were critical. He made it plain before the hearing that he favoured making a recommendation and that a conditional discharge would be 'going too far'. With the offer of a bed in local facilities, he said that it would take a lot to persuade him that the patient was not suffering from psychopathic disorder.

---

[21] Although the patients might both have come within the classification of psychopathic disorder under the 1959 Act, with the exclusion of sexual deviancy under S1(3) of the 1983 Act, the evidence to support their legal labels became thin. S1(3) of the 1983 Act states that no person 'may be dealt with under this Act as suffering from mental disorder, or from any other form of mental disorder described in this section, by reason only of promiscuity or other immoral conduct, sexual deviancy or dependence on alcohol or drugs'.

Following a deliberation lasting less than four minutes, the tribunal recommended immediate trial leave to a supervised halfway house. The legal member reasserted his view that this was 'not the kind of case to get tough [about] and force the Home Secretary's hand'. He described the IPs' evidence as impressive, yet believed that it was up to the patient to prove he was not psychopathic. He stated, 'he's too dangerous to take the risk'. Notably, the medical member's reservations about whether the patient could be said to be suffering from psychopathic disorder, rather than personality disorder, were never put to the RMO. Was this omission also due to the inexperience of the legal member? Finally, although the lay member argued that it was impossible for the patient to prove he was not psychopathic, his view that the risk was worth taking was clearly not going to find favour with the legal member and he put it forward only tentatively. Instead, he pressed for urgent transfer.

The legal member's confused reasoning emerged when he wrote the decision. There was no mention of the criteria under S72(1)(b)(ii) and the clerk had to rectify this. Furthermore, the legal member proceeded to use the standard format—despite the concurring medical evidence that the patient was not a danger. His decision noted merely that the tribunal had 'preferred' the evidence of the RMO to that of the two IPs.

The decision was undoubtedly outcome-oriented. Given the easy option of recommending trial leave to an available bed, the members of the tribunal were not prepared to allow the independent evidence to outweigh the cautious approach advocated by the RMO. Similarly, they were not prepared to give themselves the opportunity of making a different decision by adjourning to hear the evidence from the other IP who was prepared to accept the patient with conditional discharge status. Although the legal member subsequently tried to justify their decision by saying that they couldn't have discharged because the Home Secretary had not seen one of the IPRs, and that the tribunal couldn't order a conditional discharge to a hostel which was part of a hospital, both of these matters could have been resolved through adjournment.

Indeed, since the tribunal frequently adjourn in order to allow the Home Office to comment or present evidence to them, it can be argued that the tribunal, or rather its legal member in this case, actively structured (or limited) their options. From the start the legal member clearly had no intention of doing anything other than making a recommendation. Even though the tribunal's decision used both the terms 'immediate' and 'strongly urge', the patient remained in hospital some nine months later, the Home Office apparently having failed to take any action. The futility of tribunal recommendations was thus underlined.

Yet in the parallel case of Patient 22B the tribunal, despite the opposition of the Home Office, found themselves able conditionally to discharge the patient. Although the medical evidence had implied that the patient was 'no longer suffering', which should have resulted in an absolute discharge, everyone was of the opinion that conditional discharge would be in the patient's interests; it had been suggested that he might otherwise be subject to 'decompression sickness'—problems with adjusting to life in the community after a long period of incarceration. The tribunal resolved this potential dilemma by finding that the patient was not suffering from psychopathic disorder *of a degree* which made it appropriate for him to be detained for treatment, but found liability to recall justified. Clearly, they had structured their options in quite a different manner to the tribunal for Patient 33A.

D. *Diagnostically Difficult Cases*

Ten cases fell into this subgroup, although, as has already been shown, other patients created similar diagnostic problems. They help to illustrate the two tentative explanations offered earlier for the differential use of reclassification, namely (i) the duality between the legal classification of psychopathic disorder and the psychiatric diagnosis of personality disorder, and (ii) the differential nature of the symptomatology to be sustained to satisfy the legal definition of psychopathic disorder as opposed to a diagnosis of mental illness.

In five cases there was little impetus for the tribunal to consider the question of discharge, because the patients were currently disturbed, admitting either to experiencing violent fantasies or to the inability to express or control their anger. In some cases the patients were themselves not seeking discharge.

Patient 2A was the exception to the rule that patients 'progress' from diagnoses of mental illness to those of psychopathic disorder. She had a disturbed history, long-standing personality difficulties, and several court appearances for theft, arson, and wounding. She was admitted to Acheland following threats to kill. At the tribunal hearing, the patient readily acknowledged that she had wanted to attack people in response to her 'bad thoughts', but was unable to distinguish whether these were auditory hallucinations or intrusive thoughts. Either way, she said they had not been present for some time. An IPR submitted to the tribunal, whilst not refuting the diagnosis of psychopathic disorder, noted that there was an important mental-illness component, which appeared to have been responding to neuroleptic medication. The RMO agreed with the IP's formulation, but had not changed her classification since he had 'not wished to burden her with an additional label'. In their decision the tribunal added a classification of mental illness whilst making no further changes in the circumstances of her detention. What is interesting is the level of confusion this generated. The representative told the patient that she had been reclassified from psychopathic disorder to mental illness, and that this was to be seen as progress, when this was not the case. No evidence had been submitted to justify removing the label 'psychopathic' and none was likely to be persuasive anyway.

Although in the majority of cases the precise legal classification made no difference to the tribunal's decision as to whether further detention was merited, it could have implications for future tribunal hearings. In the three cases below, it should have been a critical factor in the determination of the decision.

For Patient 26A, there was a direct conflict in diagnosis. This was crucial to the question of whether the patient could continue to be detained. An IP asserted that the patient had suffered from a short-lived psychosis from which he was now fully recovered and should therefore be discharged. The RMO who, pre-trial, had diagnosed the patient as suffering from a 'progressive psychotic illness' maintained at the tribunal hearing that he suffered from psychopathic disorder. He cited the patient's refusal to co-operate further with psychotherapy, his 'short fuse', and, implicitly, the absence of any psychotic symptomatology as supporting evidence. He believed that because the underlying personality disorder was still present there was a risk of similar offences recurring.

At the hearing, the conflict in diagnosis was not properly examined. The patient objected to the judge sitting on his case because he had presided at his hearing ten months previously. An application to have the tribunal differently constituted was turned down. The patient, his representative, and his IP, took no further part in the hearing. Not surprisingly, the tribunal favoured the evidence of the RMO—supported by the medical member's view that the patient had committed the offence in a state of clear consciousness and that this seemed to fit more closely with a diagnosis of psychopathic disorder than with one of a psychotic episode.[22] Interestingly, a subsequent tribunal with a different judge presiding made a deferred conditional discharge on the grounds (i) that the patient was no longer suffering from mental illness, and (ii) that the patient was not suffering from psychopathic disorder of a nature or degree to justify detention for treatment.

Patient 36A had initially been diagnosed as 'floridly psychotic' and 'sliding into schizophrenia'. His apparent recovery without medication, followed by conditional discharge, might have cast some doubt on this diagnosis. However, two years later, following his sexual harassment of a neighbour, he was readmitted, still with a classification of mental illness. But, there was no active symptomatology; rather he suffered from 'a severe personality disorder, characterized by extreme immaturity, for which he has compensated with fantasies of violence and by transvestism of a fetishistic kind' (RMO). An IP similarly noted that he showed 'no features of mental illness'. There was no diagnostic clarity in the RMO's report, but in oral evidence to the tribunal he equated the patient's condition (a schizoid personality with sexual deviation) with a personality disorder and further stated that a personality disorder could be equated with psychopathic disorder. This somewhat circuitous route provided the tribunal with the grounds for reclassification. Without this testimony, they were confronted by a patient legally detained as suffering from a mental illness, but whom neither the RMO nor the IP considered to be mentally ill. Yet, given over five years stable behaviour, with no evidence of violence or even irresponsibility, some doubt might have been raised about whether his particular personality disorder could indeed be described as psychopathic disorder. But the sequence of the decision-making—is he mentally ill? should he be reclassified

[22] Since the IP did not give oral evidence, he could not back up his assessment that he could find no evidence of 'a severe personality disorder'. Yet, the tribunal's reasons noted that the IP had made no direct reference to the classification of 'psychopathic disorder' in his report. If this were even a partial basis for the tribunal rejecting his assessment, it would ap-pear somewhat harsh because the RMO maintained a similar distinction. Namely, in his written reports, he merely asserted that the patient suffered from a severe personality disorder, i.e. he satisfied the clinical definition.

to psychopathic disorder?—meant that the evidence for his 'psychopathic disorder' was not fully examined. Once again, the RMO's oral evidence solved what might otherwise have been a real problem for the tribunal. Transfer to his catchment area secure unit, to be opened in the following six months, was agreed.[23]

The final case illustrates many of the difficulties discussed by Grounds (1987*a*) which arise when offenders are transferred from prison almost at the end of their sentences—otherwise known as being 'ghost-trained'. Patient 20B had been convicted of a comparatively minor offence. He was transferred to Bendene as suffering from psychopathic disorder on the advice of a psychiatrist who considered him 'an extremely dangerous young man'. Although Bendene had also assessed him and reached the conclusion that he was *unsuitable* for treatment, he was none the less transferred there on the advice of the Hospital Managers (DHSS). The restrictions on his discharge quickly expired and the RMO was faced with the difficulty of having to find not only that he suffered from psychopathic disorder within the Act, but also that he was treatable within its terms—otherwise discharge should have been effected under S16(2).

The tribunal were presented with four conflicting views. A case conference report found the patient 'sensitive, obsessional, ruminative'. He clearly had personality difficulties, but psychometric testing and his earlier history swayed them against a finding of psychopathic disorder; they certainly did not consider him to be treatable. The medical director of Bendene submitted a report indicating that he was showing signs of becoming treatable, and that his RMO was not satisfied that he was not psychopathic. An IPR maintained that the patient was psychopathic and that his personality was characterized by 'a low tolerance to frustration, immaturity and on occasions a tendency to violence'. He was particularly concerned about the lack of control over discharged S37 cases and favoured continuing detention. Another IPR, requested by the hospital, found the patient 'more neurotic than psychopathic in the commonly used sense' and described him as

---

[23] It is interesting that a previous tribunal had recommended transferring the patient to his catchment area *local* hospital. The RMO had done nothing about this, because he believed that the patient 'would need more supervision than is now commonly available at conventional psychiatric hospitals'. This illustrates well the powerlessness of the tribunal to see through its recommendations without the support of the patient's RMO.

vulnerable, immature, inadequate, and of low self-esteem. This IP recognized 'dangerousness' to be the hidden agenda. He asserted that those responsible for the patient's original transfer probably worked in the sequence 'dangerous–due for release–psychopathic––treatable' rather than 'psychopathic–treatable–dangerous'. He too none the less urged caution, saying that it was too soon to say that the patient was not psychopathic and not treatable. Again this illustrates the necessity for *more* evidence if the negative is to be successfully asserted.

Not surprisingly, the tribunal found against discharge. They argued that the patient, who had admittedly been a management problem (understandable in the circumstances), was 'disturbed and destructive and in the view of the Tribunal, psychopathic'. Moreover, they failed to equate a refusal to co-operate in treatment with non-treatability; they believed he needed therapy to help him develop social skills and to mature. Their cautious findings predominantly reflected those of the experts who did not have to have the responsibility for treatment and, in this respect, they may have been able to be more optimistic about the patient's likely progress. Yet again, the tribunal had rejected part of the official hospital view, in order to adopt a more cautious strategy.

IV. CONCLUSIONS

Moral imperatives abound in decisions concerning the future of offender patients. Tribunals are as prey to them as anyone else. One of the reasons therefore for detailing individual cases has been to attempt to resolve the conundrum present for any observer of the tribunal's proceedings; namely, that each decision appears internally consistent, is usually difficult to disagree with, and is sometimes seemingly unavoidable. However, by placing side by side a series of tribunal decisions, it becomes evident that the grounds on which detention is justified shift from case to case. In this context, individual decisions and the moral imperatives employed to justify them appear less persuasive.

The first rationalization concerns the patient's need for treatment. Curiously, although treatment considerations may be employed to rationalize further detention, treatability is not, in the cases of restricted patients, a necessary prerequisite to continued detention. As the Home Office argued, even where a patient suffering from psychopathic disorder was not thought to be benefiting or likely to benefit from treatment, this was not a relevant consideration. The principal relevance of treatability is to the initial decision to detain; it is largely not a relevant statutory consideration in the decision to discharge. Indeed, for patients suffering from psychopathic disorder the attractions of treatment are less compelling than for those diagnosed as mentally ill. None the less, under S72(1)(b) tribunals have to be satisfied that the broadly defined 'medical treatment' in hospital is not appropriate.

Yet, the potential benefits of treatment do enable tribunals to accommodate decisions which result in offender–patients remaining in confinement as reluctant clients. Where treatment needs are not actively expressed by patients, or are not so overridingly obvious that no sane tribunal would discharge, a decision to continue to detain and treat clearly has to be justified. Defending the advantages of compulsory treatment of admittedly limited efficacy (Grounds 1987a), where patients *are* capable of understanding the nature, purpose, and likely effects of the treatment in question, is difficult. Where the direct advantages to the patient are not clear-cut, an alternative strategy is to highlight the effects of treatment on the future diminution of risk. This undoubtedly constitutes the 'hidden agenda' at most tribunals dealing with offender-psychopaths. Yet, employing the prediction and prevention of anticipated harm as a basis for justifying continued detention is not only outside the tribunal's statutory remit, it is also wholly problematic (Gottfredson and Gottfredson 1988). Moreover, there is little or no specific evidence that treating psychopathic disorder *per se* reduces the likelihood of reoffending (Grounds 1987a).

The two moral justifications for treatment in confinement, benefit to the patient and benefit to society, tend to become confused. Moreover, although the medical experts may be best qualified to offer opinions on the first issue, that of likely benefit to the patient, they should not claim any especial expertise in the second, namely the likely diminution in future offending. Yet, the cases demonstrate, time and again, that it is the medical experts, whether they be the RMOs or the medical members of the tribunal, who hold sway.

Indeed, the opinions of key individuals, namely the RMO, the medical member, and the legal member, constitute one of six factors which appear to have influenced the tribunals' decisions.

Curiously, although any of these three professionals could potentially block discharge, none alone could ensure that it took place. The second factor concerns the passage of time. Had the offender passed the appropriate threshold to enable a decision to be made realistically about his release?[24] The seriousness of the behaviour was the third critical factor. The tribunal looked harder and needed more evidence to be convinced where the potential behaviour amounted to more than 'stealing a Mars bar from Woolies'; the criterion for satisfaction shifted. Equity could be used as a basis for promoting discharge in the absence of positive therapeutic prognoses, but only where the anticipated behaviour was sufficiently trivial to be tolerated and dealt with by the penal system. Fourth, there was the question of evidence. In some cases the evidence favouring discharge appeared to be irrefutable or unavoidable—but even this feature could be militated against given sufficiently serious behaviour and a constructive search by the tribunal. This constituted the fifth factor—the tribunal's intentions. Tribunals were capable of actively constructing a case for discharge or producing reasons to justify not discharging. Their strategies could result in preconceived perceptions of constraint encompassing either decision. Finally, there was the concept of future control. Being able to release a patient on the leash of conditional discharge was an option, but again, only where the anticipated offence was not too serious. Otherwise tribunals would delay and face the prospect of direct discharge if it arose.

The subgroup of fourteen 'classic dilemmas' undoubtedly crystallized many of these issues because of the requirement that tribunals justify decisions not to discharge, seemingly in the face of the evidence. Here their reasoning abounded with the issue of uncertainty and how it could be resolved. 'What will happen if?' was a problem tribunals commonly faced. Many of the questions they posed themselves were, in all practical senses, unanswerable. Such as: what will happen if this patient is frustrated in his attempts to establish a relationship with an adult woman, or, alternatively, a satisfactory adult homosexual relationship? Tribunals also asked questions that could only be answered with an unsatisfactory level of certainty. Hence: has this patient's sexual drive diminished? Does this patient still have violent sexual fantasies? Psychometric and psychophysiological testing could

[24] See for example Maguire *et al.* (1984), Dell and Robertson (1988) and Hawkins (1983*b*).

increase levels of certainty that such features persisted, but could not reliably establish their absence. Similarly, observations of a patient's behaviour over an extended period of time might indicate the absence of abnormal aggression or serious irresponsibility, but it could not establish beyond doubt the non-continuation of a particular underlying disorder of mind. The Home Office's view (Patient 47B) was that 'only a substantial period of stable behaviour and attitude in (a non-secure environment) could offer reasonable satisfaction that a diagnosis of psychopathic disorder could no longer be applied'. With such pre-requisites, neither unescorted day parole nor trial leave in a regional secure unit would suffice. Thus, tribunals could only genuinely test out the validity of patient's recovery by discharging into the community and waiting. Representatives sometimes asked that their clients be put to this ultimate test. However, there was a clear reluctance on the part of the tribunal to take what were frequently perceived to be such unacceptable risks; the seriousness of these patients' index offences militated against this. Furthermore, without a clinical recommendation there was no prospect of it, and even with one, or several such recommendations, no certainty that they would necessarily be followed.

Both the Home Office and the tribunal clearly preferred the concept of stepped progression, allowing patients' behaviour to be monitored as they moved through increasingly less secure environments. Although such schemes might permit tribunals to make decisions about which they felt more confident, since they had no power to enforce recommendations for trial leave or transfer, they could not guarantee that the opportunity to make those decisions would come about. As a result, tribunals were occasionally faced with the invidious choice of having to make a decision on the basis of evidence about which they felt uncertain, or to make a recommendation with no certainty attached to its fruition.

Mainly, tribunals did not find themselves faced with a choice at all. Since imputations of potential dangerousness were easy to make, even in the context of long periods of trouble-free behaviour, and impossible to refute satisfactorily, any case which raised the spectre of potential problems invoked a cautious approach from the tribunal. Rarely did tribunals find it necessary even to spell out why it was that they felt a patient was dangerous—it was sufficient merely to note that the patient's RMO had given evidence to that effect. In cases of genuine uncertainty, difficulties in satisfying the statutory criteria could be used to justify a decision not to discharge. However, resort to a strict interpretation of the statutory criteria by those seeking the discharge of patients, for example, on the grounds on non-treatability in S37 cases, did not appear to have much impact on the tribunal. This was in notable contrast to the manner in which the Home Office would invoke the statutory criteria in relation to the treatability of restricted psychopaths as a non-relevant criterion for continuing detention. Representatives' recourse to arguments about equity similarly received short shrift.

Finally, it emerged that the Home Office were opposed to any relaxation in levels of security where doubt existed about potential risk to the public. Their arguments had several layers, each of which might be brought into use as the likelihood that the tribunal might decide to discharge became greater. The most common concerned the generalizability of behaviour occurring in a secure environment; others included the need for unanimity amongst the medical opinions, the insufficiency of even a substantial batch of psychological tests, and the requirement for a supporting opinion from the Advisory Board. Furthermore, even given a consensus in the evidence, the Home Office believed that the tribunal were justified in taking a different view to that offered to them. Hence, uncertainty could be generated where none obviously presented itself in the opinions (if not the evidence) of those testifying before the tribunal. Uncertainty always favoured caution. Since it could rarely be resolved satisfactorily, it is not surprising, particularly among the subgroup of 'serious psychopaths', that so few decisions went beyond 'no discharge'. Wider questions about the potential effectiveness of any safeguard for the liberty of detained psychopaths are not readily answerable. The existing arrangements are open to criticism if the tribunals only ever endorse the views of the RMOs. But, given the problems associated with the release of this group, whether any other outcomes could have resulted, or indeed, would have been sought by those with the discretion to impose them, is arguable.

7. Patients with Classifications of Mental Illness

Mental illness is not defined by the Mental Health Act 1983. But, unlike psychopathic disorder, there are universally agreed signs and symptoms of its presence. These would include abnormality in one or more of the following areas: mood, perception (hallucinations and/or delusional misinterpretation of events), cognitive functions (delusional beliefs, impairment of intellectual functions—memory or orientation), and form and/or content of speech (thinking so disordered as to impede communication with others or to prevent reasonable self-appraisal).[1] Most psychiatrists would have little difficulty diagnosing as mental illnesses the major psychoses, including schizophrenia, manic-depressive and depressive illnesses. These are also the disorders which most commonly occur as a basis for compulsory treatment.

From the perspective of the tribunals, the schizophrenias and the depressive illnesses create different problems. In schizophrenia, which most commonly occurs as a process illness, the tribunal's dilemma frequently revolves around whether the patient has sufficient insight to be relied upon to continue to take medication, which in turn usually prevents a relapse. For the depressives, where the illness may be both intermittent and transient, and where there may be no immediate symptoms, three questions are uppermost. Is the patient still suffering from the disorder, but his condition is in remission? Or has he made a full recovery? And is the patient likely to be placed again in the same stressful environmental situation which may have contributed to the onset of his original illness? It is important to recognize that it is possible to argue persuasively that patients have recovered from depressive illnesses, whereas it is almost impossible to refute the underlying existence of either the 'psychopathic' disorders or, as will emerge, the schizophrenic illnesses.

Indeed, it was more common for tribunal discharges to occur in

[1] A more precise closed definition is given in Appendix II of *A Review of the Mental Health Act 1959*, DHSS (1976).

cases where patients had been suffering from a depressive illness. Of the 40 matched patients reviewed, 6 of the 9 who were discharged were diagnosed as having suffered from depressive illnesses. Yet, of the 23 patients who were neither discharged nor recommended for transfer or trial leave, 18 were suffering from schizophrenia.

These mentally ill patients presented a marked contrast to the psychopathic group. Treatment programmes were, by and large, much more effective and there were well-known patterns of improvement.[2] Also, uncertainty over diagnosis was rare. It arose mainly in relation to the extent of recovery, where disputes would occur over whether the patient's symptoms were sufficient to sustain the diagnosis. Similarly, could an isolated abnormality of insights about past beliefs or actions alone be taken as a sign of mental illness? A final area of doubt concerned whether the neuroses, manifestations of anxiety or depression in their less severe forms, should be classed as mental illnesses.

Given the greater certitude with which diagnoses generally were made, it is curious that the RMOs' reports went into much greater detail about the patients' symptoms. Perhaps the explanation lies merely in the contrasting absence of overt symptomatology in many of those with diagnoses of psychopathic disorder. Certainly, the severity of the symptoms in the mentally ill group contributed both to the confidence with which diagnoses were made, and to the probability of patients demonstrating their illnesses through the most innocent of remarks which they made to the tribunal. In spite of this, RMOs would occasionally attempt further to substantiate their diagnoses at hearings, by intentionally 'bringing out' the severity of patients' symptoms or by illustrating their lack of insight. It was almost as if they believed their professional assessment of the patient would be insufficient to convince the tribunal.

1. RECURRENT THEMES IN THE TRIBUNALS' REASONING

A. *Insight*

Insight may be defined as 'having a correct attitude to a morbid change in oneself'. Whether a patient showed insight into the

[2] As a result, non-medical issues, such as time for crime concepts arose less frequently (with the exception of those patients who committed very serious offences, but seemingly made a rapid recovery from depressive disorders).

reasons for his offence(s) and into his condition, was regarded as crucial, by both RMOs and tribunals. Usually, patients needed to demonstrate insight on a number of levels; first, and obviously, that they accepted they were ill at the time of the commission of their offence; secondly, that they remained ill (even if their symptoms were controlled by medication) and/or that they recognized that there was a good possibility that they would become ill again if they stopped taking medication. RMOs and tribunals therefore needed to be assured (*a*) that patients understood why they needed to take medication, (*b*) that they were likely to have to do so for some time, if not indefinitely, and (*c*) that they showed no reluctance—even if not positive enthusiasm—for this course. When all of these criteria were met, patients would additionally have to show some stability in these beliefs, in order to demonstrate that they were genuine, and to have been free of disturbed periods in hospital. The opinion was further expressed that since loss of insight was usually the first symptom to recur when a patient's condition deteriorated, there was a significant risk associated with discharging even apparently stable patients. With loss of insight, patients would not necessarily recognize that they were becoming ill again nor accept their need to seek help. Even patients who gave the requisite assurances, would not be too readily believed unless they were to be closely supervised. Thus, the genuineness of a patient's insight was difficult to establish, and even if the tribunal were satisfied of this, it would remain vulnerable. Its prominence as a factor in the tribunal's decision-making derives principally not from its application as an index of the patient's recovery, but from its interrelationship with future control over the patient's condition. Hence, it was insight into the need for medication which was crucial.

B. Medication and Stability

Another marked contrast with the psychopathic groups concerned the relative lack of stability in these patients' histories, and sometimes in their condition between the time at which reports were prepared by the RMOs and their performances at the hearings. A number of the patients had long-standing psychiatric histories with repeated admissions to local hospitals in the years preceding their index offence. Often these periods of illness would be associated with an unwillingness to accept medication—particularly among those patients suffering from schizophrenic illnesses. Where the index offence resulted in the patient being diagnosed as suffering from mental illness, the periods of stability which interspersed their disordered behaviour would occur within the confines of the secure hospital.

Sometimes patients would ask to come off medication to see whether their stability could be maintained, and RMOs would endorse this approach. Other patients would refuse to continue with medication and, if their RMOs insisted on its necessity, a second opinion would need to be sought from the Mental Health Act Commissioners. Sometimes a tribunal would suggest that a patient be tried without medication. Occasionally a RMO would take the initiative. Whatever the impetus, patients would have medication-free periods in hospital. These were usually (but neither invariably and certainly not immediately) followed by a deterioration in their condition and a reactivation of acute symptoms.[3]

C. Remorse

Another criterion deemed important by both the tribunal and the RMOs related to whether patients showed remorse for their offences. Not only did patients have to say that they were sorry, but it was also necessary for them to sound as if they meant it. A desire to see the appropriate emotive content is understandable. However, invariably to expect it was somewhat curious. For those patients suffering from chronic schizophrenia, an inability to show appropriate affect is symptomatic of their underlying mental state. Inappropriate affect and particularly negative affect, with apathy and lack of motivation, characterize the chronic state. Indeed, such patients rarely show any of the positive symptoms of schizophrenic illnesses (delusions, hallucinations, etc.).

It is important to stress that many of the patients had committed offences of serious violence; sixteen resulting in death—eleven of these involved close family and five 'strangers'. For those who had committed lesser assaults outside the hospital environment,

[3] The RMOs' assertion that tribunals would not discharge patients who were actively ill, even if not a danger to themselves or others, is broadly borne out. Even though patients' acute phases could be predictably brought under control by long-acting medication (which *per Hallstrom* can be administered on an outpatient basis), tribunals did not discharge patients until they had demonstrated considerable stability.

family members also constituted the most common victims. It was sometimes hard to distinguish patients' remorse from the grief and guilt arising out of the direct harm they had inflicted on their families. Furthermore, as the offences often involved the use of readily obtainable weapons—kitchen knives, hammers, etc.—the prospect of their repetition was understandably extremely worrying. Finally, unlike the psychopathic group, no case involved any overt sexual element. However, where patients' delusions entailed aspects of morbid jealousy, and/or where patients had caused the death of spouses or lovers, it was evident that complex emotional issues, sometimes of a sexual nature, had been raised.

D. *The Absence of Disorder?*

Although the indices of the presence of mental illness are more clear-cut than for the psychopathic group, it is apparent that the criteria used to assess the extent of recovery are, if not as nebulous, at least fluid. Insight, remorse, the cessation of delusions and hallucinations are criteria largely not open to objective quantification, but depend upon what the patient chooses to say about himself and his intentions. As a result, the tribunal's decisions will be dependent on the opinions of those who know the patient best; independent assessment (whether by the tribunal or an IP), particularly where the patient's condition is known to fluctuate on a day-to-day basis, will not readily outweigh the views of the RMO.

Finally, the diagnostic confusion so prevalent in the psychopathic group is not apparent. Although many mentally ill patients clearly suffer additionally from personality disorders (the presence of severe illness of any kind frequently distorts normal relationships), rarely are these sufficiently significant to amount to a clinical diagnosis of personality disorder. Moreover, the presence of continuing symptoms of mental illness negates any necessity to attach a legal classification of psychopathic disorder. Reclassification occurs primarily in a context of remission or recovery, where a classification solely of mental illness cannot be sustained because of the absence of symptoms, yet the gravity of the patient's offence and the likelihood of its repetition prompts a desire for detention to be continued.

II. THE TRIBUNALS' DECISIONS: OUTCOME MEASURES

Table 7.1 *Tribunal outcomes in the cases of 40 patients with diagnosis of mental illness detained at Acheland and Bendene*

	Discharges (% in brackets)	Other Advice[a] (% in brackets)	No Discharge (% in brackets)
Acheland	3 (17)	4 (22)[b]	11 (61)
Bendene	6 (32)	1 (5)[c]	12 (63)

a transfer or trial leave recommended
b excludes two cases adjourned (one patient died, one to be discharged by RMO).
c excludes one case withdrawn

Although the differences are less pronounced than for the psychopathically disordered patients, Bendene tribunals retained their preference for discharging the mentally ill, whilst Acheland were more likely to recommend to the Home Secretary that there be some change in a patient's circumstances (see Table 7.1). The proportion of cases in which the tribunal merely recommended either transfer or trial leave, was less than for the psychopathically disordered (14 per cent of the total in contrast to 25 per cent).

Again, the tribunals overwhelmingly followed the courses which the RMOs advised, namely in nine out of every ten cases. In three cases they went beyond the views of the RMO—twice to discharge (where they were supported by IPRs) and once to recommend transfer in an unrepresented case (in the knowledge that this was not likely to have any real impact). In one case the tribunal disagreed with the RMO in order to be more cautious.

It was apparent that many of the patients, particularly those in subgroup A (no discharges below), had no immediate prospect of being discharged. Applications were frequently for changes in the patients' circumstances which the tribunal had no power to effect—for example, transfer to another ward in the hospital, or indeed to a hospital in another country. Some patients merely wished to manifest their sense of grievance; even so, public hearings were rare.

Although thirty-two of the cases were represented, in thirteen of these it was not thought necessary to seek IPRs. It was also not unusual for the style of representation to be low key or for the representative to submit that his client 'did not reach the statutory criteria' (Patient 61A) or that he had 'no particular submission to make' (Patient 20A).

In fifteen of the nineteen cases where IPRs were submitted (one was excluded because the case was adjourned), the views expressed were broadly in accord with those of the RMOs. In one of the three cases where the IPR took a different view to the RMO, the tribunal preferred the more cautious course advocated by the RMO and, in the other two the tribunal accepted the advice of the IPs.

III. THE TRIBUNALS' DECISIONS: RATIONALE

For the purposes of discussion, the tribunals' reasoning in the forty cases is divided into three subgroups: (A) straightforward no discharge cases; (B) intermediate decisions—where the tribunal acted primarily not as decision-makers, but as negotiators or brokers. These cases illustrate a series of key themes which inhibit or frustrate the tribunals in the enforcement of their powers. The group includes three cases which were withdrawn or adjourned and a further five where there were specific recommendations for transfer or trial leave; (C) discharged cases or recommended for discharge.

A. No Discharge Cases

With the exception of four patients on S37 orders, all of this group of nine women and thirteen men were restricted cases. The bulk of the group remained very ill and their cases were easily resolved by the tribunal. They will be dealt with only briefly. They illustrate the readiness with which the statutory criteria for continued detention may be satisfied given first, the presence of illness; secondly, patients' obvious lack of insight into their disorders; and thirdly, their unresponsiveness to medication. Patients could be characterized as 'hopeless and helpless'. The tribunal found them tragic and recognized that their own role was cosmetic.

Patients in this subgroup frequently condemned themselves in terms either of what they said to the tribunal or what they failed to say. Two patients were electively or effectively mute, whilst a third was so thought-disordered that her speech was largely unintelligible to the tribunal. Others underlined in evidence their clear lack of insight. For example, Patient 20A was described by the RMO as 'one of our more disabled patients' and 'a significant and serious danger to anyone who became the centre of his persecutory beliefs'. He was suffering from paranoid schizophrenia and had additionally experienced deterioration of his intellect. Although the patient said all the right things about his willingness to continue with medication, the tribunal did not believe him. His argument that his offence had occurred on the spur of the moment (he had taken a knife from his kitchen, got into his car, driven at and knocked down a neighbour and his children, got out of the car, and stabbed his neighbour to death) did not impress the tribunal. Nor did his assertion that there would be no chance of the offence occurring again: 'What I did was unique ... I was under extreme stress ... I can't see myself attacking someone in broad daylight again'. His complete lack of insight was, to the tribunal, confirmed by his remarks that 'It's not as if I planted a bomb or put them in an acid bath', and that the children would be all right because their father was 'probably insured'. The tribunal considered his attitude to his offence 'irrational, bizarre and inappropriate'. Their reasons for refusing discharge did not seek to give him any hope for the future.

It was also evident that the information patients volunteered was assessed in interaction with the nature of their previous actions. Where, for example, patients' offences had been associated with their delusional or bizarre beliefs and these beliefs persisted, patients were considered to pose a real risk. Sometimes the danger to others was generalized, but other cases involved named individuals or specific groups. For example, Patient 7B believed that, because of their mental condition, some people were no use to society and therefore not fit to live. He had been convicted of the manslaughter of a 61 year old fellow patient. The continuation of his delusional beliefs about the elderly and handicapped, combined with a refusal to accept that he was ill, made him an obvious danger. Even where patients denied that 'troublesome thoughts' persisted, if they failed to recognize the need for continuing medication, they just as effectively damned themselves. Patient 28A illustrates this point. On a large dose of anti-psychotic medication, the patient told the tribunal that she continued to hear voices, but that these no longer bothered her because she knew they were 'only voices' and she no longer felt impelled to carry out their instructions. Although she volunteered to continue to take her medication for as long as the hospital wanted, she told the tribunal that she no longer needed it as she had recovered. The tribunal concluded that she had failed to recognize the connection between her medication and her improved response. They left the case in the RMO's hands.

Although this cautious approach was typical, it is understandable—all of this subgroup of patients had been assaultive, and eight of them had caused the death of others. Where the assaultive or disruptive behaviour was persistent or where patients were in a deteriorated condition there was commonly a requirement for continuing security or intensive nursing. Since these were not so readily available in other facilities, prolonging a patient's stay in a Special Hospital was the most likely option. Some of the group had anyway been transferred from local facilities as 'unmanageable', frequently following attacks on staff or other patients there. Thus, there were real problems in identifying other potential locations for them. Moreover, patients were seemingly often unaware of these difficulties and expressed wholly unrealistic expectations about their own futures. For example, Patient 10A was a deteriorated schizophrenic. He was a large man, described in his absence by his RMO as 'extremely fierce and very unpredictable'; he appeared at the hearing flanked by two nurses from Acheland's high security unit, so that the tribunal were left in no doubt as to his 'unpredictability'. The patient was on a combination of major tranquillizers, which his RMO described as 'keeping things steady if not having much curative effect'. The case was tragic because the patient told the tribunal that he wanted to go to his father's home, but the RMO had privately informed them that his family were terrified of him. Clearly, the patient was to be a 'long-term customer' at Acheland.

The specific nature of patients' illnesses was also an important criterion in assessing their suitability to be moved on. Some of the chronic schizophrenics no longer showed positive symptomatology, but the negative sequelae were all too apparent. Apathy, negative affect, and an inexorable deterioration in their intellect and level of functioning meant that these patients would require extended care. Whether these symptoms were attributable solely to a natural progression in their illnesses, or had been exacerbated by the lengthy exposure to medication which their conditions had required, was almost academic; their futures were bleak.

Similarly, those with more active symptomatology could fluctuate in their day-to-day rationality and in the desires they expressed. Unpredictability in behaviour, consequent on instability in a patient's condition, was a cause of concern to the tribunal and RMOs alike. However, it posed particular difficulties for the former where they were required to assess the patient at a specific point in time. In this respect, a patient's performance at the hearing was not taken as definitive. In the case of Patient 16A the medical member of the tribunal reported that the patient had refused to be interviewed by him only days earlier and had been behaving in a paranoid manner on the ward. Yet his behaviour at the hearing was unremarkable.

Only three patients could be regarded as exceptions to this litany of despair. Patients 19A and 23B were unusual because the tribunal were clearly favourably disposed towards their future transfer. Both had committed their offences whilst suffering from psychotic illnesses with quasi-religious delusions. Patient 19A was unusual because he made a good impression on the tribunal despite the horrific nature of his offence (he had fractured the skull of an elderly woman, attempted to gouge her eyes out, causing blindness in one eye, and had also killed her pets). The patient had been suffering from an acute paranoid schizophrenic illness, in which he was plagued by thoughts about evil and a desire to destroy it. His response to medication had been good, but he had had one serious relapse whilst in hospital. Although his insight had improved, he remained, according to the RMO's report, reluctant to take medication. The RMO believed that if the patient were to be discharged 'he would default on treatment almost immediately'. Peculiarly, the patient did not seem to have experienced the expected inexorable deterioration of personality. He was articulate, charming, and polite at his hearing, maintaining that he needed the medication to keep his illness 'at bay'. His brother gave evidence to support this change of heart. The RMO was not entirely convinced, stating that it was an artificial environment in which to assess the genuineness of his co-operation. Moreover, despite the patient's assurances that he would avoid matters relating to the occult if he were to be discharged, the RMO was uncertain whether such interests were a symptom or a cause of his deterioration. He wished to proceed cautiously. The tribunal concurred, but hoped that 'in the near future' the patient could be transferred to a secure unit.

The final case in this section, that of Patient 24A, was unusually complex. It involved a young man who had recently killed with excessive violence. Yet, it appeared from the reports that the RMO did not believe that the legal criteria for his continuing detention were satisfied. Ultimately the tribunal did not discharge. How did this resolution come about?

The patient suffered from epilepsy. At the time of his trial numerous psychiatrists testified that he did not suffer from mental illness, or from any of the other three forms of mental disorder within the 1983 Act. It was agreed, however, following *Sullivan* [1983] 1 All ER 590, that his epileptic automatism constituted a (temporary) disease of the mind amounting to insanity. The patient was accordingly found not guilty by reason of insanity to the charge of murder. An order was made under S5 of the Criminal Procedure (Insanity) Act 1964. This required no particular diagnostic classification.

The hidden agenda at the tribunal undoubtedly concerned the patient's potential for future offending. He had been detained for only twelve months following the original offence. There was no evidence to suggest that the patient might not similarly reoffend. Yet, legally, this could not be a legitimate consideration if the patient could not be classified under S1(2) of the 1983 Act.

Before the tribunal hearing written evidence was submitted by his RMO setting out the medical and legal difficulties. The RMO stated that 'there have at no time been any symptoms of a mental illness' adding that most psychiatrists reserved the term mental illness for the major psychoses such as schizophrenia and manic-depressive illness. But he tentatively suggested that it could be argued that the patient satisfied the legal definition of psychopathic disorder, because he had a persistent disorder of mind (due to his epilepsy) which had been associated with violence and he also had a history of irresponsibility, as shown by his previous abuse of alcohol and drugs.

An IPR submitted to the tribunal contested this diagnosis of psychopathic disorder on the grounds that (i) epilepsy was not a disorder of mind, (ii) epilepsy was not persistent, (iii) evidence (apart from the epilepsy) for psychopathic disorder was slender, i.e., his early life was not typical of those with personality disorders. But the IPR, like the RMO, indicated that if the patient were to be discharged, it should be conditionally. His behaviour during epileptic attacks was sufficiently worrying for there to be a clear need to supervise his medication.

The Home Office, who were represented by counsel at the hearing, made a long submission arguing that the patient fell within the legal definition of psychopathic disorder. They also contended that since 'mental' and 'of the mind' could be regarded as coterminous, as could 'disease' and 'illness', the patient could additionally be classified as suffering from mental illness. They cited *W. v. L.* [1974] QB 711 in support of their argument that the words 'mental illness' should be construed in the way that ordinary sensible people would construe them; hence the patient's recent offence, his epilepsy, his addiction to drink and drugs, and his underlying hostility to his mother made him 'obviously mentally ill'. It appeared as if the tribunal were going to be faced with a clear conflict of evidence, and a confusing complexity of psychiatric, legal, and lay definitions of the various terms at issue.

In the event they were greatly assisted by the RMO, who substantially revised his opinion by the time of the hearing. He argued that, although there had been no change in the patient's condition since he wrote his report, his 'understanding of his condition [had] changed'. He still maintained that there were no psychotic symptoms, but now argued that the patient suffered from symptoms of a neurosis, principally anxiety and depression, and that these amounted to a mental illness. He further stated that he did not believe that the patient could be properly supervised in the community, and therefore he invited the tribunal to continue to detain him—but on the grounds of mental illness, not psychopathic disorder. However, when questioned by the judge, who insisted that he apply his mind to the legal definition (the RMO had argued that most psychiatrists would not recognize the patient's condition as psychopathic disorder), the RMO agreed that the patient could be said to satisfy the legal criteria for psychopathic disorder. The judge also put to the RMO the World Health Organization's description of epilepsy as a disease and a psychosis. The RMO rejected the suggestion that the patient suffered from a process psychotic condition, but agreed that he did have attacks which put him out of touch with reality and hallucinations which could be called psychotic.

Finally, the representative submitted that the only evidence the tribunal had to go on in respect of the patient's mental illness was the changed opinion of the RMO and, since the patient's aggression arose out of his epilepsy, which was a disease of a brief paroxysmal nature and intermittent rather than persistent, he could not be described as psychopathically disordered within the terms of the Act. He argued that although it might be advisable to continue to detain him for treatment, in order to do so it would be necessary to strain and distort the concepts of psychopathic disorder and mental illness far beyond what had been intended by those who had drafted the Act.

The tribunal in their reasons were ultimately to argue: (i) that the patient suffered from epilepsy which manifested itself as an acute confusional state which could be described as a transient organic psychotic condition (*WHO*, 9th Revision International Classification of Diseases); (ii) that the epilepsy combined with certain definite neurotic symptoms to cause a persistent mental illness (currently reasonably controlled by medication); (iii) that the patient's former severe abuse of alcohol amounted almost to a disease (the medical member of the tribunal was an ardent teetotaller); and (iv) that his history and present state indicated that he might additionally be suffering from a persistent disorder of mind which resulted in serious irresponsibility. The tribunal concluded that they were satisfied that the patient was suffering from mental illness and that they were not satisfied that he was not also suffering from psychopathic disorder.

The case illustrates a number of features already discussed. First, the weight attached to oral evidence seemingly overrides both written submissions and contradictory written testimony by the same author; in this respect the revised opinion of the RMO was convenient to the tribunal. Moreover, negligible weight was attached to the report of the independent psychiatrist since he did not attend the hearing to give oral evidence. Secondly, the clear risk which could have arisen had the patient been discharged meant that the outcome, not to discharge, had a certain inevitability associated with it. There was an arguable preparedness to dispense with the legal niceties. In the event, it was not necessary to resort to the Home Office's arguments about 'the common man', but this does not negate their submission. Even the representative was seemingly prepared to collude in an interpretation of the term mental illness which would ensure that his client received supervision under a conditional rather than an absolute discharge, if he were to be discharged at all. Finally, the case illustrates the opposite side of the argument most commonly found in cases involving psychopathic disorder. Psychiatrists routinely find themselves in the dilemma of having patients in their care who are clearly personality disordered, but who do not fit the legal definition of psychopathic disorder making them eligible for detention and treatment—to permit this requires the lawyers to stretch the definition of psychopathic disorder. In this case, the patient did not clinically merit a diagnosis of personality disorder, but, when pressed by the judge, the RMO was prepared to state that the patient fitted the fine detail of the legal definition (one which, as a clinician, he would not readily recognize). Hence, the dual flexibility of psychiatric and legal definitions enables psychiatrists and lawyers to ensure that those whom they feel should be detained, can be so detained. The tribunal had, unusually in this case, to draw on the fine print of the statutory criteria, supported by the evidence of the RMO, in order to satisfy themselves that the patient could continue to be detained. Yet again, in order to ensure a particular outcome, the process of review was itself affected, in this instance unusually requiring a minute (rather than the more usual sparing) examination of the evidence.

B. Intermediate Decisions

In these nine cases the tribunal attempted to go beyond a straightforward no discharge decision; in five cases making specific recommendations. In restricted cases they have no power to do this. Moreover, the likelihood of these recommendations having much impact is limited.

The cases illustrate a series of problems which repeatedly frustrate or are seen to limit the tribunal's effectiveness in the informal arena in which they operate as negotiators or brokers. The first cases concern the impact which the conditions imposed by other bodies, such as the receiving institutions or government departments, can have on the tribunal's decision. Aside from the Special Hospitals, no institution is obliged to provide patients with beds. The other principal theme concerns the tribunal's own preparedness to put ends before means—in achieving what the tribunal perceive to be the best all round outcome, there is a tendency for them to neglect the fine detail of their statutory powers.

(i) Systemic problems The cases already discussed highlight the difficulties tribunals experience where patients lack insight or have unrealistic expectations about their futures. However, even where patients had an appropriate appraisal of their own needs, obtaining

the required placements was not always straightforward. Some of these difficulties stemmed from the reluctance of RSUs to accept patients before they had demonstrated stability within conditions of special security. RSUs wished to be confident that patients would neither abscond nor occupy their beds for unduly prolonged periods (more than 18–24 months); both of these fears could lead to delay in patients moving on from the Special Hospitals (Snowden 1986). However, difficulties could also arise where patients wished to be moved to hospitals outside the country. Patient 11A exemplifies the systemic difficulties the tribunal experience in such cases.

The patient was stabilized on medication and thought to represent a 'minimal risk' provided his medication was continued; he wished to return to Ireland. Acheland accepted that he did not require the conditions of special security they offered. Instead, there were plans to transfer him to a secure hospital in Ireland. But the tribunal were informed that this hospital would be prepared to assist with a bed only if the patient were first discharged from his order under the 1983 Act. This created obvious jurisdictional problems. Acheland considered that it would be irresponsible to discharge him absolutely without supervision. In their deliberations the tribunal agreed that the patient was no great danger to anyone, but in the absence of any positive plan to move him to Ireland they could not reach a decision. They adjourned, in the expectation that this might promote progress in the plans for the patient's return.

They were, however, to be disappointed. During the subsequent five months the RMO seemingly took no steps to pursue transfer, despite being repeatedly pressed by the patient's solicitors. Ultimately, the tribunal took the unusual course of writing directly to the RMO, making it plain that they expected him to take the necessary action to implement their requests. Even this proved ineffective. The patient died in Acheland without any real progress having been made.

(ii) Departmental pressure: Home Office   Although in the case of Patient 11A the systemic difficulties stemmed primarily from an intransigence on the part of both hospitals about which the tribunal were in no position to take official action, the difficulties in the case of Patient 35B were even more complex. Here the problems could be attributed primarily to the role of the Home

Office. The patient had committed an unprovoked assault on a stranger whilst experiencing persecutory delusions (there was a recurrent history of both psychiatric difficulties and assault). He had responded well to medication and within nine months was assessed as showing no evidence of mental illness. The RMO had initially recommended transfer to an interim secure unit, but could not obtain the permission of the Home Office for the patient to have unescorted days out from Bendene, which the unit required before they were prepared to accept him. The RMO subsequently recommended, partially in order to avoid a stalemate, that the patient be conditionally discharged to a hostel, for he was not considered to be a danger to himself or others.[4] When the tribunal met, they lent the RMO their support by making a deferred conditional discharge, subject to appropriate after-care arrangements including the provision of a hostel place. However, it emerged that the only hostel which was prepared to offer the patient a bed, wished him first to spend three to six months in the ISU. This view echoed those of other hostels which had been approached—they unanimously agreed that unescorted leave in the community from a controlled environment was a prerequisite. An impasse existed. When the tribunal reconvened, the only course open to them, if they were not to discharge absolutely or discharge conditionally without conditions, was to follow the recommendations of the Home Office. These were that the patient should first successfully complete six months trial leave at the ISU, prior to transfer there. They would then be prepared, in principle, to recommend conditional discharge to the hostel provided the patient first spent a period of successful trial leave there. This might be regarded as a refined example of the stepped approach to discharge. The tribunal rescinded its deferred conditional discharge and recommended the course set out by the Home Office as being in 'the best interests of the patient with the least risk to the community'.[5] Clearly, they felt they had little choice, despite the following factors: the patient had shown no positive signs of mental illness for some years, his medical

[4] However, his RMO did believe that he might be a danger towards any women with whom he formed a liaison in the future, although his morbid jealousy, if it developed, would be likely to do so slowly, and be obvious to his supervisors.
[5] Notably, in rescinding the deferred conditional discharge the tribunal followed a course which it was subsequently found by the House of Lords not to be empowered to do (see *Campbell* in Appendix 3).

requirements were for 'monitoring', he had considerable insight, he was motivated to take his medication and he was not considered a danger.

(iii) Departmental pressure: DHSS Patient 50B had a suggested history of epilepsy, but no recent attacks. Like Patient 24A above, he was a young man who had killed with excessive violence. The motivation for his offence had never been clear, and for some years prior to abreaction, he had been unable to recall details of the offence. A previous tribunal had recommended his transfer to a RSU and he had been accepted there as 'highly suitable'. However, permission for the transfer was not given by the Home Office. His RMO questioned both the nature of his supposed mental illness (there had been no evidence of overt mental illness or epilepsy for some years) and the need to detain him in secure conditions. He recommended in his report to the tribunal that the patient be conditionally discharged. This appraisal did not meet with the approval of the DHSS, who were prepared only to back the patient's trial leave at the RSU. They wrote to the RMO and asked that their views, as the Responsible Authority, replace his. They also wrote to the chairman of the hospital management team to ensure that the tribunal were similarly informed. It subsequently transpired that the RMO revised his submission to the tribunal, to the effect that he firmly recommended the patient's trial leave at the RSU, but no longer felt that conditional discharge was in the best interests of the public or the patient. He had clearly been exposed to some pressure.

The Home Office were represented at the hearing. They indicated that the Home Secretary would not be prepared to allow trial leave until the patient had been referred to the Advisory Board. It was recommended that the patient withdraw his application whilst his case was reviewed; the patient agreed. However, it is arguable whether this was in his best interests. Had the tribunal reached a similar conclusion to that finally proposed by the RMO, the Advisory Board would have had recommendations from three sources for their consideration. In the event, only the recommendation of the RMO and the DHSS (possibly) would be put to them. The patient could be disadvantaged.

(iv) A lack of impetus The cases discussed above illustrate clear pressure to prevent a patient's imminent departure either by

blocking a proposed move or by prolonging the necessary arrangements. In contrast, other cases illustrate that where there is no particular motivation to move a patient on it is likely that a *laissez-faire* approach will prevail, even if it is recognized that a patient is not confined within the most appropriate conditions. Similarly, even if the tribunal go beyond the recommendations of the RMO, where they confine themselves to a low-key recommendation, it is unlikely to have any impact.[6]

The case of Patient 7A illustrates the first difficulty. The patient had been detained for fifteen years following an offence of a less serious nature, namely, window-breaking; he was a chronic schizophrenic detained on a S37. Looking back over the medical reports, it was clear that it was his indiscriminate homosexual behaviour which had caused the greatest concern. But, as the years had passed, he had become institutionalized and was clearly unable to look after himself. His parents were caring, but elderly and unable to support him. The RMO was pursuing transfer to a secure unit, but was not confident that he would be successful because of the patient's constant need for supervision and his grossly unacceptable behaviour (his libido had, unusually, not decreased with time). The RMO readily admitted that he felt 'guilty that he's been here so long, but there really is nowhere that will take him'. Although the patient was described as 'a social menace rather than a danger', the RMO argued that his intolerable behaviour 'could act as a focus for unrest or violence on the part of other people'. The representative was described as 'sensible', in that he sought nothing from the tribunal for his client other than that they endorse the RMO's plans for transfer. This they did, with little expectation that it would come to anything. Despite the patient's minimal need for medical treatment and arguable need for security, his continued detention in conditions of special security seemed tragically likely.

[6] The case of Patient 13A typifies the low-key approach. The patient had made a serious attack on his wife following the development of his 'pathological ideas of infidelity' and a fear of being poisoned by her. Despite medication in Acheland (over a period of nine years) he retained these delusions. The medical member described him as 'over-ripe for a move'. The tribunal agreed that he did not require the conditions of special security at Acheland, and recommended that 'consideration be given . . . to transferring him to the secure unit of a general psychiatric hospital'. Although this went beyond the RMO's view that the patient was not ready for transfer, the likelihood of it having any effect was recognized as being minimal.

(v) Means and ends: Pragmatism and the law In some cases a lack of rigour can creep into tribunals' thinking, where decisions are apparently straightforward, because patients are not asking them to exercise their powers under the statutory criteria. These cases illustrate a further nuance to the suggestion above that some cases are resolved by default primarily because of a lack of impetus. Here, a strict interpretation of the law again takes second place because the tribunal recognize that a desirable end result can be achieved through other more subtle routes. In this respect the ends triumph over the means. This is, of course, a risky strategy. If the informal resolution does not succeed, patients have lost their right of recourse to the tribunal until their next period of eligibility.

Patient 9A had committed a serious assault, whilst suffering from paranoid delusions, and had a prior history of assaultive behaviour. He had been detained for three years, was on only a small dosage of medication and experienced no current symptoms. He was thought to suffer 'not from a process illness, but from a recurring illness in remission'. He showed good insight and the tribunal was confident that he would continue to accept medication (which in his case anyway was of questionable value) and that he would seek help if he were to relapse. The patient wanted to be transferred to a local hospital where a consultant had offered him a bed and provided an IPR recommending transfer. The RMO and the tribunal both concurred with this course. Discussion of the reasons for continuing detention (in a less secure setting admittedly) were perfunctory, because there was no impetus for the tribunal to go beyond what the patient was requesting. Moreover, there was no consideration as to whether a conditional discharge might have been merited on the facts, or whether the necessary control over his stability might have readily been achieved through this route.

The case of Patient 22A was complex and there was a direct conflict in the medical evidence. The patient had been detained in Acheland for four years following a conviction for manslaughter, having strangled her daughter and attempted suicide by stabbing afterwards. The RMO believed that the offence occurred as a response to her delusional system, as part of a schizo-affective illness. He thought her illness was in 'reasonable remission in this secure setting' but felt himself 'quite unable to predict whether she had any insight into her illness or whether she would draw attention to any relapse or apparent thought pattern recurrence'. In reports, two IPs gave a different opinion, namely that she had committed the offence during a depressive illness, from which she was now fully recovered. Both recommended transfer to a local psychiatric hospital. Her representative intended to argue before the tribunal that the patient was not mentally ill; she had received no anti-psychotic medication and her anti-depressant medication had been discontinued two years previously with no recurrence of symptoms. However, it was apparent that he wished the tribunal to order a conditional discharge, on the grounds that if the patient was in remission there might be a relapse. He wanted her to be transferred to a local psychiatric hospital to which she wished to go voluntarily (i.e., rather than making residence at the local hospital a condition). The tribunal regarded this as inconsistent, in that they did not believe that they had the power to make a conditional discharge to another hospital and that the representative's plan would put the hospital in an impossible position.[7] Furthermore, if conditional discharge was sought the tribunal would have had to adjourn so that the second IPR could be submitted to the Home Secretary.

At the hearing, it emerged that the RMO's views had changed substantially and that he was prepared to recommend that the patient be transferred to a local hospital, from which he anticipated there would be an early discharge. This change of heart prevented a thorough examination of the conflict in the medical evidence, peculiarly pertinent since the medical member would have agreed with the IPs that the patient had been suffering from depression rather than schizophrenia. However, he would clearly have been reluctant to challenge the views of the RMO, who he assumed would know the patient better than he did. Although the judge had made it plain before the hearing that he doubted this, the presence of illness did not become an issue at the hearing and therefore there was no necessity for the medical member to put his views.[8]

---

[7] As confirmed by *Secretary of State for the Home Department* v. *Mental Health Review Tribunal* and associated case (see Appendix 3).

[8] Since it was clear that the tribunal were going to recommend transfer with the RMO's support, the representative agreed not to make a submission on the presence of illness. However, he wished the tribunal to record that there was a substantial body of evidence that this was not an illness in remission, but rather an episodic incident which might never recur. This argument did not find especial favour with the tribunal, who found it hard to distinguish between the

This case illustrates two notable points. First, the representative was, in the final analysis, as prepared as the tribunal to place ends above means. Despite the fact that he may well have succeeded on a submission under S72(1)(*b*)(i)—particularly in respect of nature or degree—no submission was made once it was plain that the desired result could be readily obtained without further delay. Secondly, the significant departure by the RMO from his report in evidence to tribunal illustrates the facilitative effect a forthcoming tribunal can have, particularly where a patient is supported by independent opinions which conflict with that of the RMO. In the absence of a hearing, there can be no way of knowing for how much longer the RMO might have found himself 'quite unable to predict' in respect of this patient.

C. Discharges

In this subgroup of nine patients the tribunal discharged or recommended discharge in every case. All but the first were cases of some complexity. Patient 41B, a S37 case, illustrates most starkly the impact tribunal review can have, given their willingness to exercise their powers in contradiction to the views of the RMO. Patient 41B had been detained for only a short period following a minor offence. An IPR noted that there were no formal signs of mental illness and the RMO's report stated that he 'would have no hesitation in discharging' as soon as adequate arrangements for his after-care had been made. In response to this evidence the tribunal discharged the patient, to take effect in two weeks from the date of the hearing. This had the effect of placing critical pressure on the RMO to ensure that after-care *would* be speedily arranged. The case contrasts markedly with a very similar one falling into the previous subgroup where the tribunal adjourned. The RMO in that case had stated that as soon as suitable arrangements had been made he intended to discharge.

(i) Against the grain: Declining to be cautious Two cases, those of Patients 5B and 24B were curious because in each instance there was evidence which could have been cited to support a decision

two descriptions of ill states, since either could recur. However, they did note that the patient had been symptom-free without medication for a considerable time and 'that any illness has been in long term remission'. They made a 'strong recommendation for speedy transfer'.

not to discharge. Yet in each case the tribunal took the seemingly riskier course. The case of Patient 5B was particularly controversial in that although the RMO and an IPR were recommending conditional discharge, the Home Office and the DHSS wanted the patient transferred to conditions of lesser security. The latter both believed that the patient might represent a danger to his wife. The patient had retained fixed delusions of infidelity verging on morbid jealousy about her, but, as these had been unaffected by years of medication, the RMO thought they were likely to remain so. The patient showed no evidence of any other thought disorder or perceptual disturbance. The RMO argued that there was accordingly no need to detain him for treatment. The tribunal noted that the patient's illness was well controlled by medication and that the injections could be effected without hospital treatment. The relatives, who were to provide accommodation for the patient, impressed the tribunal as caring and responsible. Nothing obviously stood in the way of discharge. One point is, however, noteworthy. The IPR contained the phrase that the patient 'does not believe that he had been, or is, ill and cannot understand why people have said of him he is either paranoid or a schizophrenic'. Such an admission by the patient, demonstrating the much sought after lack of insight, might, in the context of the specific risk to his wife, have prevented a decision to discharge. Indeed, had the patient's original offence been more serious, it would almost certainly have resulted in the patient being categorized amongst the 'hopeless and helpless'. However, in the circumstances of this case the tribunal drew no attention to it in their reasons.

Patient 24B had been detained for twelve years. He had assaulted his mother, intending to cause serious injury, but had in fact inflicted only superficial wounds. An IPR made the point that the patient had been detained for a period longer than that which the average domestic homicide would have served. The patient's paranoid schizophrenia had responded slowly to medication and he appeared before the tribunal largely as a chronic case, although the specific delusions about the offence had been retained. At the hearing the medical member of the tribunal, the RMO, and the IP all agreed that the patient's illness was controlled by a weekly depot injection and that provided he continued to receive the medication there was no need for him to be detained in hospital. Similarly, all agreed that he was not a danger to himself or others.

They made a deferred conditional discharge and the patient subsequently went to a hostel.

This was also somewhat curious. First, the IPR noted that the patient had told him a version of events surrounding the offence which departed substantially from the recorded facts, and secondly, the IP had asserted that it would not be safe for him to live with his parents. Potentially, he could have been perceived as a specific danger to them. The Home Office had been opposed to discharge and favoured transfer, thus adding to the support for this option. Perhaps the tribunal were swayed by two factors; hostel accommodation had been obtained for the patient and approved by the RMO, and secondly, the patient's sister attended the hearing and both she and the patient impressed the tribunal with their 'sensible and realistic attitude towards the patient's illness and need to have a weekly injection'. Again, the presence of supportive relatives seemed to have had a significant impact.

(ii) Muddied waters: The unavoidability of evidence and law Patient 8A had been convicted of the multiple manslaughter of members of his family. The circumstances of his offence were thus both horrific and tragic, but there was also the spectre of repetition. Good evidence existed that the patient had suffered from a depressive illness at the time and, indeed, had attempted suicide. He was classified as suffering from mental illness, namely depression, but medical reports from the hospital noted that there had been 'no evidence of affective or psychotic illness' during his time there. They variously described him as 'opinionated', 'uncompromising', 'cold and unemotional', and as showing 'only minimal remorse'. Other reports noted the 'excessive violence' he had used on his victims and that he was 'very controlled', 'aloof', and that his attitudes had not changed much during his seven years in Acheland. Moreover, it was suggested that because of his 'self-contained' nature, it was impossible to assess 'with any reasonable degree of accuracy as to his dangerousness if released'. Prediction of dangerousness was thus one hidden agenda. Indeed, even the Home Office's observations noted that, 'The Home Secretary does not accept that a patient's good behaviour within the protected environment of a special hospital, necessarily indicated a fitness for discharge.' All of these observations are remarkably evocative of the descriptions of patients suffering from

psychopathic disorder. Although there was no suggestion that Patient 8A did so suffer, and indeed his early history would count against such a diagnosis, there were clear suggestions that he had 'an immature personality'. There were therefore, within the reports, indications of some personality difficulties. Thus, it might be argued that, although the patient was detained as suffering from mental illness, the hospital and the Home Office, who were both opposed to discharge, were seeking to employ arguments before the tribunal which were normally reserved for patients suffering from psychopathic disorder. These have been found exceptionally difficult to refute. As a result, there was some confusion as to the precise reasons for continuing detention.

The tribunal considered the case both unusual and troubling. The RMO presented evidence that the patient showed no signs of mental illness, but was opposed to discharge or transfer on the basis that the patient might break down under emotional stress and behave violently. A hospital psychologist's report similarly noted that there were no signs of depression, that the patient appeared to be well and had showed appropriate remorse; and concluded that it was 'difficult to see what more could be achieved by keeping [him at Acheland]'. Thus, the RMO and the psychologist concurred about the absence of illness, but the RMO employed arguments about potential risk to justify continuing to detain him. An IPR said there was no evidence of mental illness and none 'to suggest that he could in any way be classified as a psychopath'. His view about the potential risk flatly contradicted that of the RMO for he did not believe that the patient posed any threat to society at large; the IPR recommended conditional discharge to a hostel. The tribunal were, therefore, presented with concurring medical opinions on the facts, but directly conflicting views about dangerousness and the appropriate course to take.

The tribunal, like the IPR, found the patient remorseful and realistic. They noted that he had manifested no symptoms of mental illness in Acheland *and* that no medication had been required. The evidence, in their view, similarly negated any question of psychopathic disorder. They also (unnecessarily) found that the patient satisfied the criteria for discharge under S72(1)(*b*)(ii), in that he was not considered to require medical treatment for his health or safety or for the protection of others. They made a decision to defer conditional discharge until a suitable hostel place could be found. In so doing, and not granting an absolute discharge, the tribunal privately accepted that they had bent the rules, and that they had done so because of the horrific nature of the offences. Although they did not believe it would be necessary to recall him, they thought it appropriate that he should remain liable to be recalled because this created the most appropriate conditions for his release.[9] Again, a pragmatic view had triumphed.

This case is most unusual because the tribunal went beyond the recommendations of the RMO and discharged against his advice. However, it could be maintained that, given the content of his evidence, they were legally bound as a minimum to take this course. They did not see the patient as posing an unavoidable risk, because they did not believe he would reoffend. Therefore, it cannot simply be argued that it was the influence of a strict legal approach which led them to adopt the course they did. The interesting question remains; had they agreed with the RMO that the patient did pose a risk, would they have none the less discharged on the grounds that it was unavoidable *because* he satisfied S72(1)(*b*)(i)?

In the case of Patient 49B the tribunal found itself constrained to adhere to a legalistic approach because of the absence of contradictory evidence. The case was complex—with many of the difficulties stemming from diagnosis at the time of trial. The patient had been convicted at a second trial of double manslaughter (of his wife and his wife's lover) on the grounds of provocation. He had none the less been given a S37/41 with a diagnosis of mental illness, because of depressive features, including several unsuccessful suicide attempts, in his history. He had been detained for three years. At the hearing, four IPRs were submitted, all of which contended that the patient was no longer suffering from mental illness. The RMO, supported by another psychiatrist from Bendene, submitted a report confirming not only that there was no evidence of current mental illness, but also that the patient had been on no medication for eighteen months and

[9] The patient was not actually discharged for some months; difficulties were experienced in finding him a hostel place and there was some suggestion that the hospital had dragged their feet in this matter. The tribunal had to make it plain to them that they did not consider the patient a risk and that therefore they were not bothered about the levels of security at the various hostels suggested. Eventually, when no hostel place was forthcoming, the tribunal discharged the patient to a private address into the care of two people who were prepared to accommodate him and who had made a 'very favourable impression' on the tribunal.

had remained symptom-free during that period. The tribunal noted the opposition of the Secretary of State, but in the absence of the Home Office being represented or calling any expert evidence to support their views, the medical evidence stood uncontradicted. The tribunal found themselves 'unable to attach much weight to the Secretary of State's observations' and conditionally discharged, bearing in mind that the patient might be 'vulnerable to depression when adjusting to the stresses of life in the community'.[10]

(iii) Outcome triumphing over evidence   Patient 41A constituted one of those rare cases where the tribunal went beyond the recommendations of the RMO, in this instance supported by the oral evidence of two IPs. The diagnosis was critical in respect of determining whether the patient satisfied the statutory criteria and should arguably have been the principal point at issue. However, in practice, pragmatism was again pre-eminent, with the decision ultimately being geared to ensuring that supervision of the patient could be maintained.

The patient, who had been convicted of the manslaughter of his wife, had been detained in Acheland for two years on no medication and was symptom-free.[11] The two IPs argued that the offence had been committed whilst the patient was suffering from a depressive illness, complicated by morbid jealousy of his wife, amounting to a delusional state. Neither believed that the patient still suffered from any mental disorder within the meaning of the Act, although they disagreed about whether the patient was in good remission or had experienced a complete recovery. Both did agree that the patient should be conditionally rather than absolutely discharged, because they favoured continued supervision, and to guard against the unlikely possibility that he might relapse. The RMO, who admitted to the tribunal that he had interviewed the patient only once (and it could thus be argued that he had no better knowledge than either of the two IPs), believed that the patient had suffered, and continued to suffer, from schizophrenia. He was opposed to discharge or transfer of any kind. When

---

[10] Dismissing written submissions by the Home Office was not out of keeping with the perspective held by some tribunal judges; namely, that where the Home Office make a purely paper-based assessment of the patient, their views were to be treated with some caution.

[11] The patient had already spent two years in prison before his life sentence was quashed by the Court of Appeal and replaced with a S37/41.

challenged about why the patient had shown no new symptoms despite the absence of medication, he argued that the patient suffered from 'paranoid schizophrenia in effect'; that he retained his delusions about his wife; and that he would be likely to develop further symptoms in years to come. These, he stated, could take fifteen to twenty years to develop. He argued that the patient had not been started on a course of medication because he, the RMO, 'wouldn't embark on a medication programme which would cut across this hearing'. The tribunal were not impressed with his evidence. They preferred that of the two IPs who claimed that the patient had regained his insight. The patient told the tribunal, 'I can't be sure *now* whether she was unfaithful . . . I have a different perspective . . . whatever she did or didn't do, I was ill. I had become very possessive, but I was depressed and she was all I had.' There was thus a direct conflict in evidence between the RMO and the two IPs and between what the patient told the tribunal and what the RMO claimed he had told him.

Before the tribunal hearing the medical member had expressed the view that he believed that it was too early 'to predict with safety' and that more observation of the patient was required. Yet, following presentation of the evidence, he revised his view. The patient had impressed the tribunal: they believed that his recent Christian conversion was genuine (and not evidence of spreading psychosis) and that he did not represent a danger. However, they took the view that it was appropriate that the patient remain liable to be recalled and that he be closely supervised. Three reasons underpinned this: the recency and gravity of the crime; the need to ensure his recovery was maintained outside the stable environment of Acheland; the possibility (even though remote) of the patient becoming deeply emotionally entangled with another woman and becoming depressed again. They accepted that he had sought help promptly when, in the past, he had been depressed. They accordingly reached the view that his depressive illness was in remission (i.e., not full recovery), but that it was not of a nature or degree for it to be appropriate for him to be liable to be detained for treatment—and it was therefore possible for him to remain liable to recall.[12] They made a deferred conditional discharge. A

[12] The judge and the medical member both took the view that if he was not ill, he could only be discharged absolutely. This informal view has been contradicted in the recent case of *Kay* (Appendix 3) in which Parker LJ held that a patient would not be entitled to be discharged absolutely even if it were established that he was not suffering from any mental disorder; medical evidence had indicated that the patient was liable to relapse.

place was available for him at a Christian hostel, but psychiatric and probation supervision had yet to be arranged. The RMO remained opposed to the plan and informed the tribunal that he would tell any proposed supervising consultant that the patient was not, in his view, ready for discharge. The tribunal recognized that he might impede their plans for conditional discharge, but, as they remained convinced that the patient needed psychiatric follow-up, they were not prepared to go the whole way and discharge absolutely.

The tribunal had clearly been frustrated by the attitude of the RMO and had not found his evidence persuasive. Yet, despite the complexities of the case and the conflict of evidence, they reached their decision after only fifteen minutes deliberation. They were subsequently to admit that they may have made the right decision for the wrong reasons—i.e., out of frustration with the RMO's behaviour and attitude. Indeed, much of their discussion concerned the issue of whether the patient's wife had been unfaithful—and if so whether the patient might have entertained reasonable doubts.[13] The quality of their deliberations was arguably questionable. Might more information from social workers about his family have tipped the balance the other way?

Subsequent events proved that it was difficult to arrange psychiatric supervision without the full support of the RMO, and the decision was deferred on two further occasions. None the less, arrangements were finally made to the satisfaction of the tribunal and the views of the RMO partially accommodated, in that both the supervising psychiatrist and the probation officer appointed were, unusually, to submit regular reports to him. Although the tribunal were not prepared to say the RMO had actively frustrated them, he clearly had not facilitated matters.

Two features of the tribunal's decision are noteworthy. First, the process was essentially back to front: the tribunal were more concerned to solve the problem arising over the patient's supervision (namely, that he must have conditional, rather than absolute, discharge) than to examine whether the evidence genuinely favoured an illness in remission or full recovery—the legalistic approach. Secondly, the nub of the problem between the opposing medical views could only fundamentally be resolved with the

---

[13] Since there was good medical evidence of a previous psychiatric history with depression and there was no other evidence that his wife had been unfaithful, this seemed somewhat irrelevant.

passage of time. Did the patient's delusional state arise from a schizophrenic autonomous process, of which the morbid jealousy was the first sign and from which other paranoid delusions would subsequently develop? Or, was the delusional state essentially depressive and psychogenic? Thus, was the morbid jealousy a reflection of a personality disorder or of a chronic and continuing psychosis (both of which may not be readily amenable to change) or was it part of his psychosocial situation of depression and inactivity? The implications for the patient's likely future 'dangerousness' were patently quite different. The IPs sought to argue that the patient's attitudes and behaviour resulted from his illness, which was itself diminishing. In contrast, the RMO argued that they were more enduring features arising out of a chronic, but slowly developing, illness. The fact that the patient showed no symptoms in the short term was not conclusive either way. The patient's denial of delusions was insufficient. In such circumstances it is impossible for patients to prove normality. It was also impossible for the tribunal to be 'certain' either way. Accordingly, they must have resolved the problem by weighing the evidence. As there was scope and impetus for caution, why did the tribunal reject the cautious approach? It might reasonably be concluded that it was not the facts they weighed (because negative evidence cannot be outweighed), but the characteristics of those giving the evidence. The RMO thus undermined his own evidence; the IPs were preferred; not only were there two of them, but both were regarded as reputable because they did not provide independent reports with any obvious regularity.

(iv) Restriction direction cases: The use of advisory powers Both of the final two patients were detained on S47/49 orders following convictions for murder. The tribunals' powers in these restriction direction cases are constrained; they act only to advise the Home Secretary. In this respect, the decision made in court as to whether to impose a sentence of imprisonment (mandatory in the case of offenders convicted of murder) or a hospital order is critical in determining the subsequent opportunities for release.[14] Patients

---

[14] Of course, at the time at which this patient was sentenced, the decision was not so critical since the tribunal did not then enjoy the power to release restricted patients. Their powers were the same as for restriction direction cases, namely advisory only. See S74 1983 Act.

are set irrevocably upon a particular course which can dramatically affect their ultimate length of confinement.

The case of patient 23A was a medically straightforward one, but its resolution proved difficult because of systemic and legal problems. The patient had been convicted on two counts of murder (of her son's mistress and child). Although a psychiatrist had submitted a report to the court stating that she was suffering from reactive depression so as to impair substantially her mental responsibility for the acts, she was convicted of murder, and sentenced to life imprisonment, with a minimum recommendation of fifteen years being imposed. Within six months she was transferred to Acheland suffering from 'Psychogenic psychosis in the setting of ongoing depression', which arguably cast some doubt on the validity of the court's finding. The patient made a good recovery in Acheland; three years later her psychosis appeared to be in complete remission and she subsequently displayed no depressive symptoms. However, she continued to be subject to detention. Some years later, when the RMO began to make moves to have her transferred, he was informed that permission would not be given for this until the patient had fulfilled the retributive element of her sentence (namely fifteen years). At her tribunal hearing, the tribunal's limited powers were a matter of comment. The judge stated that all they could say would be that 'we passionately don't want her to go back to prison'. The RMO said that the patient continued in a state of excellent remission and that she was not a danger to herself or others. He further noted that she did not require any further rehabilitation, although she might benefit from some social support. This concurred with the medical member's view that he would not be opposed to her going straight out of hospital. It was agreed that there was no medical reason for continued psychiatric supervision, particularly since she would receive life licence supervision under the Criminal Justice Act arrangements. None the less, a short period at a local hospital was regarded as desirable, although not essential, to make appropriate social arrangements. However, in their reasons, the tribunal found the patient to be 'not now suffering' on the grounds that all the medical evidence was to the effect that 'she has been entirely recovered for many years'. They accordingly noted in their recommendation that she would be entitled to be absolutely discharged, but went on to recommend that she spend a short period in a local hospital and, in any event, that she should not be transferred back to prison.

Subsequent discussion confirmed that the tribunal had misunderstood the impact of their decision. Under S74(1) the tribunal can only recommend that a patient continues to be detained in hospital if they reach the decision that the patient would be entitled to a conditional discharge. If, on the other hand, they say that a patient would be entitled to an absolute discharge, and the Home Secretary rejects this advice, patients have to be transferred back to prison under S74(3) by the hospital managers. It was open to the tribunal to find that the patient was 'in remission' and therefore entitled to a conditional discharge (see the advice of the RMO above). This would have achieved the outcome desired: namely, that the patient would have been able to stay in hospital if the Home Secretary rejected their advice. Since the tribunal did not choose conditional discharge the patient risked being returned to prison.

It was fortuitous that nearly fifteen years had elapsed since the patient's conviction. Taking into account the ninety days which the Home Secretary had to consider the tribunal's advice [S74(2)(b)] the fifteen years would be complete. Given a speedy referral to the Parole Board, it could just prove possible for her to be absolutely discharged (with a voluntary stay at the local hospital), having fulfilled the retributive element in the sentence. However, this was not a calculation which the tribunal had knowingly made. Yet again, the substance of the statute had not properly been understood by the tribunal. Had the patient been represented, this risk might not have been run, because the tribunal might have been better informed of the consequences of their decision. In the event, the patient was released on life licence.

The case of Patient 109B represents a marked contrast to that of Patient 23A since the tribunal plainly were aware of the constraints imposed by the statute. The patient had been convicted of the murder of her 14 month old son. She had 'served' eight years of a life sentence, three in prison and five in various hospitals.[15] At her hearing, an IP concluded that she was no longer suffering from mental illness and did not pose a risk to the public. The RMO similarly recommended that she posed no risk and should be conditionally discharged to a hostel: in his view she had become a

---

[15] There was some diagnostic confusion, in that the patient had originally been transferred to a RSU (from prison) with a diagnosis of schizophrenia. Subsequently she experienced depressive symptoms and finally hypothyroidism was diagnosed. This may have given rise to her depression and contributed to the earlier symptomatology.

model patient. He was firmly opposed to any return to prison, as this was felt likely to result in gross deterioration to her mental health. The tribunal concluded that although she was still suffering from mental illness and in need of treatment, they did not believe that she needed to be detained in hospital for treatment. As for Patient 23A, the tribunal could have recommended absolute discharge. But, knowing that the patient had only been detained for eight years, such a recommendation would risk her having to return to prison for a further, possibly lengthy, period of incarceration. In order to avoid this detrimental course, the tribunal adopted a pragmatic strategy. They advised the Home Secretary that she was ready for conditional discharge to a named hostel, and recommended (under 74(1)(*b*)) against her return to prison. The Home Secretary rejected this advice and the patient continued to be detained in Bendene. The case is notable because the patient was being recommended for conditional discharge on the grounds of S72(1)(*b*)(ii) and not (i). Again, perhaps the tribunal's knowledge that their decision was only advisory encouraged them to adopt this course.

Both of these cases illustrate the difficulties for tribunals which arise because of the sentence imposed on patients and not because of any inherent psychiatric problems they may have. Thus, discharge decisions cannot be seen in isolation from the present sentencing structure, which diverts offenders either irrevocably into the hospital system or into the penal system, where a concurrent risk of hospital treatment arises (under the S47/49 transfer provisions). These offender-patients are arguably doubly disadvantaged since they may have their detention prolonged on either therapeutic grounds, if a determinate prison sentence expires, or on retributive or public-safety grounds, if they recover from their disorders. This theme, of the interrelationship between the sentencing structure and the function and operation of the tribunals, will be discussed further in the concluding chapter.

IV. CONCLUSIONS

For patients suffering from psychopathic disorder, problems arising out of the prediction of their future offending behaviour emerged as a key element in the decision not to discharge. As shown in the last chapter, the essence of the dilemma for tribunals stemmed from the validity of the diagnosis. Did a disorder really exist to be treated, or did the diagnosis depend principally upon the preceding unlawful behaviour? Moreover, all the time there was uncertainty about whether the disorder was a major contributory factor in the pattern of offending, there could be little certainty that a patient's recovery would result in a diminution in the probability of offending.

Yet, for the mentally ill patients who formed the basis of this chapter, the relationship between diagnosis and offence, if not causal, was of considerably greater strength.[16] Hence, the greater 'identifiability' of disorders, combined with the demonstration that treatment had been reasonably effective, and partial recovery established, meant that tribunals could be more content about the concomitant reduction in future risk. In this context, for patients who had achieved a satisfactory stability in their recovery, the tribunal focused not on whether they would reoffend, but on whether control could be retained over their illnesses; any deterioration was seen as likely to increase the probability of reoffending. Therefore, the tribunal's deliberations were outcome-orientated. They concentrated on whether the patient could be successfully supervised and whether the continuation of medication could be ensured.[17]

The emphasis on these interlinked questions of outcome and control meant that, in some cases, the method by which decisions should be derived, namely weighing the evidence in the context of the statutory criteria, was arguably neglected. Indeed, the tentative conclusion may be drawn that the strength or otherwise of the evidence was not the sole or critical factor in determining whether patients were discharged. Thus, tribunal decisions were arguably pragmatic rather than legalistic. Ironically, this seeming relegation to secondary status of the process of evaluation, combined with a rejection of a 'fine detail' approach to the statute, occasionally resulted in tribunals jeopardizing the outcome they so passionately desired, as for example occurred in the restriction direction case of Patient 23A.

Of course, resort to the fine detail would occur where the tribunal wished to justify keeping a patient in confinement, as for example in the case of Patient 24A. This entailed a thorough

---

[16] See Taylor and Gunn (1984) and Monahan and Steadman (1983).
[17] Curiously, in some cases this emphasis on medication was misplaced; patients who had been detained for comparatively lengthy periods were often receiving only minimal doses.

examination of the evidence. Similarly, there was little impetus to examine contradictions in the evidence unless it was necessary to avoid a particular outcome, for example the patient's inappropriate return to prison. In these instances, tribunals showed creativity in their use of the statute. More frequently though, it was somewhat neglected. The common, if unconscious, pattern was for tribunals to arrive at a decision which they found tolerable (or, rather, not to arrive at ones they found intolerable).

The pre-eminence given to attaining the most desirable outcome also led to what constituted implicit bargaining with other bodies and individuals who had some control over a patient's destiny. Occasionally it appeared as if the adjournment procedures were being used to generate reciprocal pressure; in some cases there were seeming trade-offs occurring between outcomes which were variously tolerated. Hence, the Home Office might be opposed to outright discharge and prefer a much more progressive relaxation in security; eventually, it might be agreed by all concerned that trial leave at another institution might be commenced.

However, for the bulk of this mentally ill group, it was evident that neither prediction nor control were of the essence. The 'no discharge' cases discussed in the early part of this chapter typify a substantial proportion of the cases which tribunals review. Although they counterpoise those where genuine legal and psychiatric dilemmas arose, rarely did they constitute taxing decisions for the tribunal. Where patients were obviously ill, or were incapacitated by their dependence on medication, or were highly likely to deteriorate rapidly without medication, they readily satisfied $S72(1)(b)(i)$. Similarly, the severity of their disorders inevitably also qualified them for further detention under $S72(1)(b)(ii)$ in terms of their need for medical treatment for their *health*. There was rarely any need to consider the risk they might have posed to themselves or others in satisfying the statutory criteria for continued detention.

Moreover, the legal issues were hardly problematic. Although seventeen of the twenty-two patients in this 'seriously ill' subgroup were represented, this was of arguable benefit in respect of the outcome of the tribunal. Undoubtedly, the representatives could play a therapeutic role, by putting the patient's case and explaining the procedures. However, it was rare for them to present these cases with vigour or to make specific submission for changes in the nature of their clients' detention. Indeed, to do so, might, from their perspective, have undermined their credibility when presenting the cases of clients for whom the legal basis for continued detention was questionable.[18] There was therefore often little impetus for the tribunal to consider the possibility of discharge; unless a patient's case was being promoted either by the RMO, the IP, or the representative, tribunals would not take it upon themselves to initiate action.

[18] See generally Stephens (1985).

8. Tribunals outside the Special Hospitals

Most compulsorily detained patients are to be found in hospitals other than Special Hospitals. Moreover, the majority are detained without restrictions on their discharge. Such cases inevitably constitute the bulk of the tribunals' work, yet the problems they create differ somewhat from those already addressed. This chapter, which is divided into two parts, examines some of these difficulties. The main part of the chapter is devoted to the hearings of twenty tribunals, observed in local facilities, whilst the second section constitutes a retrospective analysis of a sample of tribunal decisions in non-restricted cases.

The tribunals' decision-making in non-restricted cases is affected in five principal ways. First, their powers are more extensive; they can discharge or recommend that patients be transferred or given trial leave. Secondly, they do not have to interact with distant decision-makers, such as the Home Office or the DHSS. In hospitals other than the Special Hospitals, local hospital managers, rather than the DHSS, fulfil the function of the Responsible Authority (see Appendix 2).[1] Similarly, in non-restricted cases the tribunals do not have to juggle with the Home Secretary's ever-pressing public safety concerns. Third, tribunals have additionally to take cognizance of the criteria of 'treatability' and, in respect of those suffering from mental illness or severe mental impairment, 'viability', in determining whether to release. Fourth, for patients detained in local facilities, there is less of a preoccupation with questions of physical security, although other concepts, relating to the desirability of maintaining control over patients in the community, are more apparent in the tribunals' reasoning. Fifth, since

[1] Although during the period of the research the Special Hospitals Committee at the DHSS undertook the day-to-day functions of the Responsible Authority, many were equally devolved to the Local Board of Managers. These Boards are likely to be superseded by a Special Health Authority, which may in turn assume responsibility for overriding the views of the RMO in those rare cases where conflict arises between the RMOs and the DHSS. Undoubtedly, the ultimate power will continue to reside in the Secretary of State at the Department of Health. (See S145(i) of the 1983 Act).

there is not the degree of stigma associated with being detained in a local hospital or secure unit, the problems are not as great when transferring patients to other facilities or into the community. Patients can be released quietly, without the tribunals feeling that their decisions are being watched. Moreover, where the tribunal are considering direct discharge there is greater potential for S117 of the 1983 Act to have some influence. S117 requires District Health Authorities and local social services to provide after-care services for detained patients discharged from hospital. Although in a context of inadequate resource provision its impact may have been limited, it should in theory have had the effect of increasing the tribunal's options (or, at the least, not inhibiting them).

The patients also provide an interesting contrast to those detained in conditions of special security because it was harder to maintain that their discharge represented an obvious or immediate danger to the safety of others. Those detained under civil provisions would not necessarily have a criminal record; the minority with restriction orders might never have been considered to require Special Hospital care; and if they had, they clearly had progressed to a stage where special security was no longer necessary. In consequence, these cases might be perceived as representing the soft end of the spectrum for tribunals. Yet, if in this arena it could be shown that tribunals still subsume the protection of individual rights to the 'greater good' arguments arising out of public safety considerations, how much more tempting must this course be for them where patients had, through their past actions, demonstrated a capacity for behaviour likely to cause concern?

Of course, there were some arguable disadvantages. Perhaps the most striking was the extent to which tribunals were forced to take responsibility for their decisions; they could not merely defer to the Home Secretary and thereby avoid those decisions which might cause them unease. As a result, some of the strategies outlined in the previous two chapters, which enabled tribunals to resolve what they perceived to be problematic decisions, were writ large in the cases of locally detained patients.

1. OBSERVED HEARINGS

The cases were made up of twelve non-restricted patients and eight with restrictions. Sixty per cent of the sample were men.

Mental illness constituted the overwhelming diagnostic classification. In consequence, the arguments presented here have the greatest parallels with those in Chapter 7. Three patients had diagnoses of psychopathic disorder (two of whom were on restriction orders), and one a diagnosis of severe mental impairment. This breakdown was approximately what would be expected given both the make-up of the total detained non-special population[2] and the discharge policies of the Special Hospitals.[3]

Of the twenty cases, one application was withdrawn,[4] one case was adjourned by the tribunal and one patient had his order discharged by his RMO less than two working days before the hearing took place. The impending tribunal, combined with an IPR concluding that the patient satisfied neither $S72(1)(b)(i)$ nor (ii) as grounds for continued detention, had clearly acted as a catalyst.[5] Of the seventeen determined cases, there were two decisions to discharge resulting in a discharge rate of 12 per cent; and in one restricted case the tribunal recommended that the patient should have trial leave.

45 per cent of the sample were automatic references (compared with the much lower rate of 22 per cent in the Special Hospital samples).[6] In at least one of these cases considerable distress was caused to the patient by the prospect of the review process; as indicated in Chapter 3, the emotional cost of enforcing some patients' rights was hard to ascertain. This problem may have been further exacerbated by the fact that automatic reviews were significantly less likely to involve legal representation (33 per cent) than those patients who had applied for a hearing (73 per cent). Moreover, the overall level of representation (55 per cent) was

---

[2] See DHSS (1987a).

[3] See Chs. 6 and 7; mentally ill patients tend to be transferred via their catchment area local hospital whilst the psychopathically disordered are more likely to be discharged conditionally or be transferred to one of the special units.

[4] The patient had started a fire in the hospital shortly before her hearing date. Her representative withdrew her application, thereby preserving her right to apply again in the same period of detention. Whether the proper procedure would have been for the tribunal to confirm with the patient her desire to withdraw, was debatable.

[5] The RMO's prediction that the tribunal would 'almost certainly' have discharged may not necessarily have been well founded; a previous tribunal had (recently) endorsed the patient's detention, on the usual grounds that they did not believe he would continue with his medication.

[6] Using a total Special Hospital sample of 91 cases—not all of the hearings observed live at Acheland were matched successfully.

considerably lower than that in the Special Hospital group (85 per cent).[7] Furthermore, the representatives were significantly less likely to have obtained an IPR; in only three cases had such a report been prepared.[8] This compared unfavourably even with the mentally ill Special Hospital patients where IPRs were prepared in 48 per cent of cases.[9] It reflected the relatively high proportion of cases which were characterized by the tribunal as 'hopeless'—particularly amongst the non-restricted subsample. As a consequence of this, the restricted and non-restricted patients are discussed separately below.

One final point is worth stressing. As with the Special Hospital patients, the tribunal overwhelmingly followed the recommendations made to them by the RMOs; namely, in 82 per cent of cases. In the three cases where the tribunal went against the RMO's advice, twice they adopted a more cautious approach, and once they were less cautious. However, this last instance arose only in respect of their advisory function, not in terms of reaching a quantitatively different decision to the RMO.

To have found these levels of concurrence in the 'local' hospital patients was particularly surprising. The RMOs' reports were of a more variable quality; their content was not infrequently sparse and sometimes of questionable relevance to the issues the tribunals had to address. The seemingly unavoidable conclusion was that the tribunals were more impressed by the source of the information than by its evidential pertinence. Thus, only those RMOs at the margins of reputability in either Special or local hospitals were likely to have their decisions questioned.

A. Non-Restricted Cases

(i) 'Hopeless' cases Five of the cases could be characterized principally by the severity of the patients' symptoms and the marginal impact had by prolonged medication. For tribunals, the spectre of what these patients might have been like without

[7] Using total Special Hospital sample of 91.

[8] Three out of a sample of 11 in comparison with 51 out of 67.

[9] Contrastingly, in 80 per cent of the sample of psychopathic patients in Special Hospitals, IPRs were obtained. As an index of the activity of the representatives, the proportions of represented cases where IPRs were sought for the non-Special Hospital groups, mentally ill sample, and psychopathically disordered sample respectively were 27 per cent, 59 per cent and 91 per cent.

medication, created sufficient grounds for ensuring that their compulsory orders continued. Moreover, three of the patients were suicidal and two physically frail, which compounded their mental disorders. One patient refused to attend the hearing; the four who did were actively deluded and insightless. The cases' speedy resolution, on average twenty minutes per hearing, was indicative of the tribunal's lack of options. Patients may have been grateful for the opportunity to air their views, but beyond this, it was hard to conclude that the tribunal had more than a cosmetic function.

Indeed, they could not always be said to have addressed the question of the necessity for compulsory measures. The case of Patient 51 is illustrative: the patient wished merely to be transferred to another local hospital where he had previously been detained. According to him, there was no violence on the wards at that hospital. However, the tribunal were persuaded by the RMO that the patient enjoyed greater freedom where he was presently detained. The patient was not represented and the necessity for compulsion was barely addressed. Yet, as the patient willingly took his medication, it might otherwise have been an issue. Arguably, the tribunal neither brought a fresh view to long-standing problems, nor acted as a check on the potential 'abuse' of compulsory procedures. What they did do, however, was to mirror the RMO's paternalistic outlook.

(ii) Borderline cases Four cases created special difficulties in respect of an earlier ruling from the High Court (hereafter known as the *Hallstrom* case).[10] In essence, the decision meant that where patients were on leave from the hospital, and therefore not in need of in-patient treatment, it would be unlawful to renew their section merely to ensure the continuation of medication in the community. Yet, this was a favourite strategy employed by RMOs to maintain therapeutic control over patients. In each of the four cases the critical issue concerned whether the patients would indeed have continued with their medication if they were not on a section. All four were spending, or about to spend, extensive periods away from the hospitals where they were nominally detained. Yet their tribunals appeared either to have been unaware of the implications of *Hallstrom* or to consider them irrelevant to

---

[10] *R* v. *Hallstrom and Morgan, Ex parte W.* and *R.* v. *Gardner and Another, Ex parte L*—before Mr Justice McCullough, Queen's Bench Division 20 Dec. 1985.

the principal issues at hand.[11] Clearly, they did not perceive it to be encumbent on them to explain to patients' RMOs the potential illegality of the courses they appeared to be advocating, if not actually proposing, at that stage.

The first two cases concerned patients whose RMOs wished to ensure future control over them in the community, by sustaining their sections. The case of Patient 49 is illustrative of how tribunals deal with such potential conflicts. The patient's section was shortly due to expire. The RMO, supported by the social worker, made it clear both that he was opposing discharge (from the section) and that he intended to renew the order. This was *not* because the patient required compulsory treatment in hospital for his own health or safety or for the protection of others. Indeed, arrangements were well advanced to establish the patient in an independent flat. Rather the RMO wished to ensure first that compulsory supervision could be maintained by a community psychiatric nurse, and secondly that he could be readmitted quickly if the need arose. His reasoning was patently of a preventive nature. The tribunal's deliberations indicated that they also endorsed this approach. However, their formal reasons placed emphasis on the patient's degree of illness and the absence of any insight, rather than being openly forward-looking.[12] Furthermore, they noted that he required treatment for his own health and safety and for the protection of others. Thus, despite the RMO apparently having failed to understand the consequences of *his* assessment, the tribunal effectively rectified this. Continued detention was legally justifiable—even if the route by which this had been achieved was innovatory.

The circumstances of Patient 45 were more stark. This patient was already on extended leave from the hospital, living in lodgings which he had found himself. His history of repeated admissions to hospital and a past reluctance to accept medication, combined with some limited aggressive behaviour, meant that his RMO also wanted to keep him on a section to ensure the continuation of medication. He accepted that the patient was willingly accepting his injections in the community. However, since his previous good intentions had not been sustained, he was opposing the discharge

[11] For further discussion, see Peay (1986).

[12] Evidence was given by the medical member that the patient did in fact have some insight, in that, although he did not accept he had been ill, he did accept that the medication prevented him from relapsing—'it stops me going down and becoming completely weird'.

of the section. Indeed, had the patient shown any persistent reluctance to accept medication, the RMO would undoubtedly have recalled him to hospital. In their deliberations, the tribunal were swayed by the medical member's view that the patient had 'a short fuse and was liable to attack people'. The tribunal decided, despite the acknowledged willingness of the patient to accept medication, that it was doubtful whether he would continue with his injections unsupervised and that danger to others would then become more likely. Curiously, the patient's period of stability in the community was insufficient to override the assumed need for him to continue to be liable for medical treatment in hospital.

In the case of Patient 55, much of the reasoning which was not explicit in 45 above emerged in the tribunal's deliberations. The case is dealt with at some length because it illustrates not only the common dilemma of what to do with the medication-stabilized psychotic, but also the essentially 'back to front' process of decision-making, which, it may be argued, underlies many of these tribunals' decisions. Thus, decisions are outcome-oriented and do not necessarily result from a logical, step-by-step application of the tribunal's decision criteria to the evidence presented. Rather, and baldly put, they reflect a process whereby the tribunal decided first what outcome it preferred and then the evidence was fitted to the criteria to ensure this result ensued.

The patient was 38, had been diagnosed as a chronic paranoid schizophrenic, and had a history of repeated, if intermittent, admissions to psychiatric hospitals over the previous seven years. At the time of his tribunal hearing he was detained on a S3; he was stabilized on intramuscular and oral medication and had been so for some six months. During this six-month period he had been on regular week-end leave from hospital, and he had also obtained a full-time job outside the hospital with employers who knew nothing of his detained status. He had worked satisfactorily in this job for two months, returning to the hospital four nights a week to sleep and to receive medication. The patient told the tribunal that he did not wish to remain on medication indefinitely, but he recognized that he had to co-operate with the treatment for some time to come. Neither his psychiatrist nor his social worker believed that he would continue to accept medication willingly if he was not 'on a section'. They predicted that without medication he would probably suffer a relapse and possibly commit violence against persons or property. In their reports to the tribunal, his caretakers made it plain that they would subsequently be seeking to renew his section 'to ensure a further period of treatment'. The tribunal did not point out to them, following the High Court ruling in *Hallstrom*, that this would be unlawful.

During the deliberation the medical member concurred with the views of the RMO that the patient would stop taking his medication as soon as he was able to do so and would relapse. The medical member drew the tribunal's attention to the fact that in similar circumstances in the past the patient had 'clearly been dangerous to others'. The legal president of the tribunal and the lay member were both of the view that the patient was in a difficult position. On balance, they believed that he probably would take his medication—after all, he had told the tribunal he would—and in any case, his psychiatrist had admitted during the hearing that he believed there were no objective criteria for deciding whether Patient 55 was telling the truth. The legal and lay members noted that the patient's psychiatrist would be doing no more than acting on a hunch when and if he decided to exercise his independent powers to release him. They out-voted the medical member, concluding that they did not believe that the patient's mental illness was of a sufficient severity to justify keeping him in hospital because 'he'd be OK if he took his medication outside'.

This should have been the end of the tribunal's deliberations, because the patient was entitled to be discharged; indeed, the tribunal were under a duty to discharge him. However, without a moment's hesitation and clearly without recognizing the implications of what they had decided, the tribunal went on to discuss whether the patient satisfied section 72(1)(*b*)(ii)—the health and safety criterion. The legal member stated that he thought it was necessary for the protection of other people that the patient should be detained. The medical member backed this up, saying, 'He gets violent and punches people.' Later he added that without medication the patient was 'a violent, dangerous schizophrenic'. At this point the tribunal clerk returned to the room; the legal member explained that he and the lay member were satisfied that the patient was 'not now suffering'. 'Well', the clerk said quickly, 'then that's an end to it.' It was only at this juncture that the legal member realized what he had done. He led the lay member back through the criteria, pointing out that if they said that the patient *was* mentally ill, then they would have to consider the next subsection. After all, he concluded, 'we all agree that it is necessary for the protection of other persons' that he be detained. Thus, the tribunal intentionally permitted public safety considerations to outweigh the patient's right to be protected from unnecessary deprivation of his liberty. At this point the discussion to all intents and purposes ended and the legal president recorded the tribunal's decision; namely, not to discharge. There was no consideration whatsoever of the discretionary powers to discharge under S72(1).

The reasons the tribunal recorded for their decision reflected matters of presentation; the tribunal had merely to demonstrate that they had properly addressed the legal criteria.[13] Indeed, since the legal criteria only required the tribunal to be satisfied that it was appropriate for him to be *liable to be detained*, it could be argued that their decision, on the face of it, did not contravene the spirit of the ruling in the case of *Hallstrom*. However, the process whereby the decision had been reached, which was, unusally, open to inspection, failed to comply with either the letter of the 1983 Act or the High Court's reasoning. The law had been improperly used as a resource for rationalizing, rather than for constraining, the tribunal's decision. If this strategy were routinely to be employed by tribunals, it might result in uninformed observers assuming that patients were detained both because they were ill and because they posed a risk.[14] Yet, the crucial factor in making this determination had been risk and not illness.

(iii) A strict application of the law?   Although at first glance the case of Patient 58 appeared to reflect a strict application of the law by the tribunal, it can be argued that the decision was also outcome-oriented. The case turned on a legal nicety: namely, whether the use of a restraint garment constituted a form of

[13] The decision recorded stated: '[The patient] is suffering from mental illness of a nature and degree which makes it appropriate for him to be liable to be detained in a hospital for medical treatment and that it is necessary for his health and for the protection of other persons that he should receive treatment'.

The tribunal was satisfied about these reasons because: '[The patient] has made considerable progress since admission largely because he has been taking his medicine regularly. He has, however, shown very little insight into his illness and therefore the need to continue to take medicine. As on previous occasions he would almost certainly stop taking it when free of constraint and this would result in danger to his health and the safety of others.'

[14] Those present at the hearing are, of course, invariably uninformed because the tribunal's deliberations are not open to review. Even if they were, it would be unusual for the decision-making process to be articulated in quite the way that it was in this case.

detention and should, therefore, be legally validated through the use of a Mental Health Act section. After lengthy deliberations, the tribunal decided that, in the context in which it was used, the harness in question constituted a therapeutic measure and was part of the patient's medical treatment (thereby utilising the Act's broad definition of medical treatment).

The patient was classified as suffering from severe mental impairment. In some respects, the extent of her incapacity assisted the tribunal in reaching their decision. First, as there was no sign that she did not consent to wearing the restraint, it did not amount to 'detention' and a formal section was therefore unnecessary. Moreover, the tribunal could be confident that she would continue to accept the 'treatment' voluntarily since, in the absence of any alternative provision for her, they could be certain that she would remain in hospital as an informal patient. In all of the cases previously discussed, despite patients' assorted assurances, the tribunal could not be sure of the desired outcome, namely, the continuing acceptance of medication. Thus, they found themselves satisfied of the second element of S72(1)(b)(i); although the patient was suffering from severe mental impairment, it was not of a nature or degree which made it appropriate for her to be liable to be detained in a hospital for medical treatment. Similarly, this patient would readily have satisfied S72(1)(b)(ii), but there was no real need for the tribunal to consider this (certainly not legally, but neither to achieve the desired outcome). The case clearly provides an interesting comparison with 55 above, where the letter of the law had to be neglected to achieve the necessary outcome. Yet in the case of Patient 58 the law had to be applied rigorously in order to ensure that the patient's section was discharged.

The decision was outcome-oriented for two reasons. Not only did the tribunal discharge in the certain knowledge that it would make no difference to the patient's continuing residence in the hospital, but they were also aware that a decision *not* to discharge would have had implications for the large number of severely impaired patients resident in local hospitals as informal patients. Many such patients were similarly subjected to a variety of restraints in their day-to-day existence. If it were necessary to section all of these patients, the resource implications for hospitals, tribunals, and the Mental Health Act Commission would be considerable.

One final feature of the case was interesting. The medical

member argued that, although severely handicapped, the patient would not necessarily satisfy the behavioural element of the definition of severe mental impairment. He interpreted 'seriously irresponsible conduct' to mean motivated behaviour along the lines of, for example, arson. The legal and lay members rejected this, stating that in their view, her unrestrained behaviour at mealtimes, where she would grab food, constituted a risk to herself of choking and was, consequently, seriously irresponsible. The medical member seemed happy to let the matter rest, but apparently only because he concurred with the main thrust of the tribunal's reasoning which would anyway result in the patient's discharge. Again, his satisfaction with the outcome made testing the process through which it was agreed upon somewhat redundant.

B. Restricted Cases

By definition, these patients had all been convicted of comparatively serious offences, even if some years previously.[15] The caution the tribunal exercised was, perhaps, more understandable than for the non-restricted sample already discussed. However, this sub-sample of restricted non-Special Hospital cases might have been unrepresentative. The statistics suggest that there is a comparatively high discharge rate by tribunals—namely, in about 40 per cent of these cases.[16] This could imply both that the Special Hospitals are unduly cautious in their decisions to transfer patients to local facilities and/or that Special Hospital RMOs are right to suspect that a different time-scale for recovery operates in such facilities—patients will quickly be discharged once transferred there. This may, of course, be a question of chicken and egg. But, as there was only one conditional discharge and one adjournment amongst these eight patients, it could be argued that the tribunals were atypically cautious, or that the cases were especially worrying.

[15] Under the 1959 Act it would only have been necessary for the court to be satisfied that the patient would be likely to cause harm if released (rather than serious harm) for them to be able to impose a restriction order. As a result, some patients received restriction orders following comparatively minor offences (see e.g., Gostin 1977, p. 182).

[16] In 1985 209 restricted hearings were held in non-Special Hospitals. There were discharges in 41 per cent of cases in comparison with a discharge rate of 11 per cent for the same year in Special Hospital restricted cases (DHSS 1985).

The former explanation seems more likely, since there were real issues to be discussed in all but two cases, one where the patient was not seeking immediate discharge and one tragically 'hopeless' case.[17]

(i) Borderline cases   In two cases the RMO was opposed to discharge. In the first, that of a Patient 57, the patient was unrepresented—his financial savings of £2,000 accrued in anticipation of the need for a deposit on a flat would have disqualified him at that time from being eligible for legal aid. Not surprisingly, there was no IPR. The patient was a chronic schizophrenic in substantial remission, well-maintained on depot anti-psychotic medication. Although he ultimately would have sought conditional discharge, he recognized the wisdom of progressing slowly with increasing amounts of freedom and weekend leave. His RMO was opposed to any dramatic change in his circumstances, principally because he did not believe that the patient would continue willingly with medication; a relapse might result in him becoming floridly psychotic and potentially very dangerous. The RMO took the view that *he* was responsible via the Home Secretary for the public's safety. Unusually, contrary evidence was given by a senior nurse at the hospital who knew the patient well. He argued that the patient was ready for discharge and could be managed if closely supervised; he believed the patient had been 'held back' too long.

Whether patients could be compulsorily medicated in the community was again a crucial issue. The patient expressed a long-term desire to come off his very small dose of medication. But the RMO, supported by the medical member, preferred that this should happen first within the confines of the hospital, if at all. It was not, however, the RMO's chosen course. In the deliberation, the medical member was firmly opposed to discharge. Whether forceful representation and an IPR might have influenced them is debatable, given the medical member's views.

The second case, Patient 43, was highly unusual since the

[17] The patient was an automatic reference and unrepresented. He was a chronic, grossly deteriorated schizophrenic, who had been detained for thirty years following indecent assaults on children; his sexual urges were reported as being 'unabated'. The tribunal found the patient to be unfit for the community, and doubted whether he would ever become fit. Quite what would happen to patients like this when this hospital shut, was a matter of some concern. Of equal concern was the scope for improvement in the quality of care provided at the hospital. The tribunal were powerless in respect of both matters.

tribunal overruled the RMO's advice that the patient remain on a locked ward. They recommended that she be transferred to an open ward, to facilitate contact with her children. Several factors may have contributed to this. The RMO readily admitted that her therapeutic relationship with the patient had deteriorated and she herself was recommending that the patient be transferred to the care of another psychiatrist; the medical member could find no signs of active symptomatology and clearly thought the RMO was being unduly cautious. Finally, the tribunal were fully aware that, in order for their recommendation to be put into effect, the Home Secretary would have to concur with this course. Thus, the RMO might still have the last word and the tribunal's decision may have been knowingly cosmetic. None the less, they did overrule the advice of a senior forensic psychiatrist who knew the patient well, on the views of an IP, who did not attend the hearing, and the medical member, who had much more limited forensic experience.

In two cases the tribunal overruled the RMO in order to be more cautious. Patient 60, diagnosed as psychopathic, was seeking unescorted day parole; in this, she was supported by her RMO. The tribunal, although noting her willing acceptance of medication and very good progress, made no such recommendation, preferring any 'progress' to be carefully supervised. In the case of Patient 56 the RMO, in conjunction with the patient's social worker, was seeking the conditional discharge of his patient to an available hostel bed. Indeed, he had been requesting the necessary permission from the Home Secretary for some months. The patient, who was stabilised on medication, had made a good recovery from a previous relapse whilst on conditional discharge. Although her insight was somewhat impaired, her RMO argued that she was as well now (if not better) as she had been when first conditionally discharged.[18] Furthermore, although she needed to continue with medication, since this was administered by depot injections, it could readily be carried out in the community.

The tribunal judge was clearly unhappy with this plan and forcibly detailed his view that it would be better for the patient to depart first from the hospital on trial leave. In arguing that

[18] Like many patients stabilized on medication, the patient's view was that if the medication was supposed to cure her, she shouldn't have to stay on it forever. Indeed, how would she know if she had been cured, until the medication was stopped? Although seemingly logical, this displayed a fundamental misunderstanding of the nature of her illness; medication controlled the symptoms, as it would, for example, in diabetes, rather than effecting a cure.

conditional discharge had failed once before, his reasoning was reminiscent of that routinely adopted by sentencers when rejecting the repeated use of non-custodial measures. Moreover, he argued that recall was easier under the trial leave provisions (a dubious proposition). Finally, he stated (incorrectly) that the tribunal had the power to reconvene, if their recommendations (for trial leave) were not complied with. The deliberation, in the context of the judge's expressed views, was something of a formality. Their decision advised trial leave.

(ii) Towards discharge: The influence of real options In the final two cases, conditional discharge was perceived as a realistic option for the patients concerned. Patient 48 was a middle-aged deteriorated schizophrenic who had been transferred from a Special Hospital five years earlier. Clinically, the patient was stabilized on depot anti-psychotic medication and there were few symptoms of active illness. His RMO was not opposed to the patient's plans to return to the West Indies, where he had extended family ties.

The tribunal accepted that the patient, who was living in an unsupervised hostel in the hospital grounds, could not be considered dangerous in any way. Although he clearly had some 'mad' ideas, he behaved well; he was only felt to require injections and some form of refuge. The tribunal were minded to make a conditional discharge, provided that they could be sure that the patient would be accompanied straight onto a boat or plane to the West Indies. In order to facilitate this, they adjourned for three months. Whether the tribunal would have been prepared to discharge, if there had been no plans for the patient to leave the country, was less clear; certainly, the lay member's argument that the patient's condition merited absolute discharge was given short shrift by the legal and medical members of the tribunal.

The tribunal in the case of Patient 65, having adjourned the case once whilst an IPR was sent to the Home Office, felt impelled to make some kind of decision. The patient, a chronic schizophrenic, had been detained for twenty-six years after she had drowned her baby. She was agreed by all concerned not to require hospital treatment. Indeed, she had remained in hospital only because there was no suitable accommodation for her outside. Her representative had been active in securing a place for her in a hostel which was due to be opened shortly. He was arguing in favour of conditional discharge since there were no medical reasons for her continued detention. The tribunal, who were keen that her departure from hospital should be managed successfully, discussed the merits of trial leave. But, the representative contended that all of the benefits that might accrue from that decision could equally be achieved through attaching appropriate conditions to her discharge, including medical supervision by her RMO, and that this would be the legally 'correct' course. The tribunal were ultimately persuaded of the merits of this over both trial leave (which raised a potential for disruption by the Home Secretary) and deferred conditional discharge (which would have left the 'need to be satisfied' about the arrangements with the tribunal rather than the RMO).

One particularly interesting point emerged. The tribunal were keen to make the acceptance of medication a condition of discharge. This was of arguable validity. If, on conditional discharge, a patient is not liable to be detained, but only liable to be recalled, has the tribunal the power effectively to enforce medication in the community? If so, it would contradict not only the spirit of the *Hallstrom* decision, but more importantly, S56(1) of the 1983 Act, which excludes conditionally discharged patients from being treated without their consent. Indeed, it would be difficult to argue persuasively that a patient who consented to medication constituting one of the unwritten conditions of his conditional discharge, had done so on a wholly voluntary basis, when it was self-evident that the tribunal perceived the continuation of medication to be a vital element in obtaining their agreement to a conditional discharge. Although this issue was discussed at a recent judicial studies day, the common view emerged that the patient's consent was implicit and that no difficulty would therefore arise in practice. However, this is arguably a complacent approach. What would have happened in the case of Patient 65 if the representative at the tribunal had explained clearly to the patient that she had the right to refuse to accept treatment at any point after she had been conditionally discharged? Had she indicated any probability of a future unwillingness to take medication, it is likely, given the tribunal's concern about its continuation, that they would have failed to find themselves satisfied of the necessary criteria for discharge. And this could have occurred despite the logical sequential necessity for the tribunal to satisfy S73(1)(*a*) *before* they considered whether any conditions could be imposed following consideration of S73(1)(*b*).

A possible solution emerged at the hearing. If the condition imposed merely required the patient to co-operate with the supervising psychiatrist, then recall, following any deterioration subsequent to a cessation of medication, could be justified on the grounds of the deterioration and not by the mere refusal to accept medication. The representative in the case of Patient 65 accordingly argued that the condition should read that the patient take 'such medication as the RMO prescribes'—which would allow for the possibility of no medication being prescribed. The decision ultimately read 'that the patient continues to take the medication prescribed by her RMO or other Consultant Psychiatrist'. Had the issue been deliberately fudged?

II. RETROSPECTIVE DECISIONS: THE USE OF S72(2)

The observational study of the twenty cases indicated that, almost without exception, where tribunals satisfied themselves in non-restricted cases of the statutory criteria under S72(1)(b) for continued detention, they did not go on to address the issues of treatability and viability in an explicit form. Hence, there was little exploration of the possibility of exercising their discretionary powers to discharge. Informal enquiries of the tribunal clerks confirmed that these observations could be generalized to the vast majority of tribunal hearings.

In order to attempt to confirm that there had been few, if any, directions to discharge patients under the tribunal's discretionary powers, and to examine the nature of the reasons given for discharge, a further study was undertaken. This comprised an analysis of all non-restricted cases for the period January 1986 to August 1986 inclusive, for the entire areas dealt with by one regional tribunal office. Methodologically, this retrospective analysis differed; instead of regarding discharge decisions as exceptional (in the sense that they were rare in the observed cases) it attempted to analyse what factors they had in common. Could it be shown that the decision criteria were capable of being applied with some consistency?

The sample consisted of 391 S3/S37 cases, recorded as determined. In thirty-five of the original cases either the RMOs discharged the patients' or orders lapsed before the hearing took place and were not renewed. A further seven cases were otherwise 'aborted', resulting in an 11 per cent wastage rate prior to the hearings.[19] In total, 349 cases were decided by the tribunal, who also discharged in thirty five cases, producing a discharge rate of 10 per cent.

The aborted case rate in this sample of S3/37 (admission for treatment/hospital order) cases was not as high as that for S2 (admission for assessment) cases.[20] There are two possible explanations for this. First, if patients are to make a rapid improvement on medication they are likely to do so within the first twenty-eight days of an assessment order; if they gain insight, they may be prepared to remain in hospital informally in agreement with their RMO. Secondly, if patients recover to the extent that their RMO anticipates that the tribunal will discharge them, he or she may accordingly reclassify them to informal status to obviate the ordeal of a hearing, both for themselves and the patients. In S3/37 cases, the longer-term orders, the position may be less clear cut; a patient's responsiveness to medication may have reached a plateau. RMOs might wish to see a stable condition maintained or believe that patients will fail to continue with medication if they are not on a section. They may, therefore, be prepared to contest the application for discharge, in order to attempt to ensure that they can maintain continuing control over their patients' well-being.

In sixteen of the thirty-five discharged cases patients were legally represented.[21] This would seem to suggest that representation is not crucial in respect of achieving discharge decisions. The observed sample discussed in the first half of this chapter clearly indicated that there was a great deal of unrewarding representation work in local hospitals. Perhaps patients who had a genuine chance of being discharged were more likely on average to obtain a representative.[22] Furthermore, in the retrospective discharged sample, there were eight IPRs supplied to the tribunal,

---

[19] This figure includes 28 cases discharged by the RMO; 7 withdrawn prior to the hearing; and 7 died, ineligible or postponed *sine die*.

[20] Aborted cases here cover those withdrawn, discharged, aborted, made informal by the RMO, invalid, or absconded. These constituted 25 per cent of S2 cases for 1984 and 35 per cent for the first half of 1985 (DHSS 1985).

[21] This representation rate of 45 per cent is comparable with the 55 per cent of cases represented in the observed hearings for the non-Special Hospital sample.

[22] Supported by the higher proportion of cases where patients had applied for review which were represented, in comparison with referred cases in the observed sample. A study funded by the Lord Chancellor's Department under the direction of H. Genn may throw further light on the impact of representation.

but none were presented in non-represented cases. The figures are, of course, small, but they seem to indicate that representation was at least partly effective in providing the impetus for an IPR which may in turn, have tilted the balance in the more marginal cases for the tribunal. However, it was clear from the observed hearings, that representation had a more limited effect where the tribunal were not disposed towards discharge. Good representation, combined with a sound legal basis for discharge, could not ensure that outcome, given the opposition of the RMO and the tribunal. It is arguable, therefore, that representation should be assessed in terms other than outcome measures, and that representatives should not merely save their best efforts for those cases where they believe that patients have a realistic prospect of discharge. If representatives only pursue their clients' wishes vigorously in such select cases, with an eye to sustaining their own credibility in front of the tribunal, they might, in the long run, do themselves and their clients a disservice.

A. Reasons for Discharge

In the thirty-five cases where the tribunal made a decision to discharge, all but one of the decisions were under S72(1)(*b*)(i) or (ii). The tribunal exercised its discretionary power to discharge *in only one case* and even this was arguably one where the patient was entitled to a statutory discharge.

The breakdown of the statutory reasons for discharge was also revealing. In only four cases did the tribunal find itself satisfied that the patient was not suffering from one of the four specified forms of mental disorder. In twenty-seven cases the tribunal found the disorder to be present, but not to be of a sufficient nature or degree to merit detention in hospital for medical treatment. In two cases, the tribunal found medical treatment not to be necessary in the interests of the patient's health or safety or for the protection of others. In the final case, the tribunal found that the previous renewal of the patient's section was unlawful (*post Hallstrom*). This was because the patient was on leave from the hospital at the time the order was renewed and therefore, the tribunal argued, could not have required in-patient treatment at the time of renewal.

Clearly, it is unlikely that the tribunal would fail to find *any* evidence of mental disorder; furthermore, where the disorder was of sufficient severity to make it appropriate for detention for medical treatment, it would only be in a tiny minority of cases that the tribunal could be satisfied that treatment was not necessary in the interests of the patient's health (a very broad criterion), or safety, or for the protection of others. Therefore, the vast majority of patients who gained their discharge from the tribunal were likely to be 'ill', but maintained on medication, manageable in the community, and arguably, comparatively harmless.

Looking at the 'reasons for reasons', which elucidate the tribunal's statutory decisions, it was also clear that in many cases there was official support for, or at least acquiescence in, the tribunal's decision. This might have emanated from either the RMO or the social worker in the case. In fifteen cases, either one or other of these parties favoured discharge, or the patient was on extended leave at home, or the RMO announced that there was no intention to renew the section. These may be regarded as safe or uncontroversial decisions. In four cases, the patient promised to remain informally in the hospital; these cases were also largely uncontroversial. And in a further three, there were obvious alternative placements for the patients outside the hospital, with supportive families or community psychiatric nurses on hand.

Finally, in six cases, patients assured the tribunal that they would take their medication if discharged, and were believed by the tribunal. Either they were sufficiently in remission for their promises to be credible, or they had actually demonstrated their willingness by currently successfully administering their own medication. The case of M, who suffered from a paranoid psychosis, is illustrative. M had been intermittently unwell for some eleven years; whilst on medication her behaviour was exemplary. Her RMO did not believe that she required in-patient treatment, but was seriously concerned that she would not continue to take medication and that her condition would deteriorate.[23] Her representative argued forcibly that since she was prepared to accept medication voluntarily (and with it she was

---

[23] The social worker's opposition to discharge was more forceful, although he employed a liberal interpretation of the concept of risk to the patient. Hence, 'I would argue that her reluctance to conduct herself according to established norms (viz, talking to visitors from behind her closed door, or refusing to be interviewed in hospitals, failing to satisfy that she has any financial security or plans for discharge, failing to pay her rent) indicate that she would be *at risk* if discharged' (emphasis added).

well) there was no need for formal detention. Her RMO maintained that her promises at the hearing were 'novel and radical' and that they would be readily forgotten. The tribunal's reasons indicated that they accepted that the patient would honour her undertaking to continue with the prescribed medication and discharged.

In the only case, A, where the tribunal exercised its discretionary power to discharge, it was clear that they had acceded to a course of action proposed by the RMO. Neither the RMO nor the IP felt that the patient (who was on leave), satisfied the criteria for continued detention. The RMO stated that his mental illness was 'not of a nature or degree' and the IP found no evidence of mental disorder at the time of the tribunal hearing. However, the RMO believed that the patient would benefit from a short period of further rehabilitation and treatment and that, if all went well, he would discharge him from his section in about three weeks. The patient's representative argued that, if both doctors felt that the patient did not satisfy the statutory criteria, he was entitled to an immediate discharge. However, the tribunal apparently felt entitled to overrule the content of the medical evidence in favour of the alternative best interests approach advocated by the RMO. They made a discretionary decision to discharge and deferred the direction for three weeks from the date of the hearing. The decision was somewhat curious. The tribunal could still have achieved the same result (a deferred discharge under S72(3)) by finding themselves satisfied that either of the statutory criteria for continued detention were not complied with. One can only speculate that the medical member of the tribunal disagreed with both psychiatrists who gave evidence—but there is no indication of this in either the transcript of the tribunal or their reasons. Either way, their strategy was facilitative.

This left six cases in which the decision was at all risky from the tribunal's perspective. Since in four of these there was persuasive support for discharge in the form of an IPR, only two decisions were not readily explicable and merit further discussion.

B. *A rigorous application of the law?*

Without having been present at the tribunal hearings it is difficult to be certain that no new and overriding evidence emerged. Similarly, patients might have significantly recovered, in comparison with their state when their reports were prepared. Recalling the numbers of patients who were regraded to informal status by their RMOs, it would certainly seem that the timing of the tribunal may be all important and, whether the RMO or the tribunal ultimately discharged, was merely a reflection of this.

Yet, in the final two cases the tribunals' decisions cannot easily be explained in terms of the patients making timely recoveries, but reflect a more rigorous application of the statute. In the case of J, the patient had experienced a fixed system of paranoid delusions, but had resisted any treatment until compulsorily admitted. This followed some superficial self-mutilation on her part. It was clear from the medical report that her condition had not improved with the limited compulsory medication she had received; moreover, the social work report indicated additional domestic difficulties. Both doctor and social worker were opposed to discharge, although the RMO recognized that, given the long-standing nature of her problems, there could be no guarantee that treatment would necessarily help her. The tribunal discharged. They accepted that she was mentally ill, but noted that they had heard no evidence to suggest she had been, or was liable to be, a danger to others. Furthermore, they did not consider that 'the evidence taken as a whole suggests that it is necessary to detain her in hospital for her own health or safety'. This decision placed the individual's right not to have her freedom unjustifiably restricted over and above a best interests approach—the desire to protect that individual from limited self-harm and potentially permit her to benefit from treatment. The underlying civil libertarian thrust is unusual with regard to the bulk of tribunal decisions. Perhaps the case may best be understood from the perspective of the legal president. He was comparatively new to this role, having previously acted as an advocate for patients. Given the findings of previous research, clearly indicating the powerful influence of the legal member of the tribunal, it would be unwise to minimize the impact that his 'poacher-turned-gamekeeper' role might have had on the outcome of the decision.

In the case of K it also seems unlikely that the patient had significantly recovered by the time of the hearing, since a stream of disturbed correspondence continued to arrive from him (at the tribunal office) up until, and after, the hearing took place. The tribunal's reasons were unrevealing, stating merely that the patient was still ill, but not of a sufficient nature or degree, and that with 'proper community support the patient would be able to maintain himself'. They noted that the patient's delusions remained as strong as ever, but there had been no recent incidents of violence. Again, the tribunal had applied the Act with uncustomary rigour—and had not allowed best interests arguments, favouring the patient's continued treatment, to outweigh their finding that he was not a danger to himself or others. Both of these cases ran against the general finding that tribunals were somewhat reluctant to discharge those who remained actively ill.

III. CONCLUSIONS

Under the 1983 Act, responsibility for the discharge of non-restricted patients is shared principally by tribunals, RMOs, and the hospital managers. In practice, and given the inevitable fluctuation in patients' conditions, which of these makes the decision to discharge is often determined by the timing of a patient's application.

Whether to discharge is a more complex issue. Notably, no body is charged explicitly with taking account of 'public interest' criteria, although, as the observed hearings illustrate, some none the less do. Moreover, although treatability, arguably the *quid pro quo* for compulsory care, is not a necessary prerequisite for the continued detention of restricted patients, poor treatment expectations or non-treatability are relevant criteria in determining whether detention can be justified in non-restricted cases. Similarly, the absence of grave disability, or of a passive risk of danger to self, should make it significantly more difficult to justify compulsory care.

But, empirically, these criteria seem to be of little relevance to the tribunal. There was no evidence that the concepts of treatability or viability were employed with any regularity; both the observed 'no discharge' hearings and the retrospective analysis of discharged cases suggested that tribunals' discretionary powers under S72 and the factors to which they should have regard under S72(2) were largely redundant. What then, were the relevant factors in determining whether patients were discharged? The answer was familiarly straightforward. Despite the relegation to tertiary status of factors concerning the probability of harm, the perception of risk remained all pervasive.

The prevention, reduction, and management of risk were the key elements and resulted in an ironic degree of consistency in the tribunals' approach. Two routes were evident, both of which shifted the emphasis to the outcome of decisions and away from the statutory criteria. Of course, tribunals would exceptionally resort to the legal criteria in order to achieve certain kinds of outcomes; the fine detail of the criteria may be employed to justify a decision *to* discharge, as in the case of Patient 58, if this is the desired outcome. In this respect, the argument advanced in Chapter 7, that the criteria are used to justify not discharging, may occasionally be turned on its head in non-restricted cases. But the motivation remains the same, namely the overpowering desire to achieve specific outcomes.

The principal routes were, first, the attainment of control over the patient's illness through medication and, secondly, control over his day-to-day whereabouts and stability through supervision and after-care.[24] In respect of both of these the law existed as a penumbra around decision-making; it was there to be drawn on to facilitate medication in the community (compulsory medication of discharged patients being strictly outside the terms of the 1983 Act) by crystallizing the alternative to a successful informal negotiation with patients. Thus, tribunals would tacitly endorse RMOs' strategies for maintaining therapeutic control and without doubt failed to see themselves in the role of advocating or clarifying to RMOs the interpretation of the law advanced by the High Court.

Paradoxically, the statutory requirements in respect of aftercare under S117 of the Act for detained patients, had done little to increase the tribunal's options or give them greater confidence when deciding whether to discharge. As Monahan (1982: 266) notes

---

[24] The tribunals' desire to keep patients on a tight rein has been reinforced by the publication of the *Report of the Committee of Inquiry into the Care and After-care of Miss Sharon Campbell* (1988) set up after the stabbing of a social worker by a patient discharged from a local hospital. The report noted that the patient was effectively allowed to 'drop out of sight'. Recommendations were made which included clarifying the duties of each relevant agency in the provision of after-care and establishing a register of designated patients living in the community. It was recommended that patients only be removed from the register on the authority of psychiatrists.

The bedrock problem of the proponents of positive rights is that we, as a society, judging by our actions rather than our rhetoric, simply do not want to foot the bill for them. The history of positive rights ... is largely one of evasion, noncompliance, interminable delay, and finally, when pressed, dumping the many to provide improved service to the few that remain.

In essence, securing positive rights has been much more difficult than merely placing them onto the statute, whilst negative rights (for example, the right not to be compulsorily medicated in the community) are readily erodable in a context where detention constitutes an alternative method of control. Thus, compulsory detention creates the impetus and obligations to provide treatment services; non-detained patients have to accept the services available. Although the onus is there to provide after-care for the discharged patient, it is extremely difficult to enforce a predetermined standard of health care.

Where, in non-restricted cases, direct discharge into the community was a realistic option, the concern to maintain therapeutic control over patients was further entwined with the issue of the patient's credibility. One of the main factors which would shift a patient from being credible and safe, to being untrustworthy and hence liable to relapse if medication ceased, was the nature of the behaviour in which the patient engaged when ill. A high-risk decision was associated with less credibility being attributed to the patient, because the consequences of making an inaccurate prediction were so much more onerous. However, this line of reasoning (patient stability plus credibility = discharge, stability minus credibility = no discharge) might be considered (*post Hallstrom*) erroneous. The tribunal are arguably not supposed to anticipate the possibility of a deterioration, but are to assess whether it is appropriate for the patient to be liable to be detained for in-patient treatment *at the time* of the hearing. Some tribunals took the view that, although the existing position would not justify the renewal of a section, they did not necessarily impel tribunals to discharge the order. This is, of course, correct, since the statutory criteria for renewal under S20(4) are not the exact mirror image of those in S72(1)(*b*). Such decisions do none the less imply that tribunals are prepared to run counter to the spirit of the decision in *Hallstrom*, as they are willing to use the implicit threat of compulsory procedures to ensure medication even where a patient expresses the intention (whether credible or not) of taking medication voluntarily and would not otherwise merit compulsory detention.[25]

However, the range of rationales employed by the tribunals in these non-restricted cases illustrate that the concept of high risk is not associated principally with harm to the individual patient. In such instances the possibility of discharge arises. Undoubtedly, the decision in the case of J above, where the evidence was 'taken as a whole', demonstrates the willingness of some tribunals to give precedence to individual rights. But if an unquantifiable risk to others existed—and even where patients had not been convicted of any offence of violence it was not uncommon for tribunals to speak of their potential for such behaviour—risk outweighed the dictates of recovery or the attractions of control in the community. The view adopted in the case of Patient 55, where public safety was enthusiastically permitted to outweigh individual rights, required the legal criteria to be ignored, neglected, or circumvented in order to keep patients in detention. The resultant balance between individual and societal rights was not atypical.

Thus, even in non-restricted cases tribunals were infected by the language of dangerousness; risk perception overlaid the assessment of illness despite its supposed formal role in coming after an assessment of the patient's medical requirements. The ill/low-risk patient might receive his discharge, but the well/perceived high-risk patient almost certainly would not. The 'great debate' surrounding the appropriateness of a dangerousness standard for civil commitment is therefore anachronistic; legal criteria had a limited impact on decisions perceived to be of this importance—decision-makers merely informally imported those they considered crucial. In this context, tagging on discretionary criteria, such as notions of treatability, constituted little more than an irrelevance.

---

[25] For example, the case of M above contrasts vividly with that of Patient 55 discussed in the first half of this chapter. Between them they illustrate the range of the tribunals' interpretations of S72, *post Hallstrom*.

9. Conclusions

> The difficulty is that most of these proposals, though comparatively easy to make the subject of regulation, are very difficult to ensure in practice; for this is just where the Law fails. It is essentially regulative and remedial, not creative or inspiring. It can deal with proven cases of abuse through the Courts or through tribunals, but it cannot create the kind of situation in which they are unlikely to occur, or ensure that the intention behind the law is fulfilled.
>
> Kathleen Jones (1980: 11)

I. THE LIMITATIONS OF LEGALISM

Writing well before the introduction of the Mental Health Act 1983, Jones (1980) argued persuasively that there were limits to what it was possible for the law to achieve in the arena of mental health. She favoured an approach in which legal restraint constituted a last resort. Good practice would be better facilitated through the sufficient allocation of resources and the creation of an appropriate working climate, wherein professional attitudes and skills could be sustained alongside the compassionate treatment of mentally disordered people. In this context, the law would 'only provide the enabling framework, the "open-textured" system, within which good policies can develop' (1980: 13). With the evolution of good practice, recourse to the law would become increasingly unnecessary.

At first sight, it would be difficult to dissent from the good sense which this incorporates. Indeed, the 1959 Act may be seen as a model for this approach; 'delegalization' had swept away the 'formalistic clutter which impeded sensible action in the face of complex human problems' (Jones 1980: 9). However, as a complete prescription, it is insufficient. Legal provisions need to be spelt out where individuals are liable to compulsory detention. Not only are patients deprived of their liberty, but, once compulsorily detained, they may find that other fundamental rights are threatened.[1] Indeed, unrestrained therapeutic zeal may itself result in abuse. Therefore, hand in hand with the 1959 Act's endorsement of professional discretion went a system of safeguards, designed mainly to protect the rights of compulsorily detained patients. Proven cases of abuse were, even according to Jones, appropriate matters for remedial action 'through the Courts or through tribunals'; they constituted attainable goals for the law.

This chapter is concerned with the extent to which the law is capable of achieving that to which it strives in theory. A number of themes recur which, in turn, have subtly affected the operation of the tribunal system. They will be addressed before presenting the implications of the empirical findings on tribunal decision-making. The first concerns the failure of the 1983 Act genuinely to embrace legalism; instead, it will be argued that the version embodied was 'watered-down'. Secondly, even if legalism had largely been embraced, this alone would have been insufficient to protect and enshrine patients' rights. It will be asserted, on the basis of the research findings, that it is wholly unrealistic to conceive of an effective legal safeguard in an inherently therapeutic environment. Contrary to Jones's assertion, tribunals do not necessarily fulfil the function of remedying abuse. Rather I would argue that the operation of the law is context-specific. Thirdly, in the quasi-legal setting in which the tribunals function, applying the law so as to protect fully the rights of individual patients is peculiarly reliant upon the willingness and inclinations of those with the statutory authority so to do. Since there is evidence that the philosophy behind the Act has not been absorbed and that some of those influential within the system have chosen to ignore or even reject it, the Act's fundamental principles are clearly endangered. The fourth theme evolves from the third. If those who operate the system start with the paternalistic assumptions that public safety and therapeutic considerations should take precedence over individual rights, then they will not only conceive of the Act as an obstacle, but also deem other determinants more critical. In

---

[1] Indeed, the 1983 Act gives doctors, in specified circumstances, the explicit power to treat psychiatric patients without their consent. However, it allows the power to apply only to patients who are detained in hospital, or who have first been detained and then given leave of absence under S17. It does not apply to conditionally discharged patients. See S56 and S63 and generally Part IV of the 1983 Act.

respect of tribunal decision-making, these concern the assessment of risk.

A. Legalism Enshrined?

The system of legal safeguards embodied within the 1959 Act was subject to much criticism. The response under the 1983 Act was to tighten selected statutory provisions, mainly those 'designed to safeguard or improve the rights of patients or potential patients' (Mental Health Act Commission 1985, para. 4: 1). The determination, by professionals, of what was in the best interests of patients was no longer to be the principal criterion in the provision of services. Rather they were to be provided as a right. Similarly, where compulsion was to be involved, it was intended that the relevant legal safeguards would ensure that 'the expert, minimally, can explain and justify his or her decision to the lay person and that there exists some objective behavioural criteria' (Gostin 1983: 38). It was argued that this generally represented a 'swing towards legal formalism' (Gostin 1983: 4).

However, the shift in emphasis that occurred did not represent a wholesale adoption of the legalistic perspective. The 1983 Act arguably steered a middle course between this approach and that at the other extreme of the pendulum—the *parens patriae* approach (Peay 1989). Moreover, unlike many jurisdictions in the United States, the shift did not go so far as to incorporate a dangerousness standard for commitment.[2]

Gordon and Verdun-Jones (1986) have argued that Gostin's dichotomy between professional discretion and the new legalism was more apparent than real. Although they agreed that developments in mental health legislation had moved towards 'the new legalism' pole, they maintained that the basic structure of what may be termed the quasi-legalistic approach had not altered significantly.[3] Bean (1986) similarly argued that although the changes introduced mirrored world-wide developments in mental health legislation seeking to 'reduce the paternalism of an earlier age, to identify the rights of the individual patient, and to reduce

[2] Smit (1987, p. 252).
[3] Hence, the extension of the tribunal system 'symbolizes the quasi-legalistic approach in that it provides an administrative, rather than a judicial mode of review and is highly susceptible to the influence of psychiatric opinion' (Gordon and Verdun-Jones, 1986, p. 76).

(albeit marginally) the power and prestige of the psychiatric experts' (1986: 14), in practice even the 'albeit marginally' turned out to be only a very minor qualification because, as Bean later asserts in respect of admission decisions, 'psychiatrists run the mental health legislation' (1986: 44). The criteria implicitly sustained the psychiatrist's position as the only figure who had all the necessary expertise to resolve issues relating to compulsion under the Act. Or, as Unsworth (1979: 110) asserted with reference to the 1959 Act, 'The use of coercion ceases to be divorcible from the need for treatment and becomes a therapeutic question.' In essence, the 1983 Act did little more than subtly embody the credibility which the medical profession enjoyed anyway in therapeutic contexts.

It can be argued that not only was a comparatively free rein given to the expression of medical considerations within the quasi-legalistic setting, but also, and in strict contrast, the intrusion of the law was minimal and its expectations moderate. The law attempted merely to ensure a modicum of procedural justice and to prevent certain kinds of things being done to the mentally disordered. It included no exhaustive principles or guidelines to control the substance of decision-making. As a result, there are many discretionary avenues down which decision-makers can go as a means of outmanœuvring the Act's essential precepts. The law, therefore, has arguably facilitated its own downfall.

B. Is the Effectiveness of the Legal Approach Context-Specific?

A number of recent Court of Appeal judgments have sought to clarify areas of the law pertinent to the tribunals' decisions, and may have acted as a countervailing influence on their more liberal interpretations.[4] Some of these judgments have undoubtedly urged a more rigorous application of the law, even where this was not seemingly in the long-term therapeutic interests of patients. Indeed, in one such appeal before Mr Justice McCullough, counsel argued that where the law was unclear, a construction should be adopted that would enable doctors to do what was in the best interests of their patients. The judge, in rejecting this assertion, stated:

[4] See Appendix 3

There is, however, no canon of construction which presumes that Parliament intended that people should, against their will, be subjected to treatment, which others, however professionally competent, perceive, however sincerely and however correctly, to be in their best interests. What there is is a canon of construction that Parliament is presumed not to enact legislation which interferes with the liberty of the subject without making it clear that this was its intention.[5]

Interestingly, the judge went on to state that his findings in no way implied criticism of either the clinical judgment or the bona fides of the doctors involved. He concluded, 'It may be (I express no view about it one way or the other) that a case should be made for granting to doctors powers to do what the doctors did in these two cases, but this is not a matter for the courts.'[6] This decision has been baldly characterized as 'facilitating the rights of patients at the expense of their care' (Peay 1986: 183). It endorsed the primacy of a rarefied legal view over a therapeutic strategy grounded in working practices: upholding patients' rights and 'doing what was correct' had arguably outweighed doing good and avoiding harm.

However, the judgment failed to have a clear-cut impact on the subsequent activities of mental health professionals and on the decisions of tribunals (see Chapter 8). This, I would argue, is because of the competing imperatives posed when considering therapeutic options in custodial settings; in the High Court these conflicting issues are subsumed by the purity of the forum. Given a clash of ideologies in an essentially therapeutic environment, it is therapeutic considerations which will hold sway. And conversely, in a purely legal context, it may be argued that psychiatric precepts will play second fiddle to legal considerations.[7] Thus, although vague legal criteria are undoubtedly malleable in their application, making the law more explicit will not, of itself, ensure a rigorous application. This raises the third issue, of the 'medium' whereby the law is applied.

[5] See Appendix 3, *Hallstrom*, p. 13, judgment transcript.
[6] Ibid p. 27.
[7] Chiswick (1985, pp. 975 and 977) has noted that when a psychiatrist examines an individual at the request of the court, 'most of the unspoken principles that govern the doctor–patient relationship are altered'. He concludes that psychiatric testimony puts 'the preservation of professional and ethical standards . . . at risk'.

C. The Impact of the System Personnel

The research findings suggest that many of those who operate the system believe that its bedrock in individual rights is not necessarily the most appropriate. Professionals working in the field were found to be either unfamiliar with the provisions of the Act, resistant to them, or, in some instances, unwilling to enforce them. Similarly, although patients' legal representatives may help to prevent sloppy thinking by tribunals, they cannot guarantee that members will necessarily give sufficient credence to the fine detail of the law. In some instances, representatives were found to collude in a negation of the appropriate legal criteria; in others, this occurred in arenas to which they had no access, for example during the tribunals' deliberations. Arguments raised by representatives based on the statutory criteria frequently failed to impress the tribunal; those based on the principles of equity received even shorter shrift. There may, therefore, be limits both to what the appeal process can achieve and, indeed, to what any changes in the statute might achieve. Without winning the 'hearts and minds' of these fulcral individuals, the Act is impotent. Arguably, changes in the system personnel, particularly by appointing those who are prepared to tolerate a certain level of discomfort to facilitate enforcement of the provisions of the Act, may be more effective than progressively hardening the letter of the law.

In the light of this, the decision to appoint judges to the tribunal appears particularly astute. By balancing changes in the law, forced upon the government as a result of the European Court's ruling in *X. v. the United Kingdom* (1981), with changes in the membership of the tribunal, the government may have favoured the impact the latter may induce. Thus, with one or two notable exceptions, the reasoning adopted in practice by the judges has not substantially departed from the traditional view of successive Home Secretaries, namely, that the discretion to release restricted patients is to be exercised cautiously, if at all. Previous research had, of course, suggested that more 'judicious' decision-making went hand in hand with greater responsibility for the decisions taken.[8] The appointment of the judges may therefore have been only a form of double insurance; none the less, it was clearly regarded as a price well worth paying.

[8] See Peay (1981, p. 176).

D. The Assessment of Risk

There is little dispute that society needs to protect those who are thought highly likely to cause themselves or others imminent harm. Indeed, even civil libertarians recognize that the moral dilemma crystallized by Darold Treffert's powerful phrase 'dying with their rights on' permeates the debate about the rights of the individual to refuse treatment and to have limits set on compulsory confinement.[9] As a bottom-line imperative, protective concepts underpin the shift towards assessments of dangerousness and their utility as a criterion for compulsion.

Although under the 1983 Act the criteria theoretically to be applied fall somewhere between *parens patriae* and the dangerousness standard, in practice it is evident that dangerousness, or the assessment of risk, none the less prevails in tribunals' decisions to release. But, if the assessment of risk were to provide the basis for compulsory measures it would be encumbent on society to 'get it right'. If there is not a real probability of risk, but rather an attributed perception of it which prompts intervention, then the moral arguments favouring it are altogether less compelling.[10] Moreover, if there were no real probability of danger then we would be infringing the liberty of a few, without any concomitant increase in the well-being of the many (except perhaps by falsely reducing their fear).

The dangerousness debate in the criminal justice sphere suggests that we are not sufficiently expert to justify indefinite detention on protective grounds. Similarly, as Webster and Menzies (1987: 202) note, psychiatrists' attributions of dangerousness are highly influential, yet they are made on the basis of 'clinical intuition' and in the 'utter absence of clear and accessible standards'. So why has dangerousness become so predominant a theme in the mental health sphere?

The explanation may lie with the presumption that it is intuitively likely that the mentally disordered do constitute a risk. As Rubin (1972: 398) noted,

Certain mental disorders [are] characterized by some kind of confused, bizarre, agitated, threatening, frightened, panicked, paranoid or impulsive behaviour. That and the view that impulse (i.e., ideation) and action

---

[9] See Treffert (1973) and also Jacob (1976).
[10] Peay (1982*b*).

are interchangeable support the belief that all mental disorder must of necessity lead to inappropriate, anti-social or dangerous actions.

Empirical evidence readily refutes the generality of this, or as Gunn (1977) puts it 'The main problem in discussing any relationship between criminal behaviour and mental disorder is that the two concepts are largely unrelated.' Indeed, for some categories of offenders given hospital orders, for example those who become depressed after the commission of their offence and before sentence, there may be no question of causality from the disorder to the offence. However, the barb remains that even the advocates of a non-relationship add the proviso that their conclusions rely on computations of criminal behaviour and mental disorder amongst groups.[11] The possibility exists that there may be an association between dangerous acts and mental disorder within any individual. It is this spectre which haunts tribunals in their reasoning. Is this individual one of those where a relationship might be proved? Criminological thinking derived from cohort studies has already suggested that, although offending is widespread throughout the community, a large proportion of serious offences may be committed by a very small minority of offenders (Blumstein, Farrington, and Moitra 1985; Home Office 1985). In this sense, attempts to evaluate risk in the individual may have some justification. But the proviso remains; it is a specific and not a generic risk. Therefore, the attribution of dangerousness in individuals, and the consequent erosion of their rights for the benefit of others, needs to be spelt out and to acquire the status of a justiciable issue; rights apply to individuals, their erosion should be determined on an individual basis and subject to strict procedural safeguards. Or, as Verdun-Jones (1988) noted, dangerousness arguably requires to be treated as a legal status in addition to a clinical one. Yet the reality of tribunals' attributions of risk is that there is no specificity as to the imminence or probability of the predicted behaviour. The present approach is tolerable neither from the perspective of natural justice nor on empirical grounds.

---

[11] See, for example, Monahan and Steadman (1983).

II. THE TRANSFORMATION OF CHOICE INTO CONSTRAINT

A. The Decisions of Tribunals

Although the absolute number of cases in the study is small, the research findings suggest that, rather than making decisions in the sense of exercising choice between real options, the tribunals invariably endorsed the recommendations made to them. While the findings do not support the assertion that tribunals were wholly constrained in these 'choices', they do reveal that the evidence as presented to them inevitably tended to support one decision or another, and that tribunals routinely acquiesced, almost irrespective of the content of the recommendation. This assessment may appear harsh, but the following may be taken as support.

1. The different rates of discharge by the tribunals serving the two different Special Hospital regions were sustained even where comparable samples were examined. Hence, similar cases were seemingly treated differently.

2. In 86 per cent of the sample cases the tribunals' decisions paralleled the recommendations made by the RMOs.[12] In those rare instances where the tribunals went against the advice of the RMOs, it was usually in order to ensure outcomes of a more cautious nature than the RMOs were advocating (69 per cent of cases). Moreover, in five of these cases, the tribunal had to go against the concurring advice of both the RMO and an IP. Since such decisions would prevent any radical change taking place in a patient's circumstances, they may primarily be regarded as 'non-decisions'.

3. The nature of the advice given by RMOs in Acheland and Bendene differed; the impact of the prevailing ethos at each location cannot be ignored.

4. The advice the RMOs offered to the tribunals did not derive irrevocably from the facts of patients' circumstances, but was, in

[12] Since the tribunals' decisions correlated with those of the RMOs it might be maintained that both groups arrived at similar decisions, but independently, because of the nature of the cases. However, given that the tribunals agreed with the decisions of the RMOs and these were, in turn, quite flexible depending on, for example, the hospital at which the RMO worked, it seems more credible that the tribunals adopted a passive role. Hence, the RMOs opinions more than merely correlated with the tribunals' decisions; they had an arguable causative impact.

turn, constructed according to both their views of the case and their professional experience. Hence, different RMOs reached different conclusions given predominantly similar evidence (as, for example, when a patient changed RMO). Also, the conclusions of two or more doctors reviewing the same case at about the same time would differ (see, for example, discordant conclusions drawn by RMOs, their colleagues, IPs, and medical members of the tribunal). Finally, the conclusion drawn by a single RMO could be changed independently of any changes in the facts of the case (where, for example, pressure was exerted by the Responsible Authority).

5. There was similarly no irrevocable connection between the evidence presented and the tribunals' outcomes. In some cases, evidence was available which, had the tribunal been so minded, could have supported an alternative decision. Indeed, on occasions the same case reviewed sequentially by two different tribunals would result in two contradictory decisions, even when the patient's condition remained stable. Hence, evidence was open to interpretation and to selection.

There is, therefore, a process of construction which occurs in any given case which starts at a point considerably prior to the tribunal hearing. The case, as presented to the tribunal, has been refined for their consideration, principally by the RMO and the patient or his or her legal representative. The tribunal's decision, like that of many other decision-making bodies hearing evidence, amounts largely to a ratification of a decision which has been structured by earlier choices (Hawkins 1986).

B. *Understanding the Reasoning Process*

In coming to an understanding of the tribunals' decision-making process it is necessary to address two questions. Why was it that so many of the deliberations were seemingly perfunctory? How did tribunals resolve conflicting evidence? Seven strategies, constituting a form of intellectual acrobatics, provided the pathways to acceptable outcomes. The first two were endemic to the tribunal's task and stemmed from the inherent nature of evidence, the criteria to be applied, and the uncertainty associated with predictive decisions. Two strategies were systemic in origin, and the final three relate to the tribunal's approach to the acquisition and evaluation of evidence.

(i) Use of the statute Almost inevitably, a legitimate basis could be found for reaching decisions not to discharge. This derived from the nature of the negative criteria tribunals had to apply under S72, which meant they could refuse to discharge if they were not satisfied that the patient was not suffering or that treatment was not necessary. Patients had to overcome one of these double negatives by establishing, on a balance of probabilities, that they did not suffer to the requisite degree. Yet, any degree of uncertainty under S72 would seemingly suffice to result in a patient remaining in confinement. Arguably, therefore, the level of certainty of which tribunals wished to be satisfied before discharging, was more akin to 'beyond reasonable doubt' than to the civil standard theoretically to be applied.

Although patients did not have to establish categorically that they were not suffering from a mental disorder, much of the dispute at tribunals none the less focused on the absence of things, rather than on their presence. For example, the absence of acute symptomatology or of recent behaviour which would satisfy the behavioural element of the definition of psychopathic disorder— 'abnormally aggressive or seriously irresponsible conduct' (S1(2)). However, even the absence of evidence that a patient was disordered did not logically imply that he was not disordered. Or, as MacCulloch (1986) has argued, it is philosophically impossible to prove the absence of a disorder.

The bases of the tribunals' thinking in this matter have been discussed at length in respect of individual cases. In essence, the episodic nature of a phenomenon like mental disorder means that the tribunal are unlikely to be confident about its absence. Thus, despite the wording of the statute, which requires that the tribunal be satisfied that the patient 'is not *then* suffering' (S72(1)(*b*), emphasis added), it was readily acknowledged that patients' symptoms could present on an intermittent basis. The possibility of relapse remained ever present (see the case of *Kay* in Appendix 3). Therefore, tribunals were reliant on the views of those who had longitudinal knowledge of the patient. But even their views could not be conclusive in respect of the absence of disorder. Where symptoms were not observed this could be either because they had not occurred during the period of observation; or because they had occurred but had not been observed; or because they would not occur as the disorder had been cured. It was difficult to be certain which explanation was correct. Furthermore, the probability of disordered behaviour being exhibited was low—patients were frequently stabilized on medication, and the opportunities for irresponsibility in a secure controlled environment were minimal. However, a single incident of, for example, aggression or deluded thinking could confirm that the underlying disorder remained. It was more common, therefore, for patients to argue not that they were not then suffering, but that they were not then suffering to the requisite degree. On this issue there was considerable scope for experts to disagree. Moreover, since the Act only urged that tribunals found themselves not satisfied of the assorted non-medical criteria, it was easy for them to accept the frequent assertion of medical need. Thus, the general tenor of the evidence presented to tribunals normally supported a finding that the patient remained in need of treatment and was legally disordered.

In other cases, where the need for treatment was less clear cut, it was only necessary for the tribunal merely to feel uncertain about the benefits of further treatment for detention to be continued. Generating uncertainty was not difficult. Frequently there would be grounds for disagreement over the continuation of the disorder or over the extent of recovery. Indeed, there could always be uncertainty (as with any predictive decision) as to whether the patient would continue with medication. Although it has been argued that this does not necessarily constitute a bar to discharge, in practice it did feature in the reasoning of tribunals.

(ii) Abuse of the statute It was ironic that the legal criteria should have been invoked in this manner to justify not discharging, because there were examples of cases where inconvenient aspects of the legislation were side-stepped. For example, the criteria of 'treatability' and 'viability' were routinely passed over as the decision not to discharge was recorded. Clearly, there was only sparse evidence that they were used as a basis *for* discharging.

It has also been argued that it was not unusual for the decision-making process of the tribunal to be, in essence, back to front; they first determined what outcome they preferred and then selected the evidence to accord with that view. In many cases, tribunals were driven to these outcome-oriented decisions by pragmatic considerations, for example, to ensure that patients would be properly supervised or that medication could be continued. In this respect, they were reluctant to relinquish therapeutic control over the patients. But, more commonly, their desires were protective;

they did not believe that patients did not constitute a real risk of reoffending, and therefore, they were prepared to endorse continuing detention—but justified it on the legally acceptable grounds that they were satisfied that the patient remained disordered and in need of medical treatment.

Although it would not be fair to assert that the tribunals' regularly abused the statutory criteria, there was evidence that considerations of risk pervaded deliberations and may inappropriately have shifted the balance between criteria relating to patients' medical needs and those deriving from concern about the public's safety. Moreover, cases were observed where such strategies were consciously pursued.

Thus, the law was complied with selectively; positively through resort to its negative criteria to achieve a negative result namely, no discharge; in contrast, its positive criteria were neglected in sustaining decisions not to discharge. The law would therefore be employed by tribunal members as a resource both for rationalizing decisions and for constraining them to their preferred options.

(iii) Lack of options Tribunals also found themselves constrained by their view that there was a lack of suitable alternative placements for patients. To some extent, what was deemed suitable was determined by the tribunal's perception of the severity of the patient's illness and his perceived likelihood of reoffending. There were examples where no hostel could be found to accept a patient. But few tribunals were prepared to take the step, seemingly logically demanded by the legal criteria, that if a patient could not be discharged to a hostel place, he should be discharged regardless. Rather, they took a step back in their reasoning and merely redefined the patient as not yet ready for discharge.

(iv) Deferral Although the tribunals were on occasions impeded by their limited powers, it was also true that these limitations enabled them to defer to other decision-makers where they perceived positive decisions as unreachable. Deferral took place either at a given point in time to the advice of sources whom tribunals saw as informed and reputable, or in order to leave the future monitoring and management of patients' progress in the hands of the RMOs. Similarly, some transfers were recommended, almost on a wing and a prayer, in the knowledge that the Secretary

of State would be unlikely to support them or the RMO unwilling to take the necessary steps to ensure a bed became available elsewhere.

(v) Quiescent patients and passive tribunals In some instances there would be no impetus from the patient for discharge. Patients sometimes applied to the tribunal out of frustration at being kept in the dark about their progress; sometimes they only sought support from the tribunal for a transfer. In other cases, passivity by the tribunal, or a reluctance on their part to seek further information, resulted in a failure to address explicitly the need for detention.

(vi) Sign-posting Under the circumstances discussed many of the tribunals' deliberations were likely to be perfunctory. Not because the decisions were not regarded as serious, nor because members failed to fulfil their responsibilities earnestly, because they did. It was merely that sometimes there were no options, and often tribunals perceived themselves as having no options. And occasionally, where there were options, the deliberations would be pre-empted by earlier 'sign-posting'. This could be at the behest of either the legal or the medical member, both of whom were capable of stamping their view upon the tribunal by making it plain at an early stage that there were points beyond which they would not go. This effectively delineated the boundaries for inaction and enhanced consensual decision-making. Earlier research (Peay 1981) had demonstrated that minimizing social interaction between tribunal members – negating 'sign-posting' – maximised conflict between members. In practice, therefore, although the observed decisions were apparently arrived at by a consensus, this arguably occurred by default. Members may have agreed whole-heartedly with the decision reached (as might be expected in the light of Asch's (1956) seminal conformity studies), but if they did disagree, they did not do so with sufficient force as to be prepared to make a stand.

(vii) Undermining the source rather than the content of evidence At the other end of the spectrum to quiescent patients were those who were prepared to fight tooth and nail through the tribunal, which they perceived as their only hope of discharge. A campaigning stance, accompanied by active representation, could

generate a great deal of evidence favouring discharge. How did the tribunals resolve these dilemmas when RMOs remained implacably opposed to discharge?

Frequently tribunals argued that the RMO, who had longstanding knowledge of the patient, knew the patient best. He always gave 'up-to-the-minute' evidence to the tribunal and this could be tested to the point of cross-examination. Independent psychiatrists were characterized as providing merely a snapshot assessment of the patient. Even if the IP overcame the credibility hurdle of being perceived as uninformed, he or she also had to establish that they were truly independent. Sustaining impartiality in the tribunals' eyes could be problematic if IPs regularly provided reports for different patients. Moreover, tribunals would occasionally characterize such evidence not only as unreliable and ill-informed, but also as 'unsafe'.[13] Thus, in only two cases in the sample did the tribunal prefer independent evidence to that of the RMO in order to discharge, and in one of these the RMO agreed with the IP on the issue of the absence of illness, but was arguing against discharge on the grounds of predicted risk.

It was also difficult for the tribunal to overrule the RMO's opinion on the basis of a single independent report, for it usually required them to follow a course which might be proved incorrect. Patients' representatives who wished seriously to promote an application for discharge had to resort to seeking more than one independent psychiatric report. It is like the story of the emperor's new clothes. When it is hard to be objective about the absence of something, it is the weight of opinion, both in terms of the numbers of alternative views and the status of those giving them, which may count, rather than their ability to verify what they say.

Another interesting aspect of the tribunal's reasoning emerges here. It has already been suggested that the medical approach enjoyed something of a head start where legal questions were addressed in what were essentially therapeutic contexts. Yet, it was not a question of medical dominance based on expert knowledge *per se*. Certainly the RMO's advice had a great influence on the tribunal's decisions. Also, his advice was invariably preferred,

---

[13] This was particularly unfortunate since some IPs had previous knowledge of patients (where for example a patient had been transferred from their local hospital). Therefore, where they made recommendations for transfer and offered the patient a bed, the tribunal should not have been too ready to dismiss their advice as partial.

where conflict arose, to that of an independent psychiatrist. Although the two are not inextricably linked, the RMO was normally attributed with having both a long-standing and an in-depth knowledge of the patient. Yet the tribunal, on occasions, allowed the advice of its medical member to overrule that of the RMO, although the former could hardly claim any greater in-depth knowledge of the patient than an independent psychiatrist. Indeed, the medical member might not even have shared an IP's forensic experience.[14] Therefore, medical expertise was weighted according not only to the source from which it came, but also to the status with which that source was attributed during the deliberation.

C. *Deliberations*

One difficulty remains with this whole analysis. In some cases tribunals seemed to be swayed in their decisions by comparatively small matters, for example, the fact that a patient's relatives were attributed with having good sense. Such matters would be given prominence in the reasons for the decision reached. But, how can it be known whether these peripheral issues were crucial in their decision-making or merely formally articulated as such, once the nature of the decision had already been determined by other matters? It cannot. And this is, of course, an impediment to those representatives who would wish to appeal against decisions. Routinely, the formal articulation of decisions was carefully phrased to ensure respectability. Yet, attendance during deliberations indicated that sometimes the routes by which decisions were made were not always wholly in accord with the 'correct' approach.

This raises an issue of natural justice. The rules of natural justice require that where the tribunal desires to proceed on the basis of a point not put before it, and which on the face of it is not in dispute, it is highly desirable, and arguably necessary, that the person whose case is being considered should be alerted to that

---

[14] Although the formal qualifications to become a medical member require only that the individual be a 'registered medical practitioner' (see Appendix 2), the Lord Chancellor invariably appoints only psychiatrists. Yet, in practice, many are semi-retired. This is in notable contrast to the views of the Butler Committee (Home Office and DHSS 1975 at para. 7.6) who expressed the hope that forensic psychiatrists would increasingly serve as tribunal members.

possibility.[15] This would then enable that person to adduce further evidence and ensure that the decision-makers had heard everything of relevance in open session. For example, in the case of *Clatworthy* the tribunal rejected the uncontradicted evidence from the RMO and an IP that the patient was not detainable under the 1983 Act. It was unclear whether the tribunal had acted on the advice of the medical member rather than on the basis of the opinions laid before the tribunal. But Mr Justice Mann noted that had the tribunal proceeded on some basis 'unknown to others but known to themselves, then I would have regarded the decision as flawed'[16]—Tribunals were alive to the relevance of this in respect of the findings of the medical member's examination of the patient. Where this contradicted the view of the RMO or an IP, tribunals usually did take steps to ensure that the applicant was aware of his findings. However, they were not as rigorous about the assessments formed by the medical member during the course of the hearing. More worrying still was the powerful impact remarks could have when made by the medical member during the tribunals' deliberations. Such off the cuff observations made at this stage could be damning, yet they would be considered unchallenged by any other medical view.

One final difficulty was evident. The medical member's qualifications for effectively overruling the RMO's medical advice have already been questioned. Yet medical members would also contribute to the deliberations in ways that went beyond their status as a medical expert. In some cases this related to the assessment of risk, where they may have been attributed by their fellow members with greater expertise than they themselves would perhaps have wished to claim. Yet on other occasions they reflected what were clearly personal preferences or even prejudices. But how were the tribunal to dissociate medical from non-medical assessments when they derived from the same source, namely their own valued medical member? Clearly, the interaction between the content of information, its source, and the context in which it was assessed was critical to the nature of the decision determined. Two questions arise. First, how could such contributions be subjected to the rules of natural justice, where they emerged in a context in which the

---

[15] For an analysis of the general principles of natural justice see Lord Diplock in the case of *Mahon* v. *Air New Zealand Ltd.* [1984] 3 All ER 201 at 210.
[16] See Appendix 3 for the case of *Clatworthy* at p. 704.

patient and his representative had no opportunity to challenge them?[17] And secondly, how could the tribunals defend a decision not to discharge, where it was reached not on the basis of a different assessment of the patient's medical needs, but in order to protect the public from what was perceived, but could not be verified, to be an unjustifiable risk?

Evidential rules and the rules of natural justice deal with the admissibility and presentation of evidence; they do not attempt to constrain the receipt or weighing of evidence since it is assumed that those with the responsibility for undertaking this task are impartial. Or rather, professional decision-makers, the judges, and those who sit on tribunals, are presumed to be impartial.[18] Moreover, it is widely assumed that the duty to act fairly requires the tribunal 'to disclose the substance of the facts to which it was going to apply its mind, and that these facts should include the professional opinion' presented by its psychiatric members.[19] But, this ruling begs the question as to what should be the import of irrelevant or personal assessments by the medical members.

Here is the nub of the problem. On the one hand we have a legal system which assumes impartiality, but recognizes its limitations in the formal sphere of the collation and presentation of evidence. Yet, on the other, there have been few responses to research findings which suggest that decision-makers are not automated weighing machines—rather they are subject to a whole series of extraneous influences which affect their decision-making skills and the decisions they reach. Indeed, since that which decision-makers bring with them to the assessment of cases—a sort of intellectual baggage made up of attitudes, beliefs, knowledge, and experience—remains relatively constant, it could have a powerful unidirectional effect on decisions.

The upshot is that tribunals, whilst seemingly embracing illness based precepts, will, on occasions, negate therapeutically derived recommendations with the overpowering pull of protective considerations based on little more than flimsy evidence. Perhaps for

[17] The course properly advocated in the Canadian case *Re Egglestone and Mosseau and Advisory Review Board*.

[18] Of course, the courts recognize that jurors may not be able to sustain an unbiased approach when presented with prejudicial or conclusory information and have therefore sought to protect them from its influence.

[19] From *Egglestone* at p. 87 (above). Notably, Griffiths, J. argued that the chairman may permit counsel to ask questions of the psychiatric members, so as to clarify any part of their reports. But, see the dissenting opinion of Trainor, J.

Special Hospital cases, where considerations of security are ever present, an element of caution is comprehensible. But, where the RMO is urging transfer or discharge, or in the cases of non-restricted patients, this situation is unjustifiable. Indeed, the paradoxical outcome may be that the doctor who has the last word, namely the tribunal doctor, may not know best medically, but his personal views may hold sway with a tribunal minded to be cautious at the expense of therapeutic considerations.

It is difficult to conceive of what might be done about this. It has already been suggested that the legal approach has limitations in therapeutic contexts. In other settings where the interests of the individual dominate, for example, in non-tariff-based sentencing decisions, the courts have largely appeared content to allow strict legal regulation to take second place to the attainment of full information.[20] Therefore, it may be encumbent on the medical professionals concerned, as Golding (1988) has advocated in respect of those giving evidence in court, to draw up a series of ethical guidlines, before they entirely erode their own credibility.

Yet, as the tribunals' decisions arguably bear a greater resemblance, in respect of their consequences for an individual's liberty, to a finding of guilt than to a decision about the most appropriate disposal, self-regulation by the professions may be insufficient. Procedural regulation stops short of deliberations. But perhaps it should not, particularly if medical members are to continue to contribute both to the evidence and to the deliberations. In the light of its evident wayward elements, there should therefore be considerably more structure to and control over the tribunals' deliberations.

There are several routes whereby this could be achieved. First, it might be possible, as happened following *Bone*, to achieve further improvement in the quantity and quality of tribunals' recorded reasons. Given that the process of decision-making cannot be open to inspection, it is vital that comprehensive reasons be required. In turn, this should make it less easy for tribunals to neglect the statutory criteria and place more emphasis on the need to justify decisions through reference to the evidence presented, thereby ensuring that presentation of the reasons does not merely conceal a choice, whether conscious or not, to fit the facts to the law. Alternatively, as under the New South Wales legislation, each tribunal member might be required to record their reasons

[20] See Ch. 2 at p. 20 (above).

separately and in writing.[21] However, it is accepted that this proposal is unlikely to find favour amongst a tribunal membership wedded to the concept of consensus decision-making. Moreover, attendance at deliberations and the recording of tribunals' decisions led me to the conclusion that the reasons given fulfilled many functions aside from clarifying and justifying the decision reached—if indeed they did that.

Secondly, a more structured approach to the deliberations might be achieved by using a standard check-list of issues to be considered. Similarly, modifying the existing form on which the decisions are recorded could go some way to ensuring that the relevant sections of the Act are given the fullest consideration in every case. Indeed, having to work through the decision-making process in an established sequential mode might help to avoid some of the more subtle departures from the spirit of the Act which are rarely spelt out in the informal atmosphere in which tribunals' deliberations take place.

Thirdly, the role of the tribunal clerks, who attend throughout the tribunal hearing and the subsequent deliberation, might be enhanced. Their role is presently ill defined, but in practice they act as a sort of Master of Ceremonies. They serve the coffee, usher in witnesses, pay their expenses, reassure patients, sort out unexpected problems, phone the Home Office when so required, and occasionally offer advice to the tribunal. Undoubtedly theirs is a very responsible position. Yet they are not legally trained. In the civil service hierarchy they are not regarded as senior appointments. Although they do build up an impressive experience of the Act and the relevant issues once in post, it is clearly difficult for them to draw to the attention of the tribunal and its legally qualified member instances where departures from the Act seem likely to occur. The observational work shows that clerks will, on occasions, speak up. However, it is not surprising that this does not invariably happen. Whether this derives from status-induced muteness, or from a lack of confidence that their interpretation is correct, or perhaps from an assumption that it is inappropriate for them to offer any advice to the tribunal, is not clear.[22] However,

[21] See generally Verdun-Jones (1986).

[22] Although the clerks are full-time functionaries of the tribunal and in particular, serve the tribunal chairmen, they are formally employed by the DHSS. Arguably a case may be made out in principle for relocating the tribunal within another government department, for example the Lord Chancellor's Department. Whether this would have any practical impact in sustaining the

consideration might valuably be given either to training clerks before they commence work or possibly to enhancing their position by requiring a legal qualification before appointment. Furthermore, since it is during the deliberation where incidental issues may creep in, unknown to patients or their representatives, and where the ultimate weighing of evidence may not bear directly on the issues explored during the hearing, it is arguable that an enhancement of the role of the clerk may have a deterrent effect on what might otherwise be errant decisions.

Although these potential routes constitute little more than tinkering, I accept that some of those experienced in the field would consider them wholly unrealistic. Even more unfortunately, the nub of the problem has still to be addressed.

D. Beyond the Legal Safeguard: Other Roles for the Tribunal

The discussion above has indicated that the extent to which tribunals provide a legal safeguard of the kind associated with courts of law may be limited. All the changes wrought in the system by the 1983 Act have not altered this fundamental conclusion; their role as a procedural safeguard has been enhanced, but their substantive function remains the same.[23] The impact of legislation has been to alter the process and not the outcome of tribunal review.

Of course, whether it is desirable that they should function in the traditional legal mode is debatable. Counsel for the tribunals and the patients in *Thomas* and *Crozier* (see Appendix 3) argued that tribunals

are not courts in the ordinary sense: but involve a meeting of experts to discuss the best interest of the patient in an informal setting, where the

---

independence of the tribunals is questionable. After all, although their independence may be erodable in theory, there is no evidence from the research that their decisions had been improperly influenced by the clerks. Indeed, where clerks offered advice, it was of considerable assistance to the tribunal members, whose involvement with tribunal matters was, by definition, intermittent.

[23] Critics of a legalistic approach to mental health, have asserted that it is concerned with procedural correctness rather than, or at a cost to, such substantive goals as psychiatric improvement. See generally Unsworth (1979). However, what is asserted here is that tribunal review may fail to effect change in a patient's legal status, even where this is merited on clinical grounds.

usual rules of evidence are ignored and the members of the Tribunal and the parties work towards a solution which is in the best interests of the patient (judgment transcript, pp. 8–9).

Mr Justice Farquharson accepted that there should be some elasticity in the tribunals' powers and their use of them, but, in his judgment the scheme of the Act 'casts the Tribunals in a judicial rather than an administrative role' (*ibid*: 10). Thus, as in the *Hallstrom* case the High Court determined that, 'the law was the law', irrespective of the inconvenience that might cause to tribunals.

Although the research has found little evidence that tribunals invariably enforce the letter of the law, the conclusion cannot be drawn that tribunals never made uncomfortable decisions. In a handful of cases the tribunal did apply the law rigorously, and discharged. In itself, this justifies retaining the edifice of the tribunal as a legal safeguard.

Perhaps of equal importance to many patients, tribunals perform a number of subsidiary functions, which endorse the justification for their retention, over and above their limited impact as a legal safeguard. As one part of a dynamic and complex system they act, most importantly, as a catalyst; the prospect or presence of review can place pressure upon other actors within the mental health system with independent responsibilities under the 1983 Act, for example RMOs or the Responsible Authority. Moreover, their informal role as a conduit for information and its clarification means that they can also be used as a resource by other actors in the system. They function therefore as negotiators or brokers, acting informally behind the scenes to 'move things along'.

With time, these informal procedures can become part of the fabric of the formal arena. For example, although tribunals have no statutory power to make them, their recommendations for transfer or trial leave in restricted cases have generally been thought to have been welcomed by the Home Office.[24] But the tribunals were disadvantaged in this informal sphere as they had no means of ascertaining whether their recommendations were acted upon. Confirmation that administrative arrangements had been introduced to ensure that recommendations do not lie fallow

---

[24] This was not always the case. During the early years of the 1983 Act a former civil servant at the Home Office had made it plain to tribunals that their recommendations would carry little, if any, weight.

within the Home Office came in a written parliamentary answer. This clarified that the Home Office not only make whatever useful comments they feel able to, at the point at which they receive the recommendations, but also ensure that a copy of the correspondence with the tribunal is sent to the RMO, as 'it is for this officer to consider the recommendation in the first instance'.[25] Furthermore, at any subsequent hearing, the Secretary of State's statement to the tribunal will explain the outcome of any recommendation made by the previous tribunal. It is too early to assess the impact of these changes. But, they will surely assist in minimizing the erosion of information and momentum that can occur where tribunals have no power to reconvene, because their recommendations carry no statutory authority.[26]

The use of tribunals as a potential lever is not without its drawbacks. Patients and RMOs occasionally found to their cost that in seeking support from the tribunal for a particular course of action, for example transfer, they might, in fact, impede their own progress. Tribunals were not always as ready as RMOs to perceive a patient as suitable for a move from conditions of special security, and their decision not to recommend such a transfer could make it harder for patients to get the Home Office's acquiescence to the plan. In such cases tribunals could act not as a lever, but as a hatchet.

Tribunals could also be used as a therapeutic tool; first, by some RMOs, as a means of settling their patients into therapy or enhancing their own insight into patients' conditions; secondly, by patients, many of whom experienced considerable frustration and anxiety about their situations or those of their fellow patients. In this respect, the tribunal hearing served a relief function—it could satisfy a patient's need for information or clarification and help to diffuse tension—elsewhere termed the 'safety-valve' function. Tribunals could therefore be regarded as therapeutic rather than curative; they made patients 'feel' better without effecting radical change in their status. Arguably, they were influenced in this more by the 'continuity of care' approach with which psychiatry is imbued than by the interventionist approach of the law.

[25] Douglas Hogg, *Parl. Debates*, HC, vol. 121, col. 265–6, 28 Oct. 1987, at 265.
[26] Notably, the impetus for these administrative changes came from judicial dissatisfaction expressed at a judicial studies day in Nov. 1986. The comparative ease with which these arrangements were introduced may provide a timely lesson for those wishing to effect changes in the tribunal system, without recourse to costly and time-consuming legislation.

Of course, problems could arise for the tribunal in the trade-offs required between their role as a formal legal safeguard and their various informal roles. The former places a premium on consistency whilst the latter require flexibility and a minimization of the tribunal's court-like procedures. Moreover, to which goals were the tribunal to look when assessing whether they were fulfilling their role? And, would highlighting their lesser effectiveness as a legal safeguard erode the laudable symbolic impact had by the existence of independent review? For example, both the appointment of the judges and the injection of a more meaningful lay element into the 1983 Act clearly fulfil an important symbolic role. As Devlin (1976) noted, judges can serve the community by removing a sense of injustice:

To perform this service the essential quality which he needs is impartiality and next after that the appearance of impartiality. I put impartiality before the appearance of it simply because without the reality the appearance would not endure. In truth, within the context of service to the community the appearance is the more important of the two.[27]

Enhancing the appearance of impartiality is an important function; patients were undoubtedly more satisfied with the new tribunals because they believed they were fairer. Yet, the research has also questioned the propriety of some of the tribunal's deliberations. In fulfilling their substantive function, both the lay and judicial members have had a more marginal impact. Where research brings this out into the open, by demonstrating a preparedness not to enforce the Act on the part of those charged with the responsibility for so doing, it risks undermining the preceding (non-medical) symbolic function which the lay and judicial groups perform. But not to do so, to fail to point out that in some cases there is a disjunction between the reality and the rhetoric, would be to fail to underline why it is that the way the law is employed is context-specific.

Thus, highlighting the tribunal's limited efficacy as a legal safeguard may erode patients' confidence in the tribunal as a forum where justice can be seen to be done. These and other tensions would suggest that there may be some merit in further differentiating the tribunal so as to provide a more sensitive forum for different categories of patient. Dell and Robertson's (1988)

[27] See Devlin (1976, p. 9).

work reveals that there are marked differences in treatment issues for psychotic and 'non-psychotic' patients. Similarly, what an articulate psychopath and a chronic mentally ill patient require from the tribunal are not likely to be the same; not all are well suited to further refinements of the adversarial process, and not all would necessarily welcome greater formality. If mental disorder comes in many shapes and sizes, perhaps the tribunal should do likewise.[28]

Therefore global assessments and their solutions may be limited in their applicability. The problems tribunals encounter with the Act depend both upon the location of patients' confinement and upon the nature of the disorder from which they have been suffering. The nature of the dilemma posed may be one of the most powerful determinants of the quality of safeguard tribunals represent. Accordingly, patients who have suffered from, for example, the depressive illnesses, may find it easier to gain their discharge through the tribunal than those diagnosed as suffering from schizophrenia. Similarly, although potential dangerousness is the hidden agenda in many decisions not to release, attributions of dangerousness are not allocated equally amongst different categories of patient. Should there therefore be a formal acknowledgement for some patients that their rights are more readily erodable on the basis of 'greater good' arguments? As suggested earlier, should predicted dangerousness become an explicit justiciable issue?

But would a more careful targetting of needs erode the tribunal's principal function as a safeguard for patient's rights—clearly erodable even under the existing set up? Moreover, does the mixture of patients actually provide the tribunal with its cutting edge? Without those patients who genuinely wish to contest their detention would the tribunal become merely a 'patients' welfare panel' and perhaps thereby trespass on the role of the Mental Health Act Commission? Finally, would not a diversification of the system require patients to identify in advance the precise nature of their applications to the tribunal? The merits of a single tribunal system with the capacity to respond flexibly are therefore considerable.

---

[28] On the basis of the research findings, the existing arrangements in automatic references clearly merit re-examination.

III. THE WAY FORWARD?

From many perspectives the tribunals could be assessed to be working reasonably well. Decision-making is approached judiciously; decisions to release may be characterized by the care, indeed caution, with which they are made. Full consideration is usually given to therapeutic considerations. Patients, as the consumers of the system, by and large, do not express dissatisfaction.

Yet, viewed from the perspective of the European Court of Human Rights, it may be that there are significant gaps between the system as it might have been hoped to operate and its practice as documented by the research findings. Of course, it may well be that the attitudes and approach of those responsible for using the legislation will only adapt slowly, and much more slowly than those who pursue change through the law might wish. Some who took part in the research, and in particular the RMOs, enjoyed even greater discretion under the 1959 Act. It was, therefore, not surprising to find that some of them clung on to chosen and well-ingrained methods of working. After all, the research took place on the heels of what were breathtaking legislative changes, especially in respect of the tribunal's role in restricted cases. It may, therefore, be too early to adopt a wholly pessimistic stance. 'Law not war' may still have its day.

Alternatively, it may be that the objectives of the 1983 Act were unrealistic; or that the interaction between the personnel appointed and the irresolvable dilemmas some patients pose, made them unrealistic. It is not inconceivable that the tribunal system is used as a resource to achieve and then justify through the back door, that which could not openly be tolerated. A conspiracy theorist might argue that some of those professionally associated with the tribunal system are content, on occasions, to allow considerations of dangerousness improperly to influence the application of the law. After all, who, apart from the patient directly involved, is liable to protest too loudly if a patient about whom predictions of dangerousness are confidently made by all concerned, is kept in 'treatment' longer than he might otherwise have been? Whether such a covert dependence on the 'good sense' of tribunals should be either condoned or relied upon, however laudable the motives, is another matter.

It is undeniable that patients who have both suffered from serious mental disorders and committed offences of a worrying nature will generate considerable anxiety when seeking their release from confinement. And it is inevitable that such decisions will be context-bound and, in part, intuitive. Or, as Grounds (1988) has asserted.

In reaching a decision in the case of an individual who has been sentenced for a grave offence, how could a conscientious tribunal entirely set aside the issue of public safety and consider discharge on the 'mental disorder' criterion alone? The task strictly enshrined in the legislation is not a reasonable one, and which of us would act any less cautiously if faced with the tribunal's dilemma?

Many of the tribunals' justifications for not releasing patients derive, of course, from the criteria which permit, indeed actively encourage, cautious application. Clearly, these could be redrawn and further legislative changes brought about. Parliament could grasp the nettle and attempt some form of substantive justice, perhaps by regulating decision outcomes. But from where would the impetus for this derive? Furthermore, could there be any guarantee, given the research findings, that positive criteria would not merely be side-stepped by those applying the legislation, if they felt that a rigorous application would lead to intolerable decisions? Although justifying a bad law on the grounds that it is sensibly enforced may, in time, bring the law into disrepute, the question remains, what is 'bad law'? Does it derive primarily from incohesive or incoherent jurisprudential principles; or from its routine abrogation by those who apply it; or because its application fails to resolve real problems—it lacks relevance to reality? Or, might it be a combination of all of these? Thus, it may not be possible to settle upon a solution until the nature of the problem has been clearly delineated, and the desired outcome agreed upon. Adopting a Shavian approach and merely setting out some of these dilemmas may be a sufficient first step. It may be for others to decide upon the route subsequently to be taken.

The first justification for circumspection derives from the recognition that the tribunal system does not exist in a vacuum. It represents only one aspect of a system of checks and balances for dealing with mentally disordered individuals. Since the research has identified the RMOs as the key figures in the sequence of decision-making, perhaps it is their decision-making skills which should properly form the focus for reform. Or, as Webster and

Menzies (1987: 202) have asserted, 'the activities of forensic practitioners deserve to be a focus of systematic evaluation quite as much as the characteristics of offenders'. Improving the decision-making abilities of RMOs might, in the long run, be a more effective route to better decisions than any action that could be taken in respect of the tribunals.

Secondly, commitment to hospital constitutes only one option for dealing with troublesome members of society. For those who have offended, their ultimate release from confinement, and the problems arising therefrom, cannot, and should not, be seen in isolation from the existing system for sentencing offenders. For this is the source of many of the difficulties which subsequently face tribunals. Similarly, any changes made to the pattern of decision-making by tribunals, such as, for example, a more rigorous enforcement of the statute, would inevitably have consequences for those making the decision to impose a hospital order in the first instance.

However, the core problem with a systems approach to mental health legislation is that there is a great deal of 'double-think' in the field, deriving partly from the range of problems encompassed by the term 'mentally disordered' and the functions it serves. Underpinning the whole approach to the field are two imperatives. First, paternalism, emanating principally from the inadequate portion of the spectrum. It produces a desire to do what is best for the mentally disordered, with the result that their aspirations and/ or rights sometimes take second place. Secondly, fear of offending. This derives mainly from the portion of the spectrum encompassing the mentally disordered serious offender, yet it may equally, in practice, readily be extended to those who have never offended and those who may never offend again. That the language of dangerousness and perceptions of risk infect considerations of the release of those who have committed serious offences may be inappropriate in terms of the 1983 Act, but it is at least comprehensible. For those kinds of considerations to be extended to non-restricted patients, and in the research sample even to civil admissions, is a matter of real concern.

Thus, the overlap between the two imperatives works to the detriment and not the benefit of both groups. On the one hand, paternalistic assumptions and the desire to treat affect the disposal of the mentally disordered offender; or, as Walker and McCabe (1973: 235) note in respect of psychopathic disorder, 'the law has offered the psychiatrist a ready-made label which will help him to get his patient through the customs-barrier of the courts if he wants to'. Whilst, on the other hand, the mentally disordered non-offender may suffer from inappropriate attributions about his likely future behaviour. For example, although the Boynton Report (DHSS 1980) noted that it was wrong to subject patients to a higher degree of security than was clinically necessary, and the 1983 Act pays some regard to the concept of the 'least restrictive alternative setting', it was evident that tribunals were occasionally prepared to override RMOs' therapeutically based recommendations on the basis of attributed risk. Similarly, hostels and local hospitals were reluctant to accept the potentially troublesome patient even where clinical interests merited a move. What is theoretically good practice and what is deemed realistic at the coal-face are not always one and the same. Yet the failure of practice to match-up to expectations is tolerated in the arena of mental health. Too much *is* done by the back door, saying one thing in the sure knowledge that another will ensue. Many indulge in these games, prompted by the best of paternalistic motives. Yet, how is the patient to ascertain the real reasons for detention if they are persistently sold as being therapeutically motivated? Therefore, the conflict between patients' interests and their rights derives partly from the confusion between the two parts of the patient spectrum; substituted interests may be justifiable for those who cannot know any better, but for patients who can and do, and who wish to contest their detention, substituted interests may frustrate the attainment of their rights.

One solution advocated has been to rationalize the system by dealing with the problematic category of psychopathically disordered offenders initially in terms of their offending behaviour. At first sight, this solution has many attractions in respect of enshrining offenders' rights, for example, not to be kept in confinement for periods in excess of those commensurate with the offences they have committed. However, it is evident that some of the specific proposals have been motivated as much by a desire to prolong protective confinement.[29] Although not all can be tarred with the same brush (for example Dell and Robertson (1988) clearly desire to bring logic and equity to the system for dealing with 'non-psychotic' offenders), the implications of any proposals for change

---

[29] See generally Peay (1988*a*).

are manifold. To illustrate, were 'non-psychotic' offenders—the psychopathically disordered of this study—to be dealt with primarily under the life-sentence arrangements, they might be in a comparable position in respect of life licence conditions and recall, but I would argue that the 'safeguards offered under the two systems' are not, as Dell and Robertson (1988: 135) assert, 'very similar'. Under the existing parole arrangements (McCabe 1985) the Parole Board only offer advice to the Home Secretary; they do not have the statutory power to order release. Moreover, prisoners are not eligible for the range of procedural safeguards offenders currently enjoy under the Mental Health Act. Even if the Parole Review Committee's recommended revisions to the existing system of parole were implemented, life sentenced prisoners were excluded from their remit.[30] Therefore, as considerations of dangerousness are an explicit parole consideration, psychopathically disordered offenders would be doubly disadvantaged if they were to be shifted into the ambit of the Parole Board; even the prospect of a rigorous enforcement of the statute would be denied to them, and they would lose the facility of 'airing the issues' provided by the mental health system's procedural safeguards.

One other implied consequence of treating the mentally disordered offender principally in terms of his offending behaviour may be a retreat from therapeutic endeavour. Moreover, even patients who nurture no desire to enforce their rights may benefit from having them pursued, as the momentum deriving from the right to receive effective treatment reveals. Thus, there are costs as well as benefits attached to a programme of rationalization. Finding the cap which fits all in the muddied central arena is not made any easier by the ready identification of the problems on the terraces. If a more honest approach is to be promoted it should go hand in hand with hesitancy.

In addition to the specific recommendations already made, two unproblematic solutions suggest themselves. First, the quality of the safeguard which tribunals represent undoubtedly depends both on the substance of the law and the abilities and inclinations of those who apply it. The latter could more easily be modified, either ideologically or professionally, if an adaptation to the Act does not occur spontaneously. Given the research findings, it would seem untenable at present to argue, as in the case of *Bone*, that it was unnecessary to offer tribunal members general guide-

[30] Carlisle Report (1988).

lines because 'people of the quality of those who form the membership of mental health review tribunals, and in particular the president of the tribunal, will be well able to apply the broad principles that I have stated to the facts of the cases before them without any further assistance.'[31] Tribunal members already receive intermittent training; but there is considerable scope for improving upon the nature and extent of this. Without doubt, attention would be merited to the role, function, and qualifications of medical members of the tribunal. Also, the role of lay members requires clarification and enhancement, not the least of which would be a formal recognition of their qualifications and of the contribution they should make to the tribunal's decision. Many so-called lay people are specialists in their own right; perhaps the label 'specialist' member would be more appropriate. Moreover, the application of non-medical criteria is an essential element in the Act's scheme for a balanced approach to mental health; lay members require the credibility effectively to promote this.

The second possibility for improvement relates to the urgent need to provide real alternatives to compulsory hospital care. The existence of such options would not only encourage tribunals to reach the decisions which they arguably should, but also enable them to feel more at ease about so doing, by reducing the risks associated with discharge into inappropriate conditions. I would, thus, concur with Sir John Wood (1985) that legal safeguards are only likely to be effective in the context of adequate resource provision. However, I would further suggest that consideration should be given to granting to tribunals the power to see through their recommendations for transfer, which would go beyond the new administrative arrangements discussed above. Without some revision of their powers in this arena they will remain, for many patients, no more than an ineffectual voice.

It is inevitable that the process of weighing the laudable yet competing objectives of patients' rights, therapeutic goals, and wide-ranging social considerations will be fraught with difficulties. Too rigid an approach—the substantive justice route—is unlikely to produce a satisfactory solution, and therefore one that will be readily employed; routine abrogation of the law is anyway undesirable. But too lax an approach cannot protect patients from unjustifiable deprivation of their liberty. Greater procedural regulation, particularly if inappropriate attributions of 'dangerousness'

---

[31] Mr Justice Nolan in *Bone*, at p. 333, see Appendix 3.

are to be made, is a necessary first step. But in the light of the research findings, this would be insufficient. Decisions to discharge are resource and reality-oriented, not rule and law-oriented; scope must be provided for tribunals to deal in these realities. Hence, if the tribunal setting is not conducive to a strict application of the law it may be that an improvement will be achieved not so much in reform of the law but in the context within which the safeguard operates and the consequences that stem from its effective use.

APPENDIX 1

Mental Health Act 1983: Selected Sections

Section 1. Definitions of Mental Disorder

1. (1) The provisions of this Act shall have effect with respect to the reception, care and treatment of mentally disordered patients, the management of their property and other related matters.
   (2) In this Act:
   'mental disorder' means mental illness, arrested or incomplete development of mind, psychopathic disorder and any other disorder or disability of mind and 'mentally disordered' shall be construed accordingly;

   'severe mental impairment' means a state of arrested or incomplete development of mind which includes severe impairment of intelligence and social functioning and is associated with abnormally aggressive or seriously irresponsible conduct on the part of the person concerned and 'severely mentally impaired' shall be construed accordingly;

   'mental impairment' means a state of arrested or incomplete development of mind (not amounting to severe mental impairment) which includes significant impairment of intelligence and social functioning and is associated with abnormally aggressive or seriously irresponsible conduct on the part of the person concerned and 'mentally impaired' shall be construed accordingly;

   'psychopathic disorder' means a persistent disorder or disability of mind (whether or not including significant impairment of intelligence) which results in abnormally aggressive or seriously irresponsible conduct on the part of the person concerned;

   and other expressions shall have the meanings assigned to them in section 145 below.
   (3) Nothing in subsection (2) above shall be construed as implying that a person may be dealt with under this Act as suffering from mental disorder, or from any form of mental disorder described in this section, by reason only of promiscuity or other immoral conduct, sexual deviancy or dependence on alcohol or drugs.

Section 72. Powers of Tribunals

72. (1) Where application is made to a Mental Health Review Tribunal by or in respect of a patient who is liable to be detained under this Act, the tribunal may in any case direct that the patient be discharged, and

> (a) the tribunal shall direct the discharge of a patient liable to be detained under section 2 above if they are satisfied
>> (i) that he is not then suffering from mental disorder or from mental disorder of a nature or degree which warrants his detention in a hospital for assessment (or for assessment followed by medical treatment) for at least a limited period; or
>> (ii) that his detention as aforesaid is not justified in the interests of his own health or safety or with a view to the protection of other persons;
>
> (b) the tribunal shall direct the discharge of a patient liable to be detained otherwise than under section 2 above if they are satisfied
>> (i) that he is not then suffering from mental illness, psychopathic disorder, severe mental impairment or mental impairment or from any of those forms of disorder of a nature or degree which makes it appropriate for him to be liable to be detained in a hospital for medical treatment; or
>> (ii) that it is not necessary for the health or safety of the patient or for the protection of other persons that he should receive such treatment; or
>> (iii) in the case of an application by virtue of paragraph (g) of section 66(1), that the patient, if released, would not be likely to act in a manner dangerous to other persons or to himself.

(2) In determining whether to direct the discharge of a patient detained otherwise than under section 2 above in a case not falling within paragraph (b) of subsection (1) above, the tribunal shall have regard

> (a) to the likelihood of medical treatment alleviating or preventing a deterioration of the patient's condition; and
>
> (b) in the case of a patient suffering from mental illness or severe mental impairment, to the likelihood of the patient, if discharged, being able to care for himself, to obtain the care he needs or to guard himself against serious exploitation.

(3) A tribunal may under subsection (1) above direct the discharge of a patient on a future date specified in the direction; and where a tribunal do not direct the discharge of a patient under that subsection the tribunal may

(*a*) with a view to facilitating his discharge on a future date, recommend that he be granted leave of absence or transferred to another hospital or into guardianship; and

(*b*) further consider his case in the event of any such recommendation not being complied with.

(4) Where application is made to a Mental Health Review Tribunal by or in respect of a patient who is subject to guardianship under this Act, the tribunal may in any case direct that the patient be discharged, and shall so direct if they are satisfied

(*a*) that he is not then suffering from mental illness, psychopathic disorder, severe mental impairment or mental impairment; or

(*b*) that it is not necessary in the interests of the welfare of the patient, or for the protection of other persons, that the patient should remain under such guardianship.

(5) Where application is made to a Mental Health Review Tribunal under any provision of this Act by or in respect of a patient and the tribunal do not direct that the patient is suffering from a form of mental disorder other than the form specified in the application, order or direction relating to him, direct that that application, order or direction be amended by substituting for the form of mental disorder specified in it such other form of mental disorder as appears to the tribunal to be appropriate.

(6) Subsections (1) to (5) above apply in relation to references to a Mental Health Review Tribunal as they apply in relation to applications made to such a tribunal by or in respect of a patient.

(7) Subsection (1) above shall not apply in the case of a restricted patient except as provided in sections 73 and 74 below.

Section 73. Power to Discharge Restricted Patients

73. (1) Where an application to a Mental Heath Review Tribunal is made by a restricted patient who is subject to a restriction order, or where the case of such a patient is referred to such a tribunal, the tribunal shall direct the absolute discharge of the patient if satisfied

(*a*) as to the matters mentioned in paragraph (*b*)(i) or (ii) of section 72(1) above; and

(*b*) that is is not appropriate for the patient to remain liable to be recalled to hospital for further treatment.

(2) Where in the case of any such patient as is mentioned in subsection (1) above the tribunal are satisfied as to the matters referred to in paragraph (*a*) of that subsection but not as to the matter referred to in paragraph (*b*) of that subsection the tribunal shall direct the conditional discharge of the patient.

(3) Where a patient is absolutely discharged under this section he shall thereupon cease to be liable to be detained by virtue of the relevant hospital order, and the restriction order shall cease to have effect accordingly.

(4) Where a patient is conditionally discharged under this section

(*a*) he may be recalled by the Secretary of State under subsection (3) of section 42 above, as if he had been conditionally discharged under subsection (2) of that section; and

(*b*) the patient shall comply with such conditions (if any) as may be imposed at the time of discharge by the tribunal or at any subsequent time by the Secretary of State.

(5) The Secretary of State may from time to time vary any condition imposed (whether by the tribunal or by him) under subsection (4) above.

(6) Where a restriction order in respect of a patient ceases to have effect after he has been conditionally discharged under this section the patient shall, unless previously recalled, be deemed to be absolutely discharged on the date when the order ceases to have effect and shall cease to be liable to be detained by virtue of the relevant hospital order.

(7) A tribunal may defer a direction for the conditional discharge of a patient until such arrangements as appear to the tribunal to be necessary for that purpose have been made to their satisfaction; and where by virtue of any such deferment no direction has been given on an application or reference before the time when the patient's case comes before the tribunal on a subsequent application or reference, the previous application or reference shall be treated as one on which no direction under this section can be given.

(8) This section is without predudice to section 42 above.

APPENDIX 2

The Tribunal Hearing: An Anatomy of Information Sources

This anatomy, presented in point form and in Fig. 1, is of the information sources normally available in the case of a *restricted* patient detained in a Special Hospital. Significant departures in the case of non-restricted patients are dealt with below. The anatomy chronicles the possible interactions between the various contributors to a tribunal hearing, but does not attempt to capture the subtlety of these interactions or the strategic deferrals in which the parties may engage. Both of these are dealt with at length in the preceding chapters.

1. The Mental Health Review Tribunal (tribunal) is usually comprised of three members, one drawn from each of the panel of legal, medical, and lay members (see Schedule 2, Mental Health Act 1983). They may discharge the patient—either absolutely or conditionally or make a deferred conditional discharge. They have *no* power to order transfer or trial leave or to make recommendations to that effect, although such advice to the Home Office is said to be taken into consideration when the Secretary of State exercises his powers (S73, Mental Health Act 1983).

2. The legal member in restricted cases would normally be a judge or Queen's Counsel 'with substantial judicial experience in the criminal courts' (Lord Belstead, House of Lords, 25 January 1982). This is not a legal bar, however, to others sitting. Schedule 2 merely notes that those appointed should have 'such legal experience as the Lord Chancellor considers suitable' (Schedule 2 (1)(*a*)). The legal member of any tribunal acts as its President and plays the key role in regard to the precise conduct of the hearing (see Chapter 5).

3. The lay member has to have 'such knowledge of social services or such other qualifications as the Lord Chancellor considers suitable' (Schedule 2 (1)(*c*)). They vary enormously in the relevance of their experience; a more accurate description would be that they number amongst the 'great, good, and wise'.

4. The medical member has to be a registered medical practitioner; invariably a psychiatrist and often semi-retired, but rarely with extensive forensic experience.

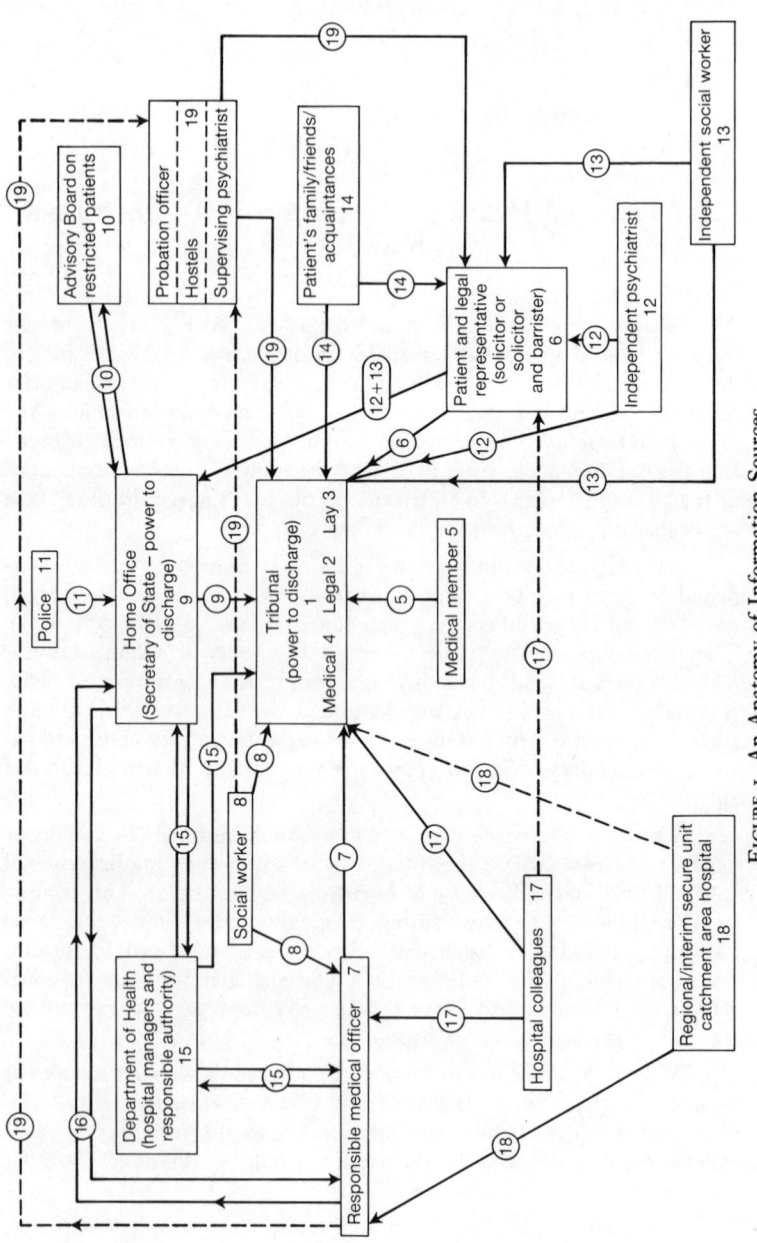

FIGURE 1. An Anatomy of Information Sources

Giving Evidence to the Tribunal

5. The medical member will, before the hearing, 'examine the patient and take such other steps as he considers necessary to form an opinion of the patient's mental condition' (Rule 11, The Mental Health Review Tribunal Rules 1983). His opinion used to be conveyed to the tribunal in private, before the hearing. It is now a more common practice for the medical member to convey only a preliminary assessment to the tribunal at this stage. Any substantial disagreement with the RMO's report should be put to the RMO in the presence of the patient. The final assessment by the medical member of the patient should be given during the tribunal's deliberations.

6. The patient (and his legal representative—solicitor or solicitor and barrister). Normally all parties giving evidence to the tribunal would do so in the presence of each other. Under Rule 22, the patient may request an interview with the tribunal before the application is determined. Evidence from the patient and the RMO may be heard in each others' absence if requested—but this is quite unusual. In such instances, the legal representative would remain present thoughout the hearing.

7. The Responsible Medical Officer (RMO) is the psychiatrist responsible for the patient's care who, in a non-restricted case, would have the authority to discharge. The RMO will also submit a written medical report to the tribunal, drawing on, where appropriate, previous reports and assessments by other members of the hospital staff caring for the patient (nurses, psychologists, occupational therapists, case conferences, etc.). This will constitute part of the 'Responsible Authority's Report'— the other parts being the social work report at 8 below, and details relating to the history of the patient's detention (see Schedule 1, MHRT Rules 1983). In restricted cases detained in the Special Hospitals the Responsible Authority has been the DHSS (see 15 below).

8. The Social Work Report. In all cases evidence would be submitted as part of the Responsible Authority's Report about the patient's social circumstances—his home and family, opportunities for employment, his financial circumstances, and the availability of community support and relevant medical facilities (Schedule 1, Part B, MHRT Rules 1983). This might be prepared either by the hospital social worker or by a local authority social worker in the patient's home area. It will be submitted along with the medical report prepared by the RMO and details of the history of the patient's detention by the 'Responsible Authority'. Only rarely in restricted cases will the author of the social-work report be called to give evidence to the tribunal, although attendance in non-restricted cases is commonplace. These reports vary enormously in their content; some giving extensive details about a patient's home circumstances, whilst others, perhaps in the cases of patients thought unlikely to

be discharged, will review briefly and in a standard format, the formal facilities available in a patient's catchment area.

9. **The Home Office.** The Home Office will always submit their written observations on the patient, in fulfilment of the statements required from the Secretary of State (Rules 6 and 32, and see Schedule 1 of the MHRT Rules 1983). In reality, these reports are prepared and day-to-day decision-making undertaken by C3 division at the Home Office. In a limited number of cases the Home Office may seek to make oral submissions to the tribunal through counsel. They are not thought to be 'a party to the proceedings' but their oral submissions will always be heard if they so request. The Secretary of State enjoys a concurrent power with the tribunal to discharge restricted patients. In addition, he has the sole authority to grant trial leave or transfer and to recall patients by warrant who have been conditionally discharged from hospital (S42(3) Mental Health Act 1983).

Evidence acquired indirectly by the tribunal

10. **The Advisory Board.** The Home Office may seek the views of the Advisory Board on Restricted Patients either before or after submitting their observations to the tribunal. The Advisory Board is comprised of a number of senior judicial and psychiatric members and others (similar in composition to the Parole Board). Their advice to the Home Secretary is confidential. Normally their advice would be sought after the hearing, but reference would none the less be made to this proposed course of action in the Secretary of State's statement. Hence, it would be indicated that before agreeing to any recommendation for transfer or trial leave, the Secretary of State would wish to refer the patient's case to the Advisory Board. The Advisory Board will normally have access to the range of papers kept by the Home Office, including police reports, witness statements, etc. They will also send one or more of the Board (usually including a psychiatric member) to interview the patient in hospital.

11. **The Police.** The Home Office may similarly seek information from the police, the DPP, and the courts about a patient's criminal records and details of their offence (witness statements, etc.) and trial. Some of this may subsequently be included in the Secretary of State's observations—at least in summary form.

12. **The Independent Psychiatrist(s) (IPs).** A patient's representative may seek psychiatric assessment of his client by psychiatrists independent of the hospital where the patient is detained. These individuals would visit the hospital, examine the patient and his case notes and compile an independent psychiatric report (IPR) for the patient's legal representative. According to its content the representative may submit the report to the tribunal. Submission would be the normal course since

both the representative's credibility and his case may be damaged if it emerges at the tribunal that an independent report has been prepared, but withheld. The representative may also wish to call the IP to give oral testimony to the tribunal. It is sometimes thought to be advantageous to seek psychiatric assessment from a psychiatrist in the patient's catchment area who might be in the position to be able to offer him a bed. Otherwise, IPs are in danger of being characterized as making recommendations without having subsequently to accept responsibility for caring for the patient. Similarly, where an IPR is in direct conflict with the conclusions of the patient's RMO, the representative may wish to seek more than one independent report.

13. Independent Social-Work Report. A representative may alternatively (or additionally) seek an independent social-work report on the patient, his family, and possible placements for him in the community. These would be prepared on the same basis as for the IPR. Only a financial restriction imposed by the legal aid committee prevents such social work reports being routinely prepared, in that representatives may be forced to choose between having either an IPR or a social-work report prepared.

12 and 13. Independent Reports prepared on behalf of the applicant and submitted by the representative to the tribunal, must also be submitted to the Secretary of State so that he may submit his comments on them to the tribunal.

14. The Patient's Family, Friends and Acquaintances. All of these individuals may provide background information to the representative. If the representative seeks to establish that the patient has changed, they may be called to give evidence directly to the tribunal. Similarly, if they are offering to provide the patient with accommodation were he to be discharged, they will be called by the representative. Patients' families may sometimes be seen by the tribunal in the absence of the patient to establish that their offer is genuine and to enable them to speak freely. Normally, close family members would remain throughout the evidence.

15. The DHSS (subsequently divided into two departments—the Department of Health and the Department of Social Security). In the Special Hospitals, the DHSS, as hospital managers, are the official 'Responsible Authority'. The relevant functions have traditionally been carried out by the Special Hospitals Committee at the DHSS. However, the situation is in flux. One Special Hospital has been managed by a specially constituted Review Board (following the recommendations of the Boynton Report (1980) Cmnd. 8073). The others similarly came under the day-to-day management of newly established Local Boards of Managers. There are also plans to establish a Special Health Authority to manage the Special Hospitals. Whatever finally transpires, it is likely that ultimate authority will remain with the Secretary of State at the DH. In general, the permission of the managers has to be sought before a patient

can be admitted to or transferred from the hospital to other facilities. It would be unusual for their views to be conveyed independently to the tribunal as they invariably concur with the views of the RMO. However, in the very rare instances where they may disagree with the conclusions of the RMO they may write to both the RMO and the tribunal to make it clear that it is their views as Responsible Authority which apply in respect of the patient's suitability for discharge (Schedule 1 Part B (3), MHRT Rules 1983). Similarly, where any dispute arises the Home Office's observations will draw the tribunal's attention to the fact that it is the views of the DHSS which must ultimately be taken into account. The Home Office will also defer to the DHSS in the first instance where requests for transfer are received from the RMO (or a recommendation for a similar course from the tribunal is received), as their agreement will be required before a patient may be removed from (or put into) Special Hospital accommodation.

16. RMO/Home Office. When a patient is assessed by his RMO as being ready for transfer, trial leave, escorted or unescorted leave, or conditional discharge, the RMO will seek, in the first instance, the views and permission of the Home Secretary for such a course (and also the DHSS, see 15 above, for transfer). The outcome of such requests will often be apparent in the submissions of either the Secretary of State or in the RMO's report. Similarly, when the Secretary of State receives recommendations from the tribunal for the patient's transfer or trial leave the views of the RMO will subsequently be sought in respect of such a course (see administrative arrangements discussed in Chapter 9).

17. The RMO's Hospital Colleagues. The RMO may seek the views of his colleagues about the patient's progress and suitability for discharge. This may include requesting written reports from the hospital psychologists, psychotherapists, nursing staff, occupational officers, etc. Some of these written reports may be submitted to the tribunal by the RMO—case conference reports and admission reports being among the most frequent. Occasionally, any of these individuals may give evidence to the tribunal at their request, or at the request of the RMO, or, unusually, be called by the patient's representative. In some cases, the RMO may seek formal medical assessment of the patient by another of his psychiatric colleagues at the hospital where the patient is detained.

18. Regional/Interim/Medium Secure Units and Catchment Area Local Hospitals. When a RMO believes that his patient is ready for transfer (and sometimes at the request of or under pressure from the tribunal) he may approach a psychiatrist at the facilities for which he believes the patient is most suited. This would normally be psychiatric facilities within his or her catchment area (i.e., the geographical area where the patient last lived or the region where he has the most ties—family etc.). Psychiatric teams (psychiatrist plus nursing staff) would then visit the patient and assess suitability for transfer to their units.

Their reports to the RMO may be submitted to the tribunal by the RMO as either supporting opinions or in explanation of why it had not been possible to transfer patients. Occasionally, patients' representatives may ask these 'second opinions' to submit reports as an independent psychiatric report (see 11 above).

19. Probation Officers/Hostels. Where a patient is thought to have a realistic prospect of conditional discharge, his RMO may seek reports from hostels which might be prepared to accept the patient with conditional discharge status. Alternatively, the tribunal might direct the RMO to seek such reports (and adjourn whilst this takes place). Occasionally, where RMOs are reluctant to see patients conditionally discharged (or positively opposed) this task might be taken on by the patient's representative. Where tribunals have made a deferred conditional discharge, the RMO and hospital social worker will usually be responsible for locating a suitable supervising psychiatrist and probation officer for the patient. Very unusually, either of these potential supervisors may be called to give evidence, if the tribunal wish to satisfy themselves that arrangements have been made to their satisfaction.

Non-Restricted Cases

The principal distinctions in non-restricted cases are:

(i) The Secretary of State plays no part in the proceedings.
(ii) The DHSS play a more limited role. The hospital managers are the 'Responsible Authority' and would therefore be specific to each individual hospital where patients are detained. (See S145(1) 1983 Act).
(iii) The RMO enjoys the discretion to discharge patients, or seek their trial leave, or transfer as he or she considers appropriate.
(iv) The legal member of the tribunal would not have to be a judge or QC, but could be an 'otherwise' qualified lawyer and member of the legal panel.
(v) The tribunal has the power to direct the patient's discharge on a future date or to recommend leave of absence or transfer to another hospital or into guardianship (S72(3) 1983 Act).

APPENDIX 3
Selected Appeal Cases
(in chronological order)

Bone v. *Mental Health Review Tribunal*, Queen's Bench Division. Judgment given by Nolan J., 14 February 1985. See also [1985] 3 ALL ER 330–4.

R. v. *Mental Health Review Tribunal, Ex parte Clatworthy*, Queen's Bench Division. Judgment given by Mann J., 4 March 1985. See also [1985] 3 ALL ER 699–704.

R. v. *Mental Health Review Tribunal, Ex parte Pickering*, Queen's Bench Division. Judgment given by Forbes J., 12 July 1985. See also [1986] 1 ALL ER 99–104.

R. v. *Hallstrom and Morgan, Ex parte W.*, and *R.* v. *Gardner and another, Ex parte L.*, Queen's Bench Division. Judgment given by McCullough J., 20 December 1985 (referred to in text as *Hallstrom*).

Secretary of State for the Home Department v. Mental Health Review Tribunal and *Secretary of State for Home Department v. Mental Health Review Tribunal for Wales*, Queen's Bench Division. Judgment given by Mann J., 22 April 1986 (referred to as *Stuttard* and *Gordon*).

Grant v. *Mental Health Review Tribunal* and *R.* v. *Mersey Mental Health Review Tribunal, Ex parte O'Hara*, Queen's Bench Division. Judgment given by McNeil J., 23 April 1986.

R. v. *Oxford Regional Mental Health Review Tribunal, Ex parte Secretary of State for the Home Department* and *R.* v. *Yorkshire Mental Health Review Tribunal and Another, Ex parte Secretary of State for the Home Department*. Judgment given by Lawton LJ, Stephen Brown LJ, and Sir John Megaw on 23 April 1986. See also [1986] 1 WLR 1180 (referred to as *Campbell* and *Lord*).

R. v. *Nottingham Mental Health Review Tribunal, Ex parte Secretary of State for the Home Department* and *R.* v. *Northern Mental Health Review Tribunal, Ex parte Secretary of State for the Home Department*, Queen's Bench Division. Judgment given by Farquharson J., 13 March 1987 (referred to as *Thomas* and *Crozier*).

Secretary of State for the Home Department v. *Oxford Regional Mental Health Review Tribunal and another*, House of Lords. Judgment given by Lord Bridge, 29 July 1987. See also [1987] 3 ALL ER 8–14 (referred to as *Campbell*).

R. v. *Merseyside Mental Health Review Tribunal, Ex parte Kay*, Queen's Bench Division, Divisional Court. Judgment of 20 May 1988.

R. v. *Nottingham Mental Review Tribunal, Ex parte Home Secretary* and *R.* v. *Trent Mental Health Review Tribunal, Ex parte Home Secretary*, Court of Appeal. Judgment given by Balcombe LJ, Woolf LJ, and Russell LJ, 15 September 1988 (referred to as *Thomas* and *Crozier* above).

Attorney-General v. *Associated Newspaper Group plc*, Queen's Bench Division, Divisional Court. Judgment given by Mann LJ and Henry J., 20 October 1988.

W. v. *Egdell and Others*, Chancery Division. Judgment given by Scott J., *Times Report*, 14 December 1988.

REFERENCES

Aarvold Report (1973). *Report on the review of procedures for the discharge and supervision of psychiatric patients subject to special restrictions*, Cmnd. 5191, HMSO, London.

Allen, F. A. (1971). 'Criminal Justice, Legal Values and the Rehabilitative Ideal. In S. E. Grupp (ed.), *Theories of Punishment*. Indiana University Press, Bloomington, Indiana 317–330.

Asch, S. E. (1956). 'Studies of independence and conformity: A minority of one against a unanimous majority'. *Psychological Monographs*, 70 (9, Whole no. 416).

Ashworth, A., Genders, E., Mansfield, G., Peay, J. and Player, E. (1984). *Sentencing in the Crown Court: Report of an Exploratory Study*. Centre for Criminological Research, University of Oxford Occasional Paper no. 10.

Bean, P. (1986). *Mental Disorder and Legal Control*, Cambridge University Press, Cambridge.

Becker, H. (1967). 'Whose Side are We on?', *Social Problems*, 14, 239–47.

Blackburn, R. (1982). 'On the Relevance of the Concept of the Psychopath', in D. A. Black (ed.), *Issues in Criminological and Legal Psychology*, no. 2, British Psychological Society, Leicester.

—— (1983). 'Are Personality Disorders Treatable?', in J. Shapland and T. Williams (eds.), *Issues in Criminological and Legal Psychology*, no. 4, British Psychological Society, Leicester.

Blair, D. (1975). 'The Medico-Legal Implications of the Terms "Psychopath", "Psychopathic Personality" and "Psychopathic Disorder"', *Medicine, Science and the Law* 15, 51–61, 110–23.

Blumstein, A., Farrington, D. and Moitra, S. (1985). 'Delinquency Careers; Innocents, Desisters and Persisters', in M. Tonry and N. Morris (eds.), *Crime and Justice: An Annual Review of Research* vi, Basic Books Inc., New York.

Carlen, P. (1983). *Women's Imprisonment*, Routledge and Kegan Paul, London.

Carlisle Report (1988). *Report of the Review Committee: The Parole System in England and Wales*, Cm. 532, HMSO, London.

Chiswick, D. (1985). 'Use and Abuse of Psychiatric Testimony', *British Medical Journal*, 290, 975–7.

Coid, J. (1987). *Psychopathology or Typology*, Paper presented to the Royal College of Psychiatrists, Forensic Specialist Section. 21 February, Stratford-upon-Avon.

Crombag, H. F. M., De Wijkerslooth, J. L. and van Tuyl Serooskerken, E. H. (1975). 'On Solving Legal Problems', *Journal of Legal Education* 27, 168–202.

Davis, K. C. (1976). *Discretionary Justice*, University of Illinois Press, Chicago.

Dell, S. (1982). Transfer of Special Hospital Patients into National Health Service Hospitals, in D. P. Farrington and J. Gunn (eds.), *Abnormal Offenders, Delinquency and the Criminal Justice System*. Wiley, Chichester.

—— and Robertson, G. (1988). *Sentenced to Hospital: Offenders in Broadmoor*, Institute of Psychiatry, Oxford University Press, Oxford.

Department of Health and Social Security (1976). *A Review of the Mental Health Act 1959*, HMSO, London.

—— (1978). Unpublished discussion paper by the Committee on Mental Health Review Tribunal Procedures.

—— (1980). *Report of the Review of Rampton Hospital* (Boynton Report), Cmnd. 8073, HMSO, London.

—— (1981). *Reform of Mental Health Legislation*, Cmnd. 8405, HMSO, London.

—— (1983). *Mental Health Act 1983: Memorandum on Parts I–VI, VIII and X*, HMSO, London.

—— (1985) *The Mental Health Review Tribunals for England. Statistics for the MHRTs in respect of Applications, References and Hearings for the Years 1982, 1983, 1984 and 1985 (until 30 June)*. DHSS, London, and supplementary tables for 1985 and 1986 (until 30 June).

—— (1987a). 'Mental Health Statistics for England for 1986', Statistical Booklet, HMSO, London.

—— (1987b). *Revised Memorandum on the Mental Health Act 1983*, HMSO, London.

—— and Home Office (1986). *Offenders Suffering From Psychopathic Disorder*, Consultation Document, HMSO, London.

De Smith, S. A. (1980). *Judicial Review of Administrative Action*, 4th edn., Stevens and Sons Ltd., London.

Devlin, P. (1976). 'The Judge as Lawmaker: The Fourth Chorley Lecture' *Modern Law Review* 39, 1–16.

Dworkin, R. (1984). 'Rights as Trumps', in J. Waldron (ed.), *Theories of Rights*, Oxford University Press, Oxford.

Fennell, P. (1977). 'The Mental Health Review Tribunal: A Question of Imbalance.' *British Journal of Law and Society*, 2, 186–219.

Fitzmaurice, C. and Pease, K. (1986). *The Psychology of Judicial Sentencing*, Manchester University Press, Manchester.

Fuller, L. (1966). 'An Afterword: Science and the Judicial Process' *Harvard Law Review* 79, 1604–28.

Garofalo, R. (1914). *Criminology*, trs R. W. Millar, 1968 edn. Patterson Smith. Montclair, NJ.

Golding, S. (1988). 'Mental Health Professionals and the Courts: The Ethics of Expertise' *International Journal of Law and Psychiatry* (in press).

Gordon, R. (1989). 'The Right to Receive Treatment', in R. Freeman and S. Verdun-Jones (eds.), forthcoming.

—— and Verdun-Jones, S. (1983). 'The Right to Refuse Treatment: Commonwealth Developments and Issues', *International Journal of Law and Psychiatry*, 6, 57–73.

—— —— (1986) 'Mental Health Law and Law Reform in the Commonwealth: The Rise of the "New Legalism"', in D. N. Weisstub (ed.), *Law and Mental Health: International Perspectives*, ii, Pergamon, New York, 1–82.

Gostin, L. O. (1975). *A Human Condition*, i, *The Mental Health Act from 1959 to 1975*. Special report for MIND (National Association for Mental Health), 22 Harley Street, London.

Gostin, L. O. (1977). *A Human Condition*, ii, *The Law Relating to Mentally*

Abnormal Offenders. Special report for MIND (National Association for Mental Health), 22 Harley Street, London.

—— (1982). 'Human Rights, Judicial Review and the Mentally Disordered Offender'. *Criminal Law Review*, 779–93.

—— (1983). 'Perspectives on Mental Health Reform'. *Journal of Law and Society*, 10, 1, 47–70.

—— (1986). *Mental Health Services: Law and Practice*. Shaw and Sons, London.

—— and Rassaby, E. (1980). *Representing the Mentally Ill and Handicapped. A Guide to Mental Health Review Tribunals*, MIND and the Legal Action Group, London.

Gottfredson, D. and Gottfredson, M. (1980). *Decision Making in Criminal Justice: Toward the Rational Exercise of Discretion*. Ballinger, Cambridge, Mass.

—— —— (1988). *Decision Making in Criminal Justice: Toward the Rational Exercise of Discretion*, 2nd edn., Plenum Press, New York.

Greenland, C. (1970). *Mental Illness and Civil Liberty*, Willmer Bros, Birkenhead.

Grisso, T. (1988). 'Conceptual Directions for Studying Dangerousness Judgements', Paper presented at the XIVth International Congress on Law and Mental Health, Montreal.

Grosman, B. (1982). 'The Prosecutor', in C. Boydell and I. Connidis (eds.), *The Canadian Criminal Justice System*, Holt, Rinehart and Winston, Toronto.

Grounds, A. (1987a). 'Detention of "Psychopathic Disorder" Patients in Special Hospitals: Critical Issues', *British Journal of Psychiatry*, 151, 474–8.

—— (1987b). 'Sections 35, 36, 37, 38 and 47: How to Choose', Paper presented to the Royal College of Psychiatrists, Forensic Specialist Section, 20–21 Feb. 1987, Stratford-upon-Avon.

—— (1988). 'A New Appraisal of Mental Health Review Tribunals', *Mental Health Trends*, forthcoming.

—— Quale, M., France, J., Brett, T., Cox, M. and Hamilton, J. (1987). 'A Unit for "Psychopathic Disorder" Patients in Broadmoor Hospital', *Medicine, Science and Law*, 27, 21–32.

Gunn, J. (1977). 'Criminal Behaviour and Mental Disorder' *British Journal of Psychiatry*, 130, 317–29

Hamilton, J. (1985). 'The Special Hospitals', in L. Gostin (ed.), *Secure Provision: A Review of Secure Services for the Mentally Ill and Mentally Handicapped in England and Wales*, Tavistock, London.

Hare, R. (1970). *Psychopathy: Theory and Research*, Wiley, New York.

Hawkins, K. (1983a). 'Thinking About Legal Decision-Making', in J. Shapland (ed.), *Decision Making in the Legal System*. Issues in Criminological and Legal Psychology, British Psychological Society, Leicester, 5, 7–24.

—— (1983b). 'Assessing Evil', *British Journal of Criminology*, 101–27.

—— (1986). 'On Legal Decision-Making.' *Washington and Lee Law Review*, 43, 4, 1161–242.

Hepworth, D. (1985). 'Dangerousness and the Mental Health Review Tribunal.' In D. P. Farrington and J. Gunn (eds.), *Aggression and Dangerousness*. Wiley, Chichester.

Hogarth, J. (1971). *Sentencing as a Human Process*, University of Toronto Press, Toronto.

References

Hoggett, B. (1984). *Mental Health Law*, 2nd edn., Sweet and Maxwell, London.
Home Office (1985). 'Criminal Careers of Those Born in 1953, 1958 and 1963', *Home Office Statistical Bulletin*, 7/85.
—— and Department of Health and Social Security (1975). *Report of the Committee on Mentally Abnormal Offenders* (The Butler Report), Cmnd. 6244, HMSO, London.
Jacob, J. (1976). 'The Right of the Mental Patient to His Psychosis', *Modern Law Review*, 39, 17–42.
Jones, K. (1980). 'The Limitations of the Legal Approach to Mental Health' *International Journal of Law and Psychiatry*, 3, 1, 1–15.
Konečni, V. J. and Ebbesen, E. B. (1984). 'The Mythology of Legal Decision Making', *International Journal of Law and Psychiatry*, 7, 5–18.
Lewis, A. (1974). 'Psychopathic Disorder: a most elusive category', *Psychological Medicine*, 4, 133–40.
McCabe, S. (1985) 'The Power and Purposes of the Parole Board'. *Criminal Law Review* 489–99.
MacCulloch, M. (1986) *Tribunals and Tribulations*, Paper presented to the Rampton Special Hospital Social with Department Conference, 'Mental Health Review Tribunals: Success or Failure?' 18 and 19 November, Buxton.
Mackay, R. D. (1986). Psychiatric Reports in the Crown Courts, *Criminal Law Review*: 217–25.
Maguire, M., Pinter, F. and Collis, C. (1984). 'Dangerousness and the tariff: The Decision-Making Process in the Release from Life Sentences', *British Journal of Criminology*, 24, 250–68.
Mawson, D. (1983). 'Psychopaths in Special Hospitals', *Bulletin of the Royal College of Psychiatrists*, 7, 178–81.
Monahan, J. (1982). 'Three Lingering Issues in Patient Rights', in B. Bloom and S. Asher (eds.), *Psychiatric Patient Rights and Patient Advocacy: Issues and Evidence*, Human Sciences Press, New York.
—— and Steadman, H. (1983). 'Crime and Mental Disorder', in M. Tonry and N. Morris (eds.), *Crime and Justice: An Annual Review of Research*, iv, University of Chicago Press, Chicago, 145–89.
Muller, D. J., Blackman, D. G. and Chapman, A. J. (eds.) (1984). *Psychology and Law*, Wiley, New York.
Nuffield, J. (1982). *Parole Decision-Making in Canada: Research Towards Decision Guidelines* Research Division. Minister of Solicitor General, Publication of the Minister of Supply and Services.
Parker, E. (1980). 'Mentally Disordered Offenders and their Protection from Punitive Sanctions: The English Experience', *International Journal of Law and Psychiatry*, 1, 461–8.
Peay, J. (1980). *'Mental Health Review Tribunals: A Study of Individual Approaches to Decision Making.'*, University of Birmingham Ph.D. thesis.
—— (1981) Mental Health Review Tribunals: Just or Efficacious Safeguards?, *Law and Human Behavior*, 5, 2/3, 161–86.
—— (1982a). Mental Health Review Tribunals and the Mental Health (Amendment) Act, *Criminal Law Review*, 796–808.
—— (1982b). Dangerousness: Ascription or Description?, in M. P. Feldman (ed.), *Developments in the Study of Criminal Behaviour*, ii, *Violence*, Wiley, Chichester.

Peay, J. (1986). 'The Mental Health Act 1983 (England and Wales), Legal Safeguards in Limbo.' *Law, Medicine and Health Care*, 14, 3/4, 180–9.

—— (1988a). 'Offenders Suffering from Psychopathic Disorder: The Rise and Demise of a Consultation Document', *British Journal of Criminology*, 28, 67–81.

—— (1988b). 'What the Doctor Ordered: But Which Doctor and Does He Know Best?', Paper presented at the XIVth International Congress on Law and Mental Health, Montreal.

—— (1989). 'Has the Mental Health Act 1983 delivered the Goods?' in P. Devonshire (ed.), *Past, Present and Future Issues for Services to Mentally Abnormal Offenders*, Special Hospitals Research Unit No. 19, forthcoming.

Prins, H. (1986). *Dangerous Behaviour, The Law and Mental Disorder*, Tavistock Publications, London.

Re Egglestone and Mosseau and Advisory Review Board, DLR 150 (3d), 86–102.

Report of the Committee of Inquiry into the Care and After-Care of Miss Sharon Campbell, (1988), HMSO, London.

Robins, L. N. (1978). 'Aetiological Implications in Studies of Childhood Histories Relating to Anti-Social Personality.' In R. D. Hare and D. Schalling (eds.), *Psychopathic Behaviour: Approaches to Research*, Wiley, Chicester.

Rubin, D. (1972). 'Prediction of Dangerousness in Mentally Ill Criminals', Archives of General Psychiatry, 27, 397–407.

Siegel, S. (1956). *Non-Parametric Statistics for the Behavioural Sciences*, McGraw-Hill, Tokyo.

Simon, F. (1971). *Research Methods in Criminology*, Research Study No. 7, HMSO, London.

Smit, J. (1987). 'Question or Quarrel? An Analysis of the Dialogue between Judge and Patient in the Involuntary Commitment Procedure', *International Journal of Law and Psychiatry*, 10, 251–63.

Snowden, P. (1986). 'Forensic Psychiatry Services and Regional Secure Units in England and Wales', *Criminal Law Review*, 790–9.

Stephens, C. (1985). 'The Role of the Representative before the Mental Health Review Tribunal' University of Brunel MA dissertation.

Stone, A. (1985). *Mental Health and the Law: A System in Transition*, Government Printing Office, Washington DC.

Sullivan [1983]1 All ER 590.

Taylor, P. and Gunn, J. (1984). 'Violence and psychosis. Part 1: Risk of violence amongst Psychotic Men', *British Medical Journal*, 28, 1945–9.

Treffert D (1973). 'Dying with their Rights on', *American Journal of Psychiatry*, 130, 1041–2.

Unsworth, C. (1979). 'The Balance of Medicine, Law and Social Work', in N. Parry, M. Rustin, and C. Satyamurti (eds.), *Social Work, Welfare and the State*, Edward Arnold, London, 104–24.

Verdun-Jones, S. N. (1986). 'The Dawn of a "New legalism" in Australia? The New South Wales Mental Health Act 1983 and related legislation), *International Journal of Law and Psychiatry* 8, 95–118.

—— (1988). 'Sentencing the Partly Mad and the Partly Bad', Paper presented at the XIVth International Congress on Law and Mental Health, Montreal.

W. v. L. [1974] QB 711.

Waldron, J. (ed.) (1984). *Theories of Rights*, Oxford University Press, Oxford.

Walker, N. and McCabe, S. (1973). *Crime and Insanity in England*, Edinburgh University Press, Edindurgh.

Webster, C. and Menzies, R. (1987). 'The Clinical Prediction of Dangerousness', in D. N. Weisstub (ed.), *Law and Mental Health. International Perspectives*, iii, 153–208, Pergamon, New York.

Wood, Sir J. (1985). 'Detention of Patients: Administrative Problems Facing Mental Health Review Tribunals', in M. Roth and R. Bluglass, *Psychiatry, Human Rights and the Law*, Cambridge University Press, Cambridge, 114–22.

X. v. *the United Kingdom*, applic. no. 6998/75 (1981). 4 EHRR 181.

Index

Aarvold Report 3, 101
Advisory Board 63, 114, 117, 125, 140, 157, 240
after-care 177, 198–9
Allen, F. A. 1
appeal 206
  appeal cases 244–5
Asch, S. E. 214
Ashworth, A. 17 n.
  et al 24 n., 79 n.
automatic referral 33, 54, 57, 178

Bean, P. 203–4
Blackburn, R. 104 n.
Blair, D. 103 n.
Blumstein, A. 208
Bone 219, 230–1
Boynton Report 229, 241
Butler Report 7–8, 216 n.

Campbell 120
Carlisle Report 230 n.
Carlen, P. 34 n.
Chiswick, D. 205 n.
Clatworthy 217
Coid, J. 34 n., 109 n.
conditional discharge 120–2, 157
  deferred conditional discharge 156
  problems with 160
  recommendations for 171–2
Crombag, H. F. M. et al 22
Crozier 221

dangerousness
  as hidden agenda 163–4
  assessment of 207–8, 228–30
  imputations of 114
  in non-restricted cases 197–8, 200
  specific risks 148–9
  see also psychopathic disorder
  unavoidable and unacceptable risks 83–4, 98
Davis, K. C. 20
decision-making
  and case construction 138

back to front 168, 182, 212–13
by Home Secretary 73, 139–40
by RMOs 68–71, 227–8
by tribunals 105–8, 146–7, 196–7, 209–10
deliberations 168–9, 183–4, 216–20
sign-posting 214
study of 19–22
tribunals' reasoning processes 210–16
Dell, S. 62, 73 n., 101, 102, 104 n., 224–5, 229–30
Department of Health and Social Security (DHSS) 5, 25 n., 81 n,, 102, 141 n., 186 n., 192 n., 229
  as responsible authority 241–2
  as source of pressure 157
De Smith, S. A. 10
Devlin, P. 224
discharges
  by Home Secretary 26–7
  by RMO 191–2
  by tribunals in mental illness 142, 146, 161–9
  by tribunals in non-restricted cases 191–3, 197–200
  by tribunals in psychopathic disorder 105–6, 124–32
  figures 26

Ebbesen, E. B. 24
Egglestone 218 n.
evidence
  of IP 87–8, 215
  of RMO 87–8, 215–16
  opposing uncontradicted medical evidence 123
  inappropriate evidence of medical member 113
  medical member's report 93–4, 125–6, 217–18

Farquharson, Mr J. 221–2
Farrington, D. 208
Fennell, P. 4
Fitzmaurice, C. 24

Index

Forbes, Mr J. 124 n.
Fuller, L. 21

Garofalo, R. 37
Golding, S. 219
Gordon, R. M. 203
Gostin, L. O. 2 n., 4, 6, 8, 186 n., 203
Gottfredson, D. vi, 19, 137
Gottfredson, M. vi, 19, 137
Greenland, C. 4
Grisso, T. 18 n.
Grosman, B. 98
Grounds, A. 135, 137, 227 et al 101
Gunn, J. 208

Hallstrom 144 n., 180–1, 183, 184, 190, 193, 199–200, 222
Hamilton, J. 58, 64, 109 n.
Hare, R. 102
Hawkins, K. 19, 21 n., 24, 210
Hepworth, D. 4
Hogarth, J. 21, 97
Hoggett, B. 2 n.
Home Office 26, 81 n., 102, 208, 240
  and absence of psychopathic disorder 122–4
  and stepped progression 139, 140
  as source of pressure 155–6
  in welcoming recommendations 222–3
Home Secretary
  and advice from RMOs 106
  and caution 89
  and protection of public 12–13, 16, 122
  powers of 6
  response to recommendations 86–7
  see also decision making and discharges
hospital order 158
  imposition 80
  lack of control over discharge 135
  sample characteristics 191–3
hostel 243
  unavailability of 118, 119–20

independent psychiatrist 87–8, 240–1
  reports by 107–8, 117, 128, 146–7, 179, 192–3
insight 142–3
  into need for medication 150
  lack of 148

Jones, K. 201
judges
  assessment of psychiatric evidence 87–9
  desire for more information 96–7

  experience of release 90–1
  influence on tribunal decision 130–1, 188–9
  interviewing of 79–80
  perception of role 82–4, 99
  style 91–2

Kay 167 n., 211
Kilmuir Rules 79
Konecni, V. J. 24

legal aid
  disqualification 187
  patients' views 47, 129 n.
legalism
  and the 1983 Act 203–4, 221–2
  effectiveness of 204–5
  limitations to 201–2
life sentence 63, 81, 170–1

McCabe, S. 228–9, 230
MacCulloch, M. 211
McCullough, Mr J. 204–5
Mackay, R. D. 88 n.
Maguire, M. et al 138 n.
Mawson, D. 32, 61, 101
membership of tribunals
  appointment of judicial members 13–15, 80–2, 224
  assessment of 29
  in restricted cases 11–13
  judicial members
  lay members 237
  legal members 237
  medical members 125, 237, 239
  regional chairmen 15–16
  training of 230–1
mental disorder
  absence of 166, 211–12
  definitions of 233
Mental Health Act 1959
  see MHRTs
Mental Health Act 1983
  admission and discharge 85
  and compulsory medication 180–3, 190–1
  and non-restricted cases 5–6
  and restricted cases 6–10
  attainment of objectives 226–7
Mental Health Review Tribunals
  absence of discretion 6 n.
  conduct of hearing 95
  criteria—for discharge 5–7, 84–5, 211

double negative 86
informal role 154, 159–61, 222–4
in non-restricted cases 176–7
lack of options 213, 231
powers of—non-restricted cases 234–5
reasoning (*see* decision-making)
restricted cases—powers 85–6, 235–6
role 3
under 1959 Act 3–5
under 1983 Act 5–6
under stress 28–9
Mental Health Review Tribunal Rules 10–11
Rule 6(4) 66, 92
Rule 11 94
Rule 12 47–8, 92, 94
mental illness
absence of 145, 165–6
absence of personality deterioration 150
and epilepsy 151–3, 157
and medication 143–4
and remorse 144–5
characteristics of part of matched sample 147–8
diagnosis 141
difficulties with 141
negative sequelae 149
patients with serious illness 147–50
relationship with offence 173
mental impairment 185–6
Menzies, R. 207, 227–8
Mental Health Act Commission 53, 203
second opinions 144
Moitra, S. 208
Monahan, J. 198–9

natural justice 10, 216–18
non-restricted cases 243
and therapeutic control 199–20
see also dangerousness and discharges
tribunal reasons for discharge 193–5

Parker, E. 59 n., 73
parliamentary answer 223
Parole Board 10, 81, 171, 230
and parole 9, 230
patients
characteristics of interview sample 33–5
interviewing of 37–8
reasons for applying for review 44–5, 55–6
recognition of need for Special Hospital care 50

views about reports 47–9
views about RMOs 38–41
views about treatment 51–2
views about tribunals 41–3
Pease, K. 24
Peay, J. 4, 5, 13, 21, 22, 29, 82 n., 95, 102, 203, 205, 214
police 240
prison
transfer from 135–6
psychopathic disorder
and equity 109–10, 111–12, 127
and length of detention 110
and maturation 115
and medication 110
and personality disorder 153–4
and psychophysiological testing 117–18
characteristics of matched sample 108–9
diagnosis and definition 102–4, 172–3
diagnostic uncertainty 132–6
difficulties with 101–2
distinguished from mental illness 104–5
reliability of clinical judgments 123–4
treatment of 137

Rassaby, E. 4
reclassification 104, 145
reports 239–43
accuracy 70–1
representation
affect of 192–3
approved 46
benefits of 46
patients' views about 45–6
research
informal contact 29–30
matching cases 27–8
methodology 23–8
objectives 22–3
plan of 30–1
restricted cases 177–9, 186–91
see also restriction order
restriction direction 169–72
restriction order
and treatability 136–7
imposition of 8–9
rights 1–2, 17, 200
and greater good 177
and interests 18
erosion of 225
positive and negative 199
Robertson, G. 73 n., 101, 102, 104 n., 224–5, 229–30

Robins, L. N. 104
RMO
  blocking change 116–20
  disclosure of reports 66–7
  in facilitating change 126–30
  recommendations of 107
  reliability of assessments 116
  role 58–64, 75–7, 239
  see also decision making and discharges
  views about tribunals 64–76, 77–8
  workload 64

secure units 242–3
sentencing mentally disordered
    offenders 9, 228
Simon, F. 21
Snowden, P. 155
social work
  independent reports 241
  reports 239
Special Hospital
  admission to 9
  images of patients 35–6
  population of Acheland 31–2
  stigma 32
  rehabilitative facilities 106–7
Stone, A. 17 n.
Sullivan 151

Thomas 221

time for crime
  patients' views 52–3
  RMOs' views 71–4
transfer
  blocking move to local hospital 73
  to Ireland 155
  to local hospital 159
  to Special Hospital 63–4
  to West Indies 189
treatability (and viability) 191, 197, 212
treatment order
  sample characteristics 191–3
Treffert, D. 207
tribunal clerks 220–1
  influence and advice 183
  patient's views 42

Unsworth, C. 204, 221 n.

Verdun-Jones, S. N. 16, 203, 208
viability (*see* treatability)

W.v.L. 152
Waldron, J. 17 n.
Walker, N. 228–9
Webster, C. 207, 227–8
W.H.O. 153
Winterwerp 7
Wood, Sir J. 231

X. v. *the U.K.* 6, 8, 11, 206